D1083628

DATE DUE

OC 30 '98			
MAY 1 2 2009			

Demco, Inc. 38-293

WELFARE, HAPPINESS, AND ETHICS

Welfare, Happiness, and Ethics

L. W. SUMNER

170
5956

WITHDRAWN
LIBRARY
MILWAUKEE AREA TECHNICAL COLLEGE
Milwaukee Campus

CLARENDON PRESS · OXFORD

1996

Oxford University Press, Walton Street, Oxford OX2 6DP
Oxford New York
Athens Auckland Bangkok Bogota Bombay
Buenos Aires Calcutta Cape Town Dar es Salaam
Delhi Florence Hong Kong Istanbul Karachi
Kuala Lumpur Madras Madrid Melbourne
Mexico City Nairobi Paris Singapore
Taipei Tokyo Toronto
and associated companies in
Berlin Ibadan

Oxford is a trade mark of Oxford University Press

Published in the United States
by Oxford University Press Inc., New York

© L. W. Sumner, 1996

All rights reserved. No part of this publication may be reproduced,
stored in a retrieval system, or transmitted, in any form or by any means,
without the prior permission in writing of Oxford University Press.
Within the UK, exceptions are allowed in respect of any fair dealing for the
purpose of research or private study, or criticism or review, as permitted
under the Copyright, Designs and Patents Act, 1988, or in the case of
reprographic reproduction in accordance with the terms of the licences
issued by the Copyright Licensing Agency. Enquiries concerning
reproduction outside these terms and in other countries should be
sent to the Rights Department, Oxford University Press,
at the address above

British Library Cataloguing in Publication Data
Data available

Library of Congress Cataloging in Publication Data
Sumner, L. W.
Welfare, happiness, and ethics / L. W. Sumner.
Includes bibliographical references and index.
1. Happiness. 2. Contentment. I. Title.
BJ1481.S87 1996 170—dc20 96-8172
ISBN 0-19-824440-1

1 3 5 7 9 10 8 6 4 2

Typeset by Graphicraft Typesetters Ltd, Hong Kong
Printed in Great Britain
on acid-free paper by
Bookcraft (Bath) Ltd
Midsomer Norton, Avon

For
my mother

PREFACE

DURING the course of my research on this book, when I was at the stage of hunting down other treatments of its central themes, I came across a reference to a book by Bill Jordan entitled *Rethinking Welfare*. Since this seemed to me an apt characterization of my own project, I eagerly anticipated reading what Jordan had to say. Alas, when I got hold of the book my hopes were quickly dashed. Jordan's aim was to rethink not welfare itself but the contributions made to our well-being by the various social spheres, public and private, within which we conduct our lives. As an amateur on these matters, I thought the book quite innovative and insightful. But it mainly served to remind me of the extent to which 'welfare' has been consolidated as a social-scientific term of art. As I quickly learned, if a book written in the post-war era includes 'welfare' in its title, then it is reasonable to expect it to deal, in one way or another, with the range of social programmes which are now standard features in modern industrialized states, and whose declared purpose is to secure a fair distribution of basic goods and services or to establish a safety net for the least advantaged.

It is therefore only fair to warn the reader at the outset that this book is not another contribution to the already enormous literature on the welfare state. It has little to say about social welfare programmes, or indeed about any matters of public policy. Its interests and concerns are neither economic nor political but philosophical. Its bearing on questions of social policy pretty well comes down to this: like all other public measures, welfare programmes are justifiable only if they ultimately contribute to welfare in its deeper and more traditional sense, the sense in which welfare is the general condition of faring or doing well, and my welfare is the same as my well-being or my interest or (in one of its many meanings) my good. That does not tell us much about how such programmes should be designed, or even whether we should prefer them to other means of promoting well-being. Those interested in such questions would therefore be well advised to look to writers like Bill Jordan for answers to them.

The project of this book is a philosophical inquiry into the nature and value of welfare. Its main conclusions can be easily summarized. The first six chapters seek the best theory about the nature of welfare. Chapter 1 develops criteria of adequacy for any such theory, while Chapter 2 sets out a basic grid for distinguishing the contenders into subjective and objective accounts. The next three chapters are extended critiques of the historically dominant accounts: objective theories (Chapter 3), hedonism (Chapter 4), and desire/preference theories (Chapter 5). The conclusion drawn from these critiques is that philosophical theories about the nature of welfare have so far been too remote from our everyday experience of it. Chapter 6 sets out to remedy this deficiency by developing a better version of a subjective theory, one which connects welfare with happiness or life satisfaction. The final chapter then defends welfarism: the thesis that individual welfare (so understood) is the only thing with final or ultimate ethical value, the only state of affairs which we have a moral reason to promote for its own sake. It concludes with some speculative remarks about the possible impact of welfarism on ethical and political theory.

This unequal division of labour between the two major concerns of the book—six chapters on the nature of welfare to one on its value—reflects my (possibly jaundiced) assessment of the current state of the argument concerning welfarism. Although there have been historical periods during which welfarism was the dominant view among moral philosophers, during this century it has been reduced to a minority opinion. Its rejection, however, has too often been based on a misrepresentation of the nature of welfare. If one begins by presupposing a crude and simplistic conception of welfare (as pleasure and the absence of pain, say, or as the satisfaction of preferences), then it is a simple matter to conclude that ethics cannot ultimately be about *that*. This victory over welfarism is cheap and hollow. However, the only way to counteract it is to show why the established theories about the nature of welfare—the ones typically taken for granted in discussions of welfarism—are inadequate, and to construct a better theory. Welfarism deserves to be tested on the basis of the best theory about what welfare is. Having located that theory, which requires an extended critical excursion, making a plausible case for welfarism is then a comparatively straightforward task.

Although welfarism tells us that only welfare matters in its own right, it dictates no particular way of using it to ground our familiar moral categories. Since utilitarians believe that our ultimate moral aim should be to maximize the sum total of welfare, they are paradigmatic welfarists. But so are egalitarians who tell us to distribute welfare equally, or maximinners who tell us to optimize the welfare of the worst off, or even egoists who tell us to secure our own personal share of it. Being a welfarist does not even require being a consequentialist, since deontologists may choose to ground their favourite rights and duties in individual well-being, and virtue theorists may do the same for their favourite virtues. It does require holding, contrary to some non-consequentialist moral structures, that the good is prior to the right. But otherwise the issue dividing welfarists from their opponents is more abstract and basic than the textbook debates among the standard moral theories. Although my own theoretical commitments tend toward consequentialism, indeed toward utilitarianism, no argument will be offered here in favour of either outcome. If it turns out that a good case can be made for welfarism, and for a subjective conception of welfare, that will be the time to ask how we should go on from these results to build a moral theory.

The themes of this book complete and complement some of my earlier projects. *Abortion and Moral Theory* (1981) included a brief analysis of the nature of welfare and a defence of welfarism (indeed of utilitarianism). Because my concerns on that occasion were primarily practical rather than theoretical, I could not give these matters the extended attention they deserved. My much fuller treatment of the same themes in this book supplies the theoretical basis for my earlier conclusions concerning the moral status of the fetus. In *The Moral Foundation of Rights* (1987) I defended consequentialism, principally against the claim that it could not make adequate sense of rights. There I prescinded entirely from the issue of the foundational value(s) to be built into a consequentialist moral framework. If the argument of that book is combined with the defence of welfarism in this one, then the overall result is part, though not all, of a case in favour of utilitarianism. What remains yet to be considered is the distinctive utilitarian idea of maximizing the sum total of welfare.

I could not have written this book without a great deal of assistance from others. My initial attempt to wrestle with these issues was undertaken in 1982–3, when I was supported by a

Killam Research Fellowship from the Canada Council and a Research Grant from the Social Sciences and Humanities Research Council of Canada. The final version of the book was started in 1986–7, when I was supported by a Leave Fellowship, once again generously provided by SSHRCC. I am very grateful to both of these agencies for the faith which they have shown in my work.

Many people have read and commented on the various treatments of these topics which I have written over the past few years. For criticisms of my earliest discussion I am grateful to Donald Evans, Joel Kupperman, Joseph Raz, Carl Wellman, and, especially, James Griffin, with whom I spent many pleasant and fruitful hours discussing issues of common concern. Readers of (some or all of) a later and very different version include David Elliot, Larry May, Andrew Moore, Peter Penz, Arthur Ripstein, and Michelle Switzer. I am especially indebted to Derek Allen, David DeGrazia, and an anonymous reader for Oxford University Press for their very thorough critiques of that version, which saved me from many avoidable mistakes, leaving only the unavoidable ones. I am also grateful to the members of my combined graduate/undergraduate seminar in ethics at the University of Toronto, who were subjected over the past few years to various stages of this work in progress and who responded by taking it seriously and helping to steer it in the right direction.

Some of the material in this book has been published elsewhere. Parts of the first three chapters appeared as 'The Subjectivity of Welfare', *Ethics*, 105: 4 (1995). An earlier version of Chapter 4 was published as 'Welfare, Happiness, and Pleasure', *Utilitas*, 4: 2 (1992), while Chapter 5 contains material from 'Welfare, Preference, and Rationality', in R. G. Frey and Christopher W. Morris (eds.), *Value, Welfare, and Morality* (Cambridge: Cambridge University Press, 1993). Finally, Chapter 7 incorporates much of 'Two Theories of the Good', *Social Philosophy and Policy*, 9: 2 (1992).

L.W.S.

Toronto
October 1995

CONTENTS

The Concept of Welfare

WHAT is welfare? And how much does it matter for ethics? These are the questions this book sets out to explore. We shall say that a fully developed answer to either question will count as a *theory* about the nature of welfare or about its value. The philosophical tradition offers us many such theories. We will try to determine whether any of them is adequate; if not, then we will need to look for something better (or perhaps conclude that a general theory is just not to be had in this area).

Our concern will be with welfare in the original meaning still preserved in the term's etymology: the condition of faring or doing well. It is in this sense that welfare attaches pre-eminently to the lives of individuals, and a person's welfare is more or less the same as her well-being or interest or (in one of its many meanings) her good. Wherein does welfare, in this sense, consist? What is it for a life to go well (or badly)? And what is the practical importance of welfare? What role should it play, say, in ethics (or politics)? These are the questions which will occupy us.

Welfare matters. On this much we all agree, at the very least when our own interest is at stake. Although most of us are highly fallible managers of our personal affairs, we generally have a fairly definite sense of when things are going well or badly for us, and a settled preference for the former condition over the latter. When we face the large decisions that shape our lives—what to work at, whom to marry, where to live, whether to have children—we either make them primarily with a view to our own well-being or, if not, come to regret this failing afterward. If the failing is persistent then our lives do not merely go badly, they also cease in a real sense to be *our* lives. At that point we need to remind ourselves that a certain degree of self-centredness is an indispensable condition for being a person or a subject in the first place. Falling below this minimum, having too little regard for one's own good, is not a virtue but a pathology, not altruism or saintliness but debasement or servility.

For most of us, especially if we are white, male, and affluent, this is not a danger; we have little difficulty rising above the threshold level of self-interest necessary in order to have an identity of our own. Our problem may then seem to be avoiding the opposite extreme: the exclusive concern for his own good which is the characteristic mark of the egoist. However, this temptation seems remarkably easy to resist (far easier than the slide the other way into the annihilation of the self). The pure egoist, indeed, seems to be exclusively the creature of textbooks in ethics or economics; with the possible exception of psychopaths, the type is virtually non-existent in real life. What renders it impracticable is our condition as social beings. Even if we picture ourselves as engaged primarily by our own well-being, we can scarcely avoid extending this concern at least to some favoured circle of others—relations, neighbours, friends, co-workers, lovers—to whom we feel closely connected. Most of us also manage to take a broader view, identifying at least intermittently with the interests of a nation or class or ethnic group or culture or race or gender. Indeed we go further still, since even the most hard-hearted among us are likely to find our sympathies aroused when we are confronted by the corrosive effects of poverty or famine or war on the lives of distant strangers. We care about their plight, simply because it is so bad for them; as would-be egoists we are dismal failures.

Welfare, whether our own or that of others, is not merely a practical concern for us—something that we seek simply because we happen to care about it. It is also a prominent feature of our common-sense morality, imposing constraints on the pursuit of our projects. The general form of these constraints is that we must show a due concern or respect for others (and for ourselves as well, in case we are not already naturally inclined in that direction). In their more specific formulations they govern virtually every aspect of our lives: decisions affecting minors must be made 'in the best interest of the child', treatment decisions protect the interest of the patient, trusts must be administered in the best interest of the beneficiary, governments must manage their affairs in the interest of the governed, and so on. Welfare is also implicated in some of the traditional virtues: prudence and benevolence, of course, but also friendship and even justice, which requires *inter alia* that we refrain from the deliberate infliction of harm on others. Indeed, were we to subtract the notions of harm and benefit from common-sense morality, there would be little left: not only little substantive content, but few of our thick ethical concepts as well.

The centrality of welfare in ethics has long been recognized by moral philosophers. It is difficult to think of any major ethical theory which does not assign an important role to protecting the interests of some favoured set of welfare subjects. Theories which share this common commitment may, of course, go on to differ in significant ways: which subjects they privilege (the members of one's society? the members of our species? all sentient beings?), what sort of protection they afford (a set of basic rights? a place at the bargaining table? inclusion in the general welfare?), and so on. One such dimension will be of particular interest for our inquiry: whether welfare is the only basic value countenanced by the theory, or is merely one among a plurality of such goods. The view that welfare is the only value which an ethical theory need take seriously, ultimately and for its own sake, we shall call *welfarism*.[1]

Welfarism is one possible answer to the question of how much welfare matters for ethics: it counts for everything. It is a highly contentious answer, largely out of favour these days. Historically, its principal defenders have been the utilitarians, who adopted welfarism as their theory of the good. But a commitment to welfarism is not necessarily a commitment to utilitarianism; a welfarist may equally be a natural law theorist or deontologist. Being a utilitarian requires being a welfarist, but not vice versa. Besides its welfarism, utilitarianism is composed of two further ingredients, each of them highly contentious in its own right: *consequentialism*, the view that the right consists in maximizing the general good, and *aggregation*, the view that the general good is the sum total of individual goods. The ethical theory which results from combining all three ingredients is very much out of favour these days, and this fact may partially account for the unpopularity of welfarism. However this may be, it would be quite wrong to reject welfarism simply because of its traditional connections with utilitarianism; if there is something seriously amiss with the latter, it might lie in one (or both) of its other defining features. The adequacy of

[1] Following Sen 1979.

welfarism as a theory of value for ethics is an issue which merits attention on its own, free of all guilt by association. Giving it this attention will be one of our aims.

We will be concerned both with the nature of welfare (what is it for a life to be going well?) and with its value (what role should well-being play in an ethical theory?). In principle, these questions could be addressed in either order. I have chosen to begin by asking what welfare consists in while prescinding as much as possible from the role it might play in our moral thinking. This order seems a natural one, since in general we expect the value of a thing to depend on its nature, rather than vice versa.

However, it does have one significant drawback. Questions about the value of welfare are, by and large, more familiar to common sense than questions about its nature. Most of us manage our ordinary lives on the unreflective assumption that well-being is worth pursuing or promoting and that ill-being (if we may call it that) is equally worth avoiding or preventing, that it is a good thing for lives to go well and a bad thing for them to go badly, that it counts in favour of some activity or condition that it is beneficial and against it that it is harmful, and so on. In all of this we are taking for granted the positive value of welfare (and the negative value of illfare). Furthermore, we generally think and act as though welfare were valuable for its own sake, or in its own right, rather than merely as a means to some further, deeper good. In doing so we assign it basic or ultimate value; we would therefore be puzzled if someone asked why welfare is valuable or demanded to be shown what it is valuable for. Surely welfare is valuable in itself, if anything is.

This is not to say that questions about the value of welfare are straightforward, or that the right answers to them are obvious; on the contrary, they are some of the deepest and most difficult issues in philosophical ethics. At every stage, however, these issues can readily be connected to the concerns of our everyday lives. In this respect, though intricate and even abstract, they remain intelligible and accessible. Furthermore, it seems obvious why tackling them will require specifically philosophical skills. The sciences, including the social sciences, have attempted to expel all questions of value from their territory. Whether or not they have succeeded in this purge, the upshot has been to relegate these issues to the domain of philosophy. Of course, it may be that evaluative questions are inherently undecidable, thus that no methodology, scientific or otherwise, is adequate to them. But if they are resolvable, the techniques needed for resolving them are, by common consent, philosophical ones. Where the value of welfare is concerned, therefore, it is easy to see why our inquiry must be a philosophical one.

The boundary between science and philosophy is harder to locate when our aim is to discover not how or why welfare matters but what it is. In general when we want to understand what something is, or what it is like, the sciences seem the obvious place to turn. It is a mysterious matter, therefore, how there could be room for a peculiarly philosophical inquiry into the nature of welfare. Worse, the question itself is mysterious. An answer to it will tell us what welfare consists in, or what is constitutive of it. But surely we must already know what welfare is, since we all seek it in our everyday lives. How, then, could a philosophical inquiry into the nature of welfare ever yield any novel results? Indeed, if we do not already agree on what counts as welfare, how could it ever yield any results at all?

1.1 THE NATURE OF THINGS

These puzzles may not be generated by any features peculiar to welfare. They might equally perplex us were we undertaking an inquiry into the nature of other things which have traditionally interested philosophers, such as mental states, or persons, or properties, or numbers. These investigations would all fall within the domain of metaphysics, which is itself a rather odd business. Consider, for instance, philosophical theories about the nature of causation. Such theories are plainly not empirical or scientific. They do not report causal connections between particular events or states of the world, and if we wish to learn about such connections we do not consult the works of philosophers. On the other hand, however, they also seem not to be merely analytic or conceptual. When we are adjudicating rival theories of causation it does not suffice to reflect on our common-sense idea of a causal relationship. This is not to say that there is nothing of importance to be learned from exploring and clarifying our concepts; most 'ordinary language' philosophy has had this modest but worthwhile aim. But no amount of explication of our conceptual framework could ever tell us what causal connections really are, as opposed to what we conceive them to be. Theories about the nature of causation purport to tell us what the world is really like, not just to remind us of our ideas about it.[2]

The fact that theories of causation are more than merely analytic helps to explain why so much argument is generally expended in order to support them, and also how they can yield surprisingly revisionist results. Consider, for instance, Hume's celebrated critique of the idea of a necessary connection between events. This idea, that if one event is the cause of another then the first necessitates the second, or has the power to make it happen, is certainly one ingredient, perhaps the central one, in our ordinary concept of causation. Hume argued, however, that there are no such connections out there in the world—or that, if there are, we could never have any knowledge of them.[3] He therefore concluded that the only ingredient in our ordinary concept which we can know to be an accurate reflection of the external world is regular succession. Whether or not Hume was right about this, he plainly thought himself to be doing more than merely analysing our idea of causation; his conclusions are a critique of the adequacy of that concept as a picture of what goes on in the world. Similarly, when other philosophers dispute Hume's account they do not accuse him of conceptual blindness or confusion. What is at issue between rival theories here is substantive, not linguistic; they disagree not about what we commonly take causation to be but about what it really is.

Theories of causation therefore seem to occupy a middle ground between the merely conceptual and the fully empirical. On the one side they presuppose a shared network of causal concepts, without which we would lack prereflective agreement concerning what is to count as a causal connection. On the other side they generalize over all such connections in all domains, telling us what must be true of any states of the world in order for them to be linked in this way. Theories of causation are answers to the question 'What

---

[2] See Mackie 1974, introduction.

[3] Mackie 1974, ch. 1 is ambivalent between an ontological reading of Hume's claim (there are no necessary connections) and an epistemological one (no such connections can be known to us). Strawson 1989 argues against the former and in favour of the latter. Both claims do more than merely analyse our concept of causation.

is it for one event to cause another?' They purport to reveal what causation consists of, or what is constitutive of it. They offer truth conditions for causal claims, or existence conditions for causal relations.

An inquiry into the nature of welfare seems to occupy this same intermediate territory. Its aim is not to tell us what is good or bad for us, or to advise us on how to attain the former and avoid the latter. If we seek such self-help guides they are readily available (indeed scarcely avoidable). But philosophers have no special expertise to offer on these questions; just as they are not biologists or physicists investigating some specific empirical domain, they are also not therapists or consultants on personal growth. However, in the same way that any particular causal inquiry presupposes some general account of what it is for one thing to cause another, any prudential advice presupposes some general account of what it is for something to benefit or harm us, thus what it is for our lives to go well or badly. If a theory of welfare is possible, it would provide this constitutive account. In doing so it would yield truth conditions for claims about, or assessments of, our interest or well-being.

This philosophical inquiry in turn presupposes that we share a concept of welfare which is rich and stable enough to support a high degree of preanalytic agreement on what is to count as faring well or badly. Only if these conceptual resources are available can we be sure that rival constitutive accounts are all theories about the nature of the same thing. But a theory of welfare will not merely explicate our ordinary concept of well-being; additionally, it will tell us what the world must be like in order for this concept to apply to it, what must be the case in order for any welfare assessments to be true. Since a theory of this sort will impose a reality test on the adequacy of our ideas, it too will be capable in principle of yielding results which are revisionist or subversive.

While there are revealing analogies between welfare and such standard objects of metaphysical inquiry as causation, they must not be pushed too far. We must, of course, allow for the possibility that welfare does not have a nature in any interesting sense, perhaps because it is too historically or culturally variable. (But then the same might turn out to be true for causation, or substance, or even numbers.) However this may be, there is one obvious difference between welfare and these other items: because they do not generally seem the right sorts of thing to have (or lack) value, theories about their nature are not usually shaped by normative or evaluative considerations. (Causation in the law may be an exception to this rule.) Where welfare is concerned, however, it may be doubted whether its nature really can be settled independently of assumptions about its value. After all, welfare is itself evaluative: it is a matter of how well a life is going. Although standards of adequacy for theories of causation may be value-free, how could this be so for welfare? How are we to keep evaluative presuppositions out of theories about the nature of welfare? What are the appropriate standards here for adjudicating among rival theories?

At the extremes two different sorts of approach are possible. The first begins by presupposing a particular theoretical framework and then goes on to test competing conceptions of welfare for their ability to play a predetermined role within that framework. The background theory could in principle be either explanatory or normative. In fact, however, philosophers who have argued from this direction have had a decided preference for normative theories, usually theories either of rationality or of morality. Let us imagine, then, some such framework with a particular niche to be occupied by welfare. If it is a theory of rationality it might take the form of prescribing that agents maximize their own welfare, while if it is a theory of morality it might require maximization of the general welfare, or the equal distribution of welfare, or maximization of the welfare of the worst off. Whatever the particular normative context, the only criterion of adequacy for a candidate conception will be its ability to play its designated role within the framework in question, which will be determined in turn by the viability of the framework when that conception is inserted into it. In this case theories of welfare are to be assessed solely for their *normative adequacy*.

The opposite procedure involves decoupling the nature of welfare from its potential role in a normative framework and testing candidate conceptions for their fit with our ordinary experience of welfare and our ordinary judgements concerning it. It will then count in favour of a conception that it is faithful to that experience and makes sense of those judgements. Call this criterion *descriptive adequacy*. Of course, if our pretheoretical concept of welfare has regions which are unsettled or disputed then no theory about its nature will be able to make sense of everyone's intuitive responses. In that event the criterion of best fit would become more complicated, and perhaps also less determinate. But the basic idea would remain that the best theory of welfare is the one which best captures our ordinary reflections and deliberative practices.

In recent years a number of treatments of competing conceptions of welfare have focused, either primarily or exclusively, on their normative adequacy.[4] In many of those discussions the issue has been posed in roughly the following way. Suppose that we share an egalitarian conception of social justice—one, that is, whose goal is that individuals have equal shares of something or other. We must then face the question: What is the stuff of which justice requires an equal distribution? In G. A. Cohen's felicitous phrase, what is the currency of egalitarian justice? Suppose that our answer to that further question is: welfare. Our theory of justice now has the more determinate goal of ensuring that individuals are roughly equally well off, or that disparities in living standards be kept to a minimum. In order to fill it out further we must go on to give an account of what we take welfare to consist in. In doing so we will need to assess different competing theories (is it the achievement of some level of functioning or flourishing? is it pleasure and the absence of pain? is it the satisfaction of desires or preferences?). In this assessment, however, we will always keep our normative objective in view: we want an account of what welfare consists in such that the requirement of an equal distribution of *that* makes for a plausible theory of justice. Our eventual choice of a theory of welfare is then entirely driven by our prior commitment to a welfarist (and egalitarian) theory of justice.[5]

It seems clear that this cannot stand as the sole test of adequacy for candidate theories. To see why this is so, suppose that after much argument and deliberation it becomes clear to you that resources are the currency of an egalitarian theory of justice. As a lover of the truth you will want to embrace this result. But suppose also that you have maintained a lifelong commitment to welfarism as a general theory of value for ethics and politics and that you are reluctant to give it up. You can achieve both of your aims by this simple procedure: first you accept a theory of justice which equates

[4] See Scanlon 1975, Sen 1980, Dworkin 1981a, Riley 1988, and Cohen 1989.
[5] Or: our rejection of welfare as the currency of egalitarian justice follows from the conclusion that there is no conception of its nature which makes equality of welfare a defensible normative ideal; see Dworkin 1981a and Cohen 1989.

it with equality of welfare and then you accept a theory of welfare which equates it with ownership of resources. By the standard of normative adequacy this must be the best theory of welfare, since *ex hypothesi* it generates the best (welfarist) theory of justice.

Although welfare is affected by resource ownership, the two are obviously not identical; something has therefore gone amiss with your procedure for selecting a theory of welfare. The problem is that your selection was driven solely by normative considerations; there was no independent control to ensure that the eventual winner would be a plausible theory of *welfare* at all. Resource egalitarianism is not a particular variant of a welfarist theory of justice; it is a rival to any such theory. This shortcoming will afflict any attempt to adjudicate among competing theories of welfare on normative grounds alone. Because the notion of welfare already has a vernacular currency it is not available as a term of art, to be defined in whatever way will best suit some favoured theoretical needs. In order to defend a conception of welfare against its competitors it is not enough to show that it has the best fit in some predetermined normative niche, and then to call this conception welfare. Whatever theoretical role we may have in mind for welfare, we will need an independent test of descriptive adequacy for theories about its nature.

If such a test is necessary, then is it also sufficient? Can theories of welfare be assessed merely for their descriptive adequacy, while holding open all questions about the normative work they might do? Can we settle the nature of welfare first and worry about its value later? There is certainly this difference between the two procedures for selecting the best theory: whereas normative criteria could not in principle be self-standing, descriptive criteria might be. But we do not yet know whether they are. Here there is no way to tell without taking a closer look at what such criteria might look like.

1.2 DESCRIPTIVE ADEQUACY

The basic test is easy enough to state: the best theory about the nature of welfare is the one which is most faithful to our ordinary concept and our ordinary experience. That experience is given by what we think or feel or know about well-being, both our own and that of others. The data which a candidate theory must fit, therefore, consist of the prodigious variety of our preanalytic convictions. We manifest these convictions whenever we judge that our lives are going well or badly, that pursuing some objective will be profitable or advantageous for us, that a change in our circumstances has left us better or worse off, that some policy would enhance or erode our quality of life, that some measure is necessary in order to protect the interest of our family or community, that a practice which is beneficial for us may be harmful to others, that we are enjoying a higher standard of living than our forebears, and so on. A theory of welfare tells us what the world must be like in order for such judgements to be correct; it offers us truth conditions for them. Its degree of fit with our ordinary experience will therefore be a function of the extent to which the truth conditions it offers can support and systematize our intuitive assessments. A theory about the nature of welfare is a proposed interpretation of our preanalytic convictions, and the best interpretation is the one which makes the best sense of those convictions.

In applying this test one of our principal assets is the richness of our welfare vocabulary. The concept of welfare is analytically connected to such cognate notions as well-being, interest, good, benefit, profit, advantage—and their various antonyms. A theory of welfare must preserve this network of analytic connections; if it fails to do so then it is an interpretation of some other concept. Since there are many such connections we will have many substitution tests for a candidate theory. Doubtless there are differences among the various items in our conceptual framework which will explain why some but not others apply in certain cases. But generally speaking a theory has given us truth conditions for welfare assessments only if it is capable of supporting all of these cognate judgements.

Our other main asset is our familiarity with welfare, which is more internal and immediate to our lives than many other items of philosophical interest. In this respect a constitutive account of welfare is less like a theory about the nature of causal relations or properties or numbers, and more like an analysis of emotion or pleasure or desire.

Even with these resources, however, the basic test of fidelity remains much too crude. Determining the fit of a particular theory cannot be a matter merely of checking its implications one by one against our intuitions, registering its various successes and failures as they occur, and then aggregating these piecemeal results into an overall score. Any such mechanical procedure will overlook important features of those very intuitions. Some of them, for instance, will inevitably be more central to our unreflective practices than others, in which case their preservation should surely count for more than the preservation of more marginal elements. The test of fidelity therefore needs to be informed by a map of our network of preanalytic convictions which distinguishes its core from its periphery. Our core beliefs about welfare are those we hold with the highest degree of confidence, or which best survive the process of challenge or reflection. One sign, therefore, that we have moved from core to periphery is that our responses become tentative or divided. In these areas of indeterminacy or dispute no test of fit is straightforwardly applicable; here any interpretation of our concept will also be a partial reconstruction of it. Further, it is also possible that some of the ingredients of our concept are confused or even incoherent, in which case any interpretation of it will also revise and reform it. Our test of fidelity seems too conservative to select among alternative possible reconstructions or revisions.

However, we need not confine the test merely to our intuitive judgements; we are also free to consider the role which welfare plays in common-sense psychology. We often explain conduct by ascribing motives which in one way or another take well-being as their object, motives such as generosity, compassion, friendship, malice, greed, and envy. Just as we can require a theory of welfare to support our ordinary assessments, so we can also require it to support our psychological explanations. Of course it need not underwrite all of them; some of our modes of explanation or interpretation might turn out to be misguided or mistaken. But it is inconceivable that all of them should turn out this way, and any theory which yielded such a result would thereby reveal that it was a theory about something other than welfare.

It is impossible to specify in advance what will count as an adequate fit with our common-sense psychology; the degree of match (or mismatch) will have to be determined for each candidate theory. But one decisive failure of fit is worth special mention. Although we often attribute selfish motives to agents, we also recognize that they are capable of altruism or self-sacrifice. We thus decisively reject the thesis of psychological egoism, which holds that all intentional action is ultimately motivated by self-interest. This fact—that my own well-being is just one possible end of action among others for me—is a core element in our ordinary concept. A theory of welfare must therefore provide no support for psychological egoism; if it implies that all intentional action is, or must be, self-interested then it has mistaken welfare for some other notion.

Fidelity to our ordinary experience has now come to embrace both our pretheoretical beliefs about well-being, whether in our own case or that of others, and also the role of these beliefs in our practical deliberations and our common-sense explanations. The further criteria of descriptive adequacy are all latent in, or derivative from, this basic test. But they deserve separate mention.

Generality. One obvious desideratum in a theory of welfare is completeness: it should give us truth conditions for all of the different sorts of welfare assessments we make. For present purposes we can sort these assessments very roughly into two groups: those which situate a subject at some particular welfare level and those which chart a subject's gains or losses (and therefore changes of level). Ascriptions of welfare levels seem to have the same logic as ascriptions of many other personal attributes, such as height or power or wealth: we presuppose some scale, appropriate for the kinds of creatures we are, on which we then locate a particular person's position or compare the positions of different persons. On the other hand, claims about the beneficial or harmful effects of some circumstance chart movements up or down such a scale, from one level to another. Both types of assessment may be either positive or negative. Someone's position on the welfare scale may be either high or low: she may be well off or badly off, fortunate or unfortunate, doing well or doing poorly. Likewise, a change of level may be either up or down: the person may gain or lose, may be made better or worse off, may be benefited or harmed.

No set of truth conditions for welfare assessments is complete unless it covers all of these categories of judgement—positive and negative, of fixed levels and of changes in level. Furthermore, it must also be able to sustain the rough discriminations of extent or degree which we make in all of them. A theory of welfare must therefore tell us what it is for one person to be much better or worse off than another, or for a particular benefit or harm to be only slight or negligible. We will discard as incomplete any theory which supports some of these modes of assessment, but can make no sense of others.

The requirement of generality has a further aspect as well. We make welfare assessments, of all of the foregoing types, concerning a wide variety of subjects. Besides the paradigm case of adult human persons, our welfare vocabulary applies just as readily to children and infants, and to many non-human beings. It is perfectly natural for me to say that my cat is doing well, that having an ear infection is bad for her, that she has benefited from a change of diet, and so on. In making these judgements it certainly seems to me that I am applying exactly the same concept of welfare to my cat that I habitually apply to my friends. A theory of welfare will therefore also be incomplete if it covers only them and ignores her.

This ideal of complete coverage, however, brings into question the boundary between the core and the periphery of our ordinary practices. Just how far beyond the paradigm case does the concept of welfare apply? All of the central ingredients in our welfare vocabulary seem straightforwardly applicable to cats, who therefore qualify as core subjects. But what about more primitive animals, such as insects, or molluscs, or bacteria? What about plants? Or machines? Or works of art? What about fetuses, or embryos? Or the brain dead? Here no straightforward version of the generality test is of any assistance. We cannot say that a theory with a wider range of application is superior just on that score, since the best account will then be the one which somehow contrives to apply to absolutely everything there is. The problem is that the range of application of our welfare vocabulary is itself indeterminate or disputed, and also that different elements of it appear to have different ranges. Some items, including the key notions of welfare and interest, seem to be at home only with creatures who qualify as subjects in the strict sense, by virtue of manifesting some form of mental life. But others, such as benefit or good, seem to apply readily to other animate or even inanimate beings. Furthermore, for each of these notions there will be some threshold area where we seem to be crossing from literal to merely metaphorical application, though of course what counts as an area of strict application for a broader notion will count as a figurative extension for a narrower one.

Like the basic test of fidelity, generality therefore presupposes a rough initial distinction between the core and the periphery of our concept of welfare. A theory of welfare would clearly be incomplete were it to exclude children or cats from the class of welfare subjects. But it would not clearly be incomplete were it to exclude paramecia or plants. Intuitively, the former are core welfare subjects while the latter are peripheral. Whereas a theory must fit the core of our concept it cannot avoid some degree of stipulation in its periphery, yielding determinate results where the application of that concept is vague and taking sides where it is in dispute. This is not to say, however, that even in this latter region a theory has a free hand. While here we cannot apply some antecedent standard of correctness, we can demand a rationale for delimiting the class of welfare subjects in a particular way and we can fault the proffered justification if it seems arbitrary or *ad hoc*. In addition, whatever its resolution of peripheral cases, a theory should offer some illuminating explanation of what makes them peripheral.

Another class of welfare subjects requires similar treatment. Thus far it has been convenient to speak as though all such subjects are individuals, though it may be unclear just which individuals they are. But this assumption is also arbitrary, since our welfare vocabulary permits us to speak without obvious strain of the good or interest of collectivities such as families, communities, classes, nations, species, and the like. Unlike idioms in which we claim to be acting in the interest of a state of affairs (such as world peace) or an abstract entity (such as honesty), our talk about collective welfare does not appear to be merely figurative or metaphorical. There thus seems little doubt that a conception of welfare which made no allowance for it whatever would be seriously incomplete. At the same time, we may legitimately wonder whether the interest of a collectivity is distinct from the aggregate interests of its constituent members, thus whether collectivities qualify as welfare subjects in their own right. Unlike viruses or pine trees, the problem raised by collectivities is not whether they lack the (physical or psychological) wherewithal to have interests of their own, but whether the interest of a collectivity is something distinct from the interests of its members (who have already been acknowledged as core welfare subjects). Since our preinterpretative intuitions do not seem to settle this reductionist issue one way or the other, we once again cannot impose a particular settlement as a condition of descriptive adequacy. But we can require a theory of welfare to assign priority to (some) individuals as core subjects, to explain why collectivities belong to the periphery of hard cases, and to provide an intelligible and principled solution to the problem of their status.

Formality. We can further expand our set of criteria by exploiting the analogy between a theory about the nature of welfare and theories about the nature of other things. A theory of causation does not tell us what causes cancer or inflation. Rather, it tells us what a causal connection between any two events consists in, or what it is for one state of affairs to cause another. That is to say, it completes the formula 'x causes y if and only if x stands in relation R to y' by proposing a value for R. It would plainly be a mistake for such a theory to confuse the conditions which constitute a causal connection between two things (the value for R) with any of the particular things capable of being causally efficacious (the values for x). An account of the nature of causation is one thing, an inventory of causes quite another.

There is an important sense, therefore, in which a constitutive account of the nature of causation must be formal or second-order. A theory about the nature of welfare must likewise be formal. It must tell us what it is for someone's life to go well or badly, or for someone to be benefited or harmed. In order to do so it must provide the appropriate relation to complete such formulas as 'x benefits y if and only if x stands in relation R to y'. It would be an equally plain mistake for a theory to confuse the conditions which constitute someone's being benefited by something (the value for R) with any of the particular things capable of being beneficial (the values for x). A theory therefore must not confuse the nature of well-being with its (direct or intrinsic) sources; it must offer us, not (merely) a list of sources, but an account of what qualifies something (anything) to appear on that list. Of course, having such an account in hand may be advantageous to us when we set about enumerating the particular conditions which contribute to well-being (for some particular set of welfare subjects), just as an analysis of the nature of causation may guide us in uncovering particular causal connections. But the nature of welfare is one thing, its several sources quite another.

We should expect many sources of welfare to vary from individual to individual, and from group to group, reflecting differences of taste or situation or constitution. Although ballet dancers and football hooligans, Amazonian aboriginals and Wall Street brokers, dolphins and giraffes may all require vastly different conditions in order for their lives to go well, a theory of welfare, because it must be both formal and general, must abstract from these contingencies of history, culture, and even biology. For it must offer a common, and comprehensive, answer to questions such as the following: 'What does the good or well-being of all of these creatures consist in?' 'What is it for their lives to go well (or badly)?' 'What is it for something to make their lives go better (or worse)?'

It should now be evident just how ambitious our requirements are. The search for a unitary theory of welfare is based on the hypothesis that, however plural welfare may be at the level of its sources, like causation it is unitary at the level of its nature. There is therefore one answer to the foregoing questions which applies equally to all the different varieties of welfare, all of its sources, and all of its many subjects. What reason could we have to accept this hypothesis? It is weakly supported, I suppose, by the linguistic facts. When we distinguish, for instance, among physical, psychological, and emotional well-being, this suggests that there is something—well-being unmodified—of which these are the several kinds or aspects. Likewise, we certainly seem to move freely around the welfare terrain, speaking of the well-being of women and men, children and adults, human beings and animals, without any consciousness of ambiguity or equivocation. But none of this evidence is sufficient to defeat the rival hypothesis that welfare is somehow different in its nature for its different varieties or occasions or categories of subjects. The assumption of the unity of welfare must therefore remain just that: an unproven regulatory hypothesis guiding our inquiry. We will not know whether or not it is justified until we either find an adequate theory or are compelled to admit failure.

Neutrality. The first two criteria of adequacy combine to yield a third. If a theory is to be general then it must apply to a wide range of creatures diverse in their natures, tastes, and forms of life. If it is also to be formal, then it must not consist merely in a list of goods considered to be indispensable to well-being, whether the list generalizes across all of these creatures or applies only to some particular variety of them. But this means that an account of the nature of welfare must not have built into it any bias in favour of some particular goods or some preferred way of life. Any such bias will inevitably violate generality—what concrete form of life could plausibly be thought to be best for all sentient beings, or all organisms, regardless of their differences? But the requirement of neutrality holds equally when attention is restricted to a particular species, such as us. Because of the formidable diversity of human cultures, patterns of socialization, tastes, and conditions of life, rich and rewarding human lives come in a variety of forms. No descriptively adequate theory of welfare can simply favour some of these possibilities over others, whether it be a preference for planning over spontaneity, for complexity over simplicity, for civilization over tribal life, for excitement over tranquillity, for risk over safety, for perpetual striving over contentment, for sexuality over celibacy, for companionship over solitude, for religious conviction over atheism, for rationality over emotion, for the intellectual life over the physical, or whatever.

To impose this condition of neutrality is not to deny that creatures of a certain nature will standardly flourish better under some forms of life than others. Surely this is to be expected; offhand, it seems likelier as the nature in question becomes more rigid, but it may well be true even for creatures as malleable as we are. But where this is so, the favoured way of life must fall out as a confirming implication of a formally neutral theory; it must not be built in as one of its presuppositions. The danger of bias is, of course, greatest in our own case, since it is tempting to shape an account of the nature of human welfare around some preferred assumption about the way in which a human life should be lived. This temptation must be resisted.

We now have four cardinal virtues for a theory of welfare: fidelity, generality, formality, and neutrality. A descriptively adequate theory will be faithful to our ordinary assessments of well-being, including the role they play in our common-sense psychology, will cover all core cases and provide a principled resolution of peripheral cases, will not confuse welfare with its sources or ingredients, and will be free of distorting bias. It should be clear by now that any comparison of candidate theories will be multidimensional. Thus there is room for a theory to satisfy some criteria better than others, and there may be no theory which fully satisfies them all. In that case picking the best theory will require balancing assets against liabilities, deciding which failures are forgivable and which fatal. This means that there will inevitably be much room for judgement, and undoubtedly some for stipulation and construction as well.

We can now return to the question we left dangling at the end of the previous section. We know that a theory of welfare cannot be selected on purely normative grounds, while ignoring all descriptive considerations. But it now seems likely that it cannot be selected on purely descriptive grounds either. If in choosing the best theory we are partly engaged in construction or stipulation, then some of this process will inevitably be guided by the normative destination which we have in mind. If we think that welfare matters, in some fairly determinate way, for ethics or politics, then we will be unable to keep this assumption from shaping our choices when our pretheoretical intuitions are uncertain or divided. (Indeed, we will be unable to determine, in any systematic way, just when our intuitions are genuinely pretheoretical.) In the discussion to follow, when I am reviewing some of the candidate theories of welfare, I have no doubt that some of my conclusions will be influenced by the role I have in mind for welfare in the framework of an ethical theory. The theories concerning the nature and value of welfare which I shall be defending are therefore more interdependent than their linear order of exposition might suggest.

None the less, that order still seems to me the right one. Normative considerations properly come into play only around the edges of our ordinary concept, in its disputed or unsettled regions. When the constraints imposed by that concept run out, or when the evidence provided by our ordinary experience is indeterminate or inconsistent, then there is a time for shaping a theory of welfare to fit some favoured normative niche. If you think, as I do, that welfare is the appropriate currency for ethics then you will wish to resolve indeterminacies and inconsistencies in such a way as to make that claim seem more, rather than less, plausible. If you are more eclectic in your ethical theorizing, or think that welfare has no place in ethics at all, then you will be pulled in a different direction. But these questions only arise for theories whose descriptive adequacy has already been established, at least for the central regions of our concept. Since welfare is a quality of our lives of which we have direct lived experience, the first question for any theory of welfare remains its fidelity to that experience. In this respect, then, questions about the nature of welfare still logically precede questions about its value.

1.3 DIMENSIONS OF VALUE

One further aspect of descriptive adequacy merits separate treatment. We have noted already that welfare differs from such metaphysical staples as causation in being inherently evaluative. To say that I am well off, or that I am flourishing, is plainly to evaluate my life. It follows that a theory about the nature of welfare will tell us what it is for our lives to have, or to lack, a certain kind of value. Lives, however, are complex things whose value can be assessed along a number of different dimensions or from a number of different standpoints. Welfare represents only one of these dimensions—one way in which a life can be going well—and it is important to distinguish it as clearly as possible from the others.

Welfare assessments concern what we may call the prudential value of a life,[6] namely how well it is going *for the individual whose life it is*. This relativization of prudential evaluation to the proprietor of the life in question is one of the deepest features of the language of welfare: however valuable something may be in itself, it can promote my well-being only if it is also good or beneficial *for me*. Since an account of the nature of welfare is descriptively adequate only if it is faithful to our ordinary concept, any serious contender must at least preserve the subject-relativity which is definitive of prudential evaluation. If it cannot manage this much then, though it might be a plausible rendering of some other dimension of value, it is not a theory about welfare at all. But surely we should be even more demanding. A theory of welfare should not only fit our ordinary concept, it should provide an interpretation of the principal features of that concept. Subject-relativity is a key ingredient in our concept of welfare, the feature which differentiates prudential value from the other modes of value applicable to lives. It is not too much to expect a theory to explicate this feature, to tell us what it means for my life to be going well not just in itself or from some other standpoint but *for me*, to explain how it is that lives can have this peculiar perspectival kind of value.

[6] I borrow this useful expression from Griffin 1986.

While subject-relativity is an essential aspect of welfare, it is also somewhat elusive. The best way to provide a preliminary sense of what it is about is to contrast prudential value with some of the other standpoints from which lives can be evaluated. Compiling an exhaustive inventory of these modes of value is out of the question (who knows how many there are?). However, three are worth special mention, in order to distinguish them from well-being.

Aesthetic value. Etymologically, the aesthetic is the domain of feeling or sensibility; we attribute aesthetic value to those objects or characteristics which we find in some respect appealing or attractive or admirable. Because there are many things to which we may be attracted, or which we may admire, there are many potential bearers of this mode of value (including human lives). It seems reasonable to suppose that the aesthetic standards appropriate for assessing a particular thing will depend on the kind of thing it is; the criteria appropriate for a novel will not fit a haiku, what we find charming in an adult may be grotesque in a child. Evaluating lives from an aesthetic standpoint will therefore require standards which are warranted by the kind of thing a life is.

What might such standards look like? Here is one possible story. A human life, we might say, is in some measure an artefact capable of being shaped and moulded by its possessor (or by others). It is therefore something which we may treat, or live, as a work of art. Because a life is a temporally extended object, or event, to shape it or subject it to conscious direction is to impose a structure on the way in which it unfolds, so that its development conforms to some conscious pattern. We need not, of course, think that only one such structure or pattern confers aesthetic value on a life. As in the case of music or architecture, there may be some who favour unity or balance or proportion, while others cultivate discord or incongruity. Perhaps there will be many ways of living the aesthetic life, sharing only the feature of having been under some degree of artistic control.

Other background stories can be imagined as well. We might say, in the spirit of G. E. Moore, that a life gains aesthetic value when it manifests aesthetic sensibility, thus a suitable degree of appreciation of the aesthetic value of (other) things in the world. This account would treat lives as second-order aesthetic objects, whose value was dependent on the recognition of first-order objects;

it would attach a high aesthetic value to being an aesthete. Alternatively, we might join Quentin Crisp in thinking that the point is to live one's life with a certain style or panache, whatever substantive ends one might choose to pursue. On this view it is not what we do that matters, but how we do it.

Because of the wide range of its possible objects, aesthetic value is unlikely to be confused with welfare. This is clearest when we are dealing with objects, such as artefacts and features of the landscape, that are not possible welfare subjects. But the distinction between aesthetic and prudential value also holds in the case of lives, which are capable of bearing both. Suppose that one or another of the foregoing accounts identifies the aesthetically valuable features of a life. From the fact that your life possesses these features to a high degree we plainly may not conclude that you are faring well. This is not (or not only) because a prudential assessment of your life is broader in its scope, taking into account conditions, such as illness or poverty, which are likely to be irrelevant from the aesthetic point of view. Although this much is true, stressing the point would leave the impression that the aesthetic value of a life is one determinant, among others, of its prudential value. The differences between the two dimensions of value, however, run much deeper than that. Knowing that your life has a high degree of aesthetic value does not just fail to tell us the full story about your level of well-being—it tells us none of the story.

Imagine that you have come to the end of a life in which you have striven to exemplify some standard of aesthetic excellence—say, one which prizes a particular kind of unity or a balance among component interests or pursuits. Looking back on this life, you are asking yourself whether you have anything to regret in it. One answer you might give is that, had you the opportunity to live it over, you might attach less importance to these aesthetic considerations, which you now regard as having been constraining and somewhat stultifying. Perhaps you think you should have taken more risks, or had more fun, or just that you should have been less grimly determined to score high on this particular scale. Whatever the details of your retrospective assessment, it is made from a standpoint distinct from the aesthetic, since what is up for debate is the proper place for the aesthetic in the conduct of your life. Abstractly, what you are now asking yourself is not how your life could have gone better from the aesthetic point of view (the problem is not that you chose the wrong standard); instead, you are asking yourself how it might have gone better for you, how it might have delivered more to you, had it been less devoted to that point of view.

It is therefore one thing for your life to contain features which augment its aesthetic value and quite another for it to be going well for you. Of course, if you have taken on the project of living an aesthetically valuable life then we should expect your success or failure in that endeavour to bear on your well-being. But the same will hold for all of your other projects: while success in one's projects is arguably an important source of welfare, scoring high in aesthetic value, just considered by itself, makes no independent contribution.

Perfectionist value. To say that something has this sort of value is to say that it is a good instance or specimen of its kind, or that it exemplifies the excellences characteristic of its particular nature. The scope of perfectionist evaluation is therefore at least as broad as that of aesthetic evaluation, since it extends to any object, natural or artificial, which can be located in an appropriate species or kind. Although the two modes of value are often near kin (we commonly find excellence appealing and praise it in aesthetic terms), the perfection of a thing is clearly a different matter from its beauty or nobility: a slug or a piece of kitsch may be a paragon of its kind despite being ugly or vulgar.

As in the aesthetic case, however, what is to count as a virtue or excellence in a thing will be determined by the kind of thing it is. A perfectionist assessment of a life is therefore likely to employ standards derived from the species to which the subject of that life belongs.[7] The derivation might take something like the following form.[8] We begin by seeking the essential characteristics of creatures of the species in question—what it is that identifies them as the particular kind of creatures they are. These will then be the characteristics whose possession at an exemplary level makes an individual member of the species a particularly good specimen of that kind. The traits or abilities so selected will count as personal excellences, conferring perfectionist value on their bearers. In our own case we might imagine that certain cognitive abilities would

---

[7] It seems unlikely that lives, abstracted from the kinds of organisms whose lives they are, themselves form a natural kind.

[8] I have adapted this account from Hurka 1993.

be included among the essential characteristics of humankind, in which case having a well-developed capacity for abstract thought or computation would score high on the perfectionist scale.

Like prudential (and aesthetic) value, perfectionist value needs a theory—an account of its nature capable of yielding operational criteria for its application. However, even in the absence of such a theory the distinction between prudential and perfectionist value is clear enough. Once again, you can easily imagine yourself, at the end of your life, taking pride in your high level of self-development but none the less wishing that you had got more out of your life, that it had been more rewarding or fulfilling, and thinking that it might have gone better for you had you devoted less energy to perfecting your talents and more to just hanging out or diversifying your interests. Whatever we are to count as excellences for creatures of our nature, they will raise the perfectionist value of our lives regardless of the extent of their payoff for us. There is therefore no logical guarantee that the best human specimens will also be the best off, or that their underdeveloped rivals will not be faring better. Like aesthetic value, the perfectionist value of a life is conceptually independent of how well it is going for its owner.

Ethical value. Under its broadest construal, the realm of the ethical is identical to that of the practical; in this sense it comprehends every mode of value relevant to the question of how we should conduct our lives, including the prudential, the aesthetic, and the perfectionist. In the modern era, however, the ethical domain has come to be understood in a more restricted way, so that it isolates those practical considerations which have to do with the impact of our choices on the lives of others. In this narrower and more social sense, which is the one I shall follow recent practice in adopting, the ethical value of a life is sharply distinct from its prudential value, since the welfare of others will be directly relevant to determining the former but not the latter. In common parlance we mark this distinction whenever we lament the ills which befall upright and decent folk, or the prosperity of the cunning and ruthless. Philosophers have, of course, long dreamed of showing that morality and self-interest coincide. But even if, contrary to all appearances, they were to succeed in this, they would thereby demonstrate only the extensional congruence of the two modes of value, not their conceptual identity.

The distinction between prudential and ethical value is an organizing principle of this inquiry, since one of its aims is to determine the ethical value of welfare itself. This question can be put in the following way. Suppose that in the normative order ethics precedes politics, i.e. that the norms specific to the political domain are grounded in deeper and more general ethical norms. Suppose further that in the structure of an ethical theory the good precedes the right, i.e. that the point of rights and duties, justice and fairness, is to advance and promote a good which is both identifiable and justifiable without reference to any of these notions. In that case the central and basic question of ethics becomes: What is this good? And one possible answer to this question is: welfare. If this is the right answer, as welfarists think it is, then prudential value is the sole ultimate bearer of ethical value, the only thing whose promotion needs, and admits of, no further ethical justification. Of course, it is no easy matter to show that this is the right answer, or even that we are asking the right question. But neither question nor answer would even be intelligible were ethical and prudential value not conceptually distinct.

Detaching these various dimensions of the value of a life leaves us with a rather disorderly conceptual landscape full of open questions: in general, the fact that a life has a high degree of one mode of value entails nothing whatever about is score along any other dimension. This is not to say that there will be no interesting or important material tendencies, but only that there are no conceptual connections among the various modes. This partition into distinct realms of value will play an important argumentative role in our assessment of theories of welfare, where from time to time it will need to be amplified. For the moment it is enough to note that prudential value is unique in determining how worthwhile a life is, or how well it is going, from the perspective of the individual whose life it is. We must therefore be wary of confusing well-being with some other measure of the quality of a life. Even the best constitutive account of a different dimension of value cannot be a descriptively adequate theory of welfare.

2

Welfare and Subjectivity

MODELS of the good life (for human beings) are as old as philosophy itself. In the western tradition extending from the Greeks to the present day, ideals which have attracted support have invoked a wide variety of concepts: pleasure, happiness, the satisfaction of desires or preferences, the fulfilment of needs, the achievement of aims or objectives, the development of capacities or potentialities, the maintenance of normal functioning, living a form of life appropriate to one's nature, and doubtless many others besides. Out of this array our aim is to locate the account which works best specifically as a theory of prudential value, the one which is most faithful to our ordinary concept of welfare and our ordinary experience.

Scrutinizing all of the possible candidates piecemeal would be a tedious and time-consuming process. Our critical task will therefore be greatly simplified if we can sort them into some appropriate categories. But which categories? The mistake to avoid here is grouping together theories by means of features which turn out, upon further analysis, to be trivial or irrelevant, since we will then be able to draw no conclusions about the category as a whole. What we need are lines of division which are *salient*, by virtue of identifying features of competing theories which bear directly (whether positively or negatively) on their descriptive adequacy. Such lines of division will themselves have explanatory power, since they will always group together theories which share some common advantage, or suffer from some common disadvantage, *vis-à-vis* their rivals. We will therefore be able to say of particular candidate theories that they are genuinely viable, or utterly unworkable, because they fall on this side of the line or that.

There may well be many salient distinctions to be drawn among theories of welfare, and many ways of combining these distinctions into an overall taxonomy. My preferred scheme begins by sorting all of the candidates into two mutually exclusive and jointly exhaustive categories: the *subjective* and the *objective*. I claim salience for this line of division because I believe there to be an interpretation of the subjective/objective distinction such that subjectivity turns out to be a necessary condition of success in a theory of welfare. If I am right then objective theories can be ruled out of consideration as a category, all of them inadequate precisely because they are objective.

This substantive thesis is, of course, highly contentious. The business of defending it will get underway in the latter part of this chapter and continue through the next. First, however, we need to develop the appropriate interpretation of subjectivity and objectivity. I invoke these notions as a means of classifying theories of welfare only with great reluctance. Along with such other persistent offenders as the real and the natural, the concept of the subjective is one of the most treacherous in the philosopher's lexicon. In different contexts and for different purposes the realm of the subjective has been delineated by means of a number of features: privacy, immediacy, incorrigibility, unverifiability, unquantifiability, relativity, arbitrariness, reliance on judgement or intuition, and immunity to rational arbitration. Since each of these features is logically distinct from all of the others, each would draw a different boundary between the subjective and the objective. None of the resultant lines of division, however, would answer to our purpose since none would be salient for theories of welfare. The problem is that, while each of these features applies to some subjective phenomena, none of them is essential to the subjective as such. What we need is a conception of subjectivity which is more primitive than any of these, one which is capable of explaining their range of application and its limitations.

2.1 SUBJECTIVE AND OBJECTIVE

Abstractly, the subjective is that which pertains to, or is characteristic of, subjects. What then is a subject? In what seems its philosophically primary sense, a subject is anything capable of conscious states or processes. Consciousness, in the sense in which it is definitive of subjectivity, must be understood very broadly so as to include not only such undeniably cognitive processes as thought or deliberation, but also perception, sensation, emotion, memory, desire, imagination, dreaming, appetite, and all of their psychic kin. This very liberal conception of consciousness must therefore be distinguished from the stricter one often utilized by psychologists and philosophers, in which it is attributed only to creatures (like us) capable of language or self-awareness. It is difficult to explain this restriction of consciousness to the human case, perhaps with the grudging admission of a few higher apes and cetaceans, as anything other than plain unadulterated anthropocentrism. The movement of thought seems to go something like this: there are forms of cognition, involving the use of linguistic symbols, which (as far as we know) are unique to us; the capacity for these processes therefore provides a useful way of delineating us from (most, if not all) other animals; a convenient way of labelling this boundary is to say that we are blessed with consciousness and they are not; therefore, consciousness requires the capacity for language.[1]

In any case, it is obvious that there is a much broader, common-sense notion of consciousness which merely requires the capacity for any form of experience, however rudimentary it might be. In this sense, a creature with no mode of awareness more developed than some variety of inner or outer sense (vision, hearing, smell, pleasure and pain, etc.) will still count as being conscious; this will certainly include many, perhaps even most, animals. Under this conception, the capacity for sophisticated cognitive processes is clearly not necessary in order to count as being conscious; the only way to fail to be conscious is to be entirely unconscious. On the other hand, this capacity is also not sufficient for consciousness, since these processes can themselves be unconscious. Depending on how demanding we choose to be about cognition, computers might count as cognitive without being conscious.

Although we are intimately familiar with the several modes of consciousness known to us, it is desperately difficult to isolate what they all have in common. On the one hand, consciousness seems

[1] The habit seems unbreakable even for those who profess to know better. For instance, Griffin 1976 begins his exploration of animal awareness in ch. 1 by equating consciousness with the having of any form at all of mental experience, and then goes on to devote most of the rest of the book to the question of animal communication. Likewise, J. R. Lucas (Kenny *et al.* 1972, ch. 8) briefly defends the possibility of consciousness without language, and then proceeds to talk at length about language.

to be an intrinsic mark of the mental.[2] On the other hand, any frontal approach to characterizing its phenomenology falls quickly into unilluminating circularity, by relying on such cognate notions as experience or awareness. We here find ourselves at one of those maddening philosophical junctures where we are perfectly certain we know what we are talking about but can find no adequate means of expressing it. We therefore resort to metaphor: what is both common and peculiar to all conscious states or processes is that there is a way they are from the inside, for the individual who has them, which is not shared by any external observer. It is to this internality of experience that Thomas Nagel points when he says that 'an organism has conscious mental states if and only if there is something that it is like to *be* that organism—something it is like *for* the organism'.[3] Alternatively: a creature has conscious states if and only if there is some way the world seems to it from the inside, some way it looks or sounds or feels.

However difficult it may be to provide helpful characterizations of the mental, we recognize it readily enough when we are confronted by its absence. We know what it is for our lives to be interrupted by periods of unconsciousness—in dreamless sleep or under anaesthesia or as the result of an injury—during which all inner and outer sense is shut off. We know what it is for unconscious states, such as beliefs or desires, to be brought to the level of recognition and acknowledgement through the therapeutic process. We also know the difference between those responses to external stimuli which are consciously mediated and those which are not. When my knee is tapped in the right spot my lower leg jerks up, whether I feel the tap or not. This reflex can therefore be intact when I am utterly unconscious. But if I grab hold of something hot I will immediately let go only if I can feel it burning me; here my response requires awareness of the pain. Finally, we can also distinguish, if only in a rough way, between those creatures which are capable of some form of consciously mediated perception and those which are not. We know, for instance, that the bee

[2] This connection is not undermined by the acknowledgement in the previous paragraph that some mental processes, such as beliefs and desires, can be unconscious. Unconscious processes are parasitic on conscious ones in two ways: (1) no process can count as mental if it is always and everywhere unconscious, and (2) no creature can count as having a mind if all of its processes are unconscious.

[3] Nagel 1979, 166.

can see and smell the flower; there is therefore a way the flower seems to it. On the other hand, though sunflowers track the sun efficiently they neither see nor feel it. Most animals have some form of consciousness, and no plant has any. But the threshold between the two domains is indistinct; we will probably be uncertain where we should locate molluscs and worms.

Having some conscious states or processes is necessary for being a subject. But is it sufficient? Subjects are normally more than random collections of scattered mental states; their lives additionally display both unity and continuity. Unity is the integration of discrete psychic activities into a single stream of consciousness or mental life; continuity is the persistence of unity over time. Philosophers have offered various accounts of what it is for different experiences (whether simultaneous or successive) to belong to the same subject. Some have sought the unifying bond in the physical organism, while others have rested content with the internal relations among the experiences themselves, or taken refuge in the postulate of a mysterious featureless ego.[4] Whatever the right account might be, our common notion of an individual subject is of a unique, enduring centre of consciousness. Like consciousness itself, this integration of a mental life is notoriously ineffable; the more we seek it the more it eludes us. Once again it is most noticeable in its absence. One striking form of internal disunity manifests itself in the phenomenon of multiple personality; here we may be doubtful whether we are dealing with one subject or many. Some forms of amnesia are capable of eroding the integrity of the self in a different way: by erasing the connecting links of long-term memory, they force their victims into perpetual reinvention of their life narrative.[5] For those of us lucky enough to be normal, these pathologies serve to remind us of the extent to which the unity and continuity of the self is a structural precondition of our ordinary lives which we need never raise to the level of reflection.

By virtue of interacting with the world around me—processing information about it, having designs upon it, being elated or disappointed by it—the particular individual who is me occupies a unique psychic position within that world. The centre of my

---

[4] These accounts have usually been intended to explicate the identity of persons. Although not all subjects are persons, some theories of personal identity might apply as well to the wider category.
[5] Oliver Sacks describes such a case in Sacks 1985, ch. 12.

perceptual, cognitive, and experiential field is the place from which I apprehend the world—literally, my point of view within it. Having some such standpoint may not be a necessary feature of subjectivity. Nagel has vividly depicted some of the mechanisms by which we can attempt to transcend our own perspective, aspiring to 'the view from nowhere'.[6] For all we know, there may exist subjects who normally operate in this transcendent mode; certainly doing so is part of one standard conception of a deity. However, even limited degrees of transcendence are difficult for us to maintain, and they are quite beyond the powers of the non-human subjects with which we are acquainted. Normally for us, and invariably for them, subjectivity is the view not from nowhere but from now-here.

The unity and continuity of an individual subject cannot be captured without resort to personal indexicals: my identity consists in the fact that some set or series of experiences are all *mine*. Likewise, the point of view of an individual subject cannot be described without resort to spatial and temporal indexicals: my perspective is the view from *here* and *now*. Of these three categories of indexical, the subjective or personal appear to be the deepest. While there seems to be no way to explicate 'I' in terms of 'here' and 'now', it is plausible to think of these spatial and temporal indicators as ultimately egocentric, marking the where and when of the subjects who employ them.[7] To take this line is to find the most primitive perspective—the one which serves as the reference point for all others—in the subject's point of view.

However this may be, the notion of being the centre or locus of an integrated and enduring mental life gives us an adequate working account of what it is to be a subject. In its philosophically primary sense, the subjective is then that which pertains in some essential way to a subject. But which way? The *Oxford English Dictionary* tells us that 'subjective' means, among other things, 'proceeding from or taking place within the subject; having its source in the mind; belonging to the conscious life'. Suppose we begin with the idea of the subjective as taking place within the subject. We are still, of course, in the grip of metaphor: the subject is not literally a location within which subjective things happen. But the most basic category of the subjective seems to embrace the

---

[6] In Nagel 1986, *passim*.   [7] See McGinn 1983, 17.

states of consciousness which belong to or constitute subjects. It is by virtue of being parts of my mental life that my memory of that summer in Provence, the dream I had last night, and the ache I feel right now in my lower back are all subjective. It is unclear whether there can be conscious states belonging to no subject whatever, but if so then they would not be (literally) subjective. The mental provides the content or substance of the subjective, but it is not identical to it.

The core of subjectivity thus consists of states attributable only to subjects. From there, however, it is but a short step to classifying as subjective certain features which common sense ascribes not to subjects themselves but to the world around them. In the first extension of the category, the feature so ascribed retains an implicit or explicit reference to the subject in question. The classic instance is external perception. As a self-conscious exercise, I can restrict myself to describing the contents of my perceptual states in purely phenomenological terms: what I am occurrently seeing, hearing, feeling, etc. But it is much more natural to speak of the way the world seems to me: the way it looks, sounds, feels, etc. In taking this step I move beyond merely reporting my inner life to characterizing the world outside me; I claim that it looks sunny, sounds noisy, feels hot. But the properties which I thereby attribute to the world remain anchored in my experience of it, by virtue of describing the ways it appears *to me*. The latent indexical, on which I will quickly fall back in the event of a challenge to my attribution, is the sure sign of the subjectivity of appearances.

The final movement away from the interior of experience carries us beyond appearance to reality, beyond the ways the world merely seems to us to the ways we take it actually to be. Some of the properties which common sense ascribes to the world seem to have little or nothing to do with the peculiar nature of our experience. Thus it is plausible to think that water would still be composed of hydrogen and oxygen even if our psychological constitution had been radically other than it is—indeed, even if we had never existed at all. But other features of the world seem to depend much more closely on the way it standardly appears to us. In the hands of philosophers in the empiricist tradition commonplace observations such as these have been worked up into a full-blown metaphysical duality, a division of the natural features of the world into two distinct inventories. Colin McGinn has drawn the contrast nicely:

There are various ways in which the mind represents the world. It is legitimate to enquire, of any way in which the world is mentally represented, whether that way is subjective or objective in nature: that is, to enquire whether the world is so represented because of the specific constitution of the representing mind or because the world as it is independently of the mind contains a feature which demands representation. Which aspects of our view of reality have their source in our subjective make-up and which reflect reality as it is in itself?[8]

In the latter category philosophers have placed what they like to call primary qualities: shape, size, mass, motion, number, etc. By contrast, secondary qualities, those which 'have their source [at least partly] in our subjective make-up', standardly include the perceptual properties of colour, sound, taste, smell, and feel. Where the latter are concerned, we have now obviously shifted to the subjective as (in the terms of the *OED*) that which proceeds from, or has its source in, the mind. An aspect of the world which is subjective in this further sense is not a conscious state of some subject, nor is it merely the way the world seems to some subject. However, despite being a state or property of the world it remains ultimately mind-dependent, since it rests on features which may be peculiar to our psychological (or physiological) constitution. As John McDowell has put it:

Secondary qualities are qualities not adequately conceivable except in terms of certain subjective states, and thus subjective themselves in a sense that that characterization defines. In the natural contrast, a primary quality would be objective in the sense that what it is for something to have it can be adequately understood otherwise than in terms of dispositions to give rise to subjective states.[9]

The realm of the subjective, in its philosophically primary sense, thus begins with experience, moves on to appearance, and ends with mind-dependent reality. It is the third stage of this progression which is germane to our purposes: if welfare is subjective then it is by virtue of being mind-dependent. However, what might be involved in this form of subjectivity is rather better understood in the classic cases of secondary qualities. To say that shape and size are primary qualities is to say that an account of their nature need make no reference to the perceptual experience of any particular subject or class of subjects. Contrariwise, to say that colour

---

[8] Ibid. 10.   [9] McDowell 1985, 113.

and sound are secondary qualities is to say that they are powers or dispositions on the part of objects with certain primary qualities to arouse certain experiences in certain circumstances on the part of creatures with a certain perceptual apparatus.[10] The place-holding 'certains' in this general formula will need to be filled out in different ways for each allegedly secondary quality. In the case of the colour red, say, the appropriate completion would doubt-less point to surface features which cause objects to reflect light of a particular wavelength, components of our optical equipment which render it capable of discriminating this wavelength from others, ambient conditions of lighting and such, and the experi-ence which we call 'seeing red'. The result will be an account which will treat being red as a disposition to evoke this experience in normal human observers under standard perceptual conditions.

The case of colour serves to illustrate that a subjective analysis of any natural property will need to furnish values for four dis-tinct variables: (1) some objective characteristic of things by virtue of which they evoke (2) some mode of experience on the part of (3) some reference group of subjects under (4) some set of normal conditions. Where perceptual properties are concerned the objec-tive characteristic will be physical, the reference group will be human beings with the standard sensory apparatus, the experience will be some mode of perception, and the normal conditions will be those which ensure the absence of distortion. But the same four slots will be filled rather differently in the cases of those non-perceptual properties which have also seemed plausible candidates for subjective analysis, properties such as boring, tempting, sub-lime, and funny.

2.2 VALUES AND SUBJECTIVITY

It is, however, in the domain of values that the notion of subjec-tivity has been most freely deployed, and most frequently abused. The claim that some particular category of values is subjective has been variously interpreted to mean that ascriptions of them to

---

[10] The classical source for this analysis of secondary qualities is Locke 1975, Book II, ch. 8. For a simple exposition of Locke's views for the special case of colour, see Landesman 1989, ch. 2. For an account of the distinction between subjective and objective analyses of colour, see Hardin 1988, ch. 2.

objects are arbitrary, variable, capricious, non-cognitive, unverifiable, and heaven knows what else. But in the strict and proper sense of subjectivity it only means one thing: that, like colours, values of this kind are mind-dependent.

Values have been prime candidates for subjective analysis partly because of their apparent motivational force. Since this has also been thought to distinguish them from the more inert natural properties, their psychological source has generally been sought not in perception or cognition but in some mode of affect. Just which mode, however, is a matter on which the several varieties of subjective theory for any given dimension of value are likely to part company. Since at this stage we are seeking a general characterization of the subjective which will apply to all possible theories of this sort, we need a neutral category which abstracts from these differences. One possible candidate, frequently resorted to in the literature, is *feeling*.[11] While this suggestion seems to be in the right general area, I think we will do better if we adapt to our purposes a proposal advanced by R. B. Perry:

It is characteristic of living mind to be *for* some things and *against* others. . . . To be 'for' or 'against' is to view with favor or disfavor; it is a bias of the subject toward or away from. . . . This duality appears in many forms, such as liking and disliking, desire and aversion, will and refusal, or seeking and avoiding. It is to this all-pervasive characteristic of the motor-affective life, this *state, act, attitude or disposition of favor or disfavor*, to which we propose to give the name of *'interest'*.[12]

Perry's explication of the notion of an interest is useful because of its emphasis on this distinctive positive/negative polarity.[13] Since values admit of the same polarity (things can be good or bad, right or wrong, beautiful or ugly, and so on), the psychological processes to which Perry points look to be likely materials for constructing a subjective theory. Furthermore, because Perry's notion of an interest generalizes over the various forms this polarity can take,

[11] See, for instance, Moore 1947, 55 ff. However, Moore also considers subjective theories which rely on cognitive states; see ibid. 74 ff. Broad 1971, ch. 9, which deals only with moral values, prefers the generic 'moral feeling' (190), which is intended to embrace sensations, emotions, and desires.

[12] Perry 1926, 115 (emphasis in original).

[13] Cf. ibid. 230 ff. Broad also emphasizes the polarity of 'moral feelings'; see Broad 1971, 191.

and the various realms of value in which it might be manifested, it seems well suited to our purposes.

Despite these evident attractions, however, we will do well to resist Perry's specific terminological proposal. Like subjectivity itself, the notion of interest is dangerously ambiguous: on the one hand my interests are the same as my concerns (what I am interested in), while on the other my interest (or self-interest) is the same as my welfare. While a theory connecting welfare with interests (in the former sense) could be illuminating,[14] one connecting it with interest (in the latter sense) would be a boring tautology. If we once begin speaking the language of interest, it is unlikely that we will be able to resist sliding from one sense to the other, in an effort to combine the significance of the first linkage with the certainty of the second. I am not suggesting that Perry himself was guilty of this conceptual shift; as far as I know, he consistently equated interests with concerns. But his project was an interest theory of value in general, where the fallacy is much less tempting. In the particular case of prudential value, we run too great a risk of trivializing subjective theories if we choose to define them in terms of the relation they construct between welfare and interest. With one slippery item already in our lexicon we cannot afford another.

We will do better to pick up another option offered by Perry and speak instead of *attitudes*.[15] The psychological notion of an attitude has preserved some of the flavour of its older physical sense, in which it indicates a bodily posture or orientation. If I have an attitude toward something then I am, figuratively, inclined one way or the other with respect to it. Speaking of attitudes thus enables us to capture Perry's notion of 'a bias of the subject toward or away from'. Generally speaking, we may say that I have an attitude toward something when the thing matters to me, or I care about it, or it is an object of concern to me, or I mind it, or (in the more formal psychological terminology) it is valenced for me. My attitude is positive (what philosophers used to call a pro-attitude) if I favour the thing or am favourably disposed toward it, negative (a con-attitude) if I view it unfavourably.

[14] For an account which explicates the notion of harm in terms of interests, see Feinberg 1984, ch. 1.
[15] As does Moore, in 1947, 96, 98, 138; in this discussion, however, he explicitly includes cognitive attitudes such as belief. However, see Moore 1922, 254, where he equates attitudes with feelings or emotions.

While this notion of an attitude or concern is still rather vague, it will suffice for the purpose of characterizing subjective theories of value as a group. As in the case of natural properties, a subjective analysis of some particular mode of value will need to fill in four slots: (1) some objective characteristic of things by virtue of which they evoke (2) some attitude on the part of (3) some reference group of subjects under (4) some set of normal conditions. There is much room for discretion in specifying all four variables. The preferred characteristic may be some way the object looks or sounds, or some function it has, or some aspect of its nature. The selected attitude might be one of wanting, or liking, or enjoying, or approving. The favoured subjects might be individual human beings, or particular societies, or the entire species, or all sentient creatures. Finally, the conditions under which the responses of these subjects are authoritative might be corrected so as to remedy factual errors, or partiality, or irrationality. Since there are many possible combinations of these various options, there are many possible varieties of subjectivism about values.[16] Furthermore, there is no guarantee that a theory well designed for one mode of value will be applicable to any other; the most plausible form of subjective theory might well be different for each dimension.

Of the four dimensions of value distinguished in the previous chapter, two are of special interest in our inquiry. When we come to ask whether welfare is the only thing which should be treated as a basic value in an ethical theory, we may need to decide whether ethical values are subjective or objective. However, this issue can safely be postponed for a while; for the moment we need concern ourselves only with the shape a subjective theory might take for the special case of prudential value. Here there seems only one plausible choice of authoritative subject. Since the prudential value of my life is its value *for me*, it seems reasonable to expect that the attitudes or inclinations which will figure in a constitutive account of my well-being will be mine. In the case of other allegedly subjective properties, such as colours, our reference point is likely to be normal human beings, or the set of creatures whose perceptual apparatus is recognizably like ours and in good working

---

[16] In his typical fashion, Broad catalogues some of the main alternatives in Broad 1971, ch. 9.

order, or whatever. Unlike colours, however, prudential 'properties' such as beneficial and harmful contain relativizing indexicals. In order to preserve this relativity, it looks as though a subjective theory will need to connect my welfare with some psychological processes in me.

As a first approximation, therefore, we may say that a theory treats welfare as subjective if it makes it depend, at least in part, on some (actual or hypothetical) attitude on the part of the welfare subject. More precisely, a subjective theory will map the polarity of welfare onto the polarity of attitudes, so that being well off will depend (in some way or other) on having a favourable attitude toward one's life (or some of its ingredients), while being badly off will require being unfavourably disposed toward it. Likewise, something can make me better off on this sort of account only if I have (or would have under the appropriate circumstances) a positive attitude (of the appropriate sort) toward it. These formulae are deliberately indeterminate, leaving room for different subjective theories to fill them out in different ways. But even at this preliminary stage two cautions are in order. The first is that a theory is subjective if it treats my having a favourable attitude toward something as a necessary condition of the thing being beneficial for me. It need not also treat it as a sufficient condition, and most subjective theories will not do so. Just as subjective analyses of colour are likely to regard it as the product of an interaction between a perceiving subject and a perceived object, subjective analyses of welfare are also likely to be relational or dispositional. The second caution is that this formula applies only to direct or immediate benefits: those whose contribution to my well-being is not dependent on their further consequences. It is a commonplace that some remote event, such as the death of a distant and wealthy relation, can be instrumentally beneficial to me without my regarding it favourably, or even being aware of its occurrence. A subjective theory tells us only that this cannot be true of the intrinsic sources of my well-being.

Subjective theories make our well-being logically dependent on our attitudes of favour and disfavour. Objective theories deny this dependency. On an objective theory, therefore, something can be (directly and immediately) good for me though I do not regard it favourably, and my life can be going well despite my failing to have any positive attitude toward it. Again it is important to note that objective theories do not merely deny the sufficiency of a reference to my attitudes in an analysis of my well-being, for most subjective theories would join in this denial. The crucial differentiating question is the necessity of such a reference. To this question subjective and objective theories give contradictory answers; the two categories are therefore both mutually exclusive and jointly exhaustive.

It might be wondered whether this strict duality is a happy result. Would we not do better to array candidate theories along a spectrum in terms of their particular mix of subjective and objective ingredients? The pure cases, if there are any, would then define the two endpoints of the continuum.[17] No doubt such a scheme is possible and it might well be useful for some purposes. However, it would not be particularly useful for our purpose. For one thing, we would lose the analogy between subjective theories of welfare and subjective theories of perceptual properties. In the latter case we can make sense of saying that within the realm of subjectivity some phenomena (such as dreams or hallucinations) are more mind-dependent than others (such as colours or textures). But saying this is not incompatible with drawing a sharp boundary between the subjective and the objective, since it will still be true of every property that it is either mind-dependent (to some extent or other) or it is not. Of course, there has to be a good reason to draw a sharp boundary and to locate it just here. In the case of perceptual properties that reason will be metaphysical; the boundary will be salient in some picture of the way the world is.

These considerations apply equally in the case of welfare. Working with a simple on/off dichotomy will not prevent us from attending to further differences among competing theories; some subjective theories may make welfare more mind-dependent, or less world-dependent, than others. However, it will locate these differences within the class of subjective theories, rather than between them and objective theories. Every candidate theory will either make welfare mind-dependent (to some degree and in some respect) or it will not. Now of course no reason has yet been given for maintaining the analogy between welfare and its perceptual counterparts; mere symmetry or tidiness is scarcely decisive. In the end the

[17] This suggestion is made in Penz 1986, 8–9.

analogy will be worthwhile only if productive, and it will be productive only if it reveals features in theories of welfare which are important rather than trivial, deep rather than superficial. But that is just to say that in the case of welfare the final defence of a sharp subjective/objective duality must be its salience. And that defence must wait until the next section.

Before setting out to construct a conception of subjectivity around the notion of a subject, I claimed that the result would be the philosophically primary sense of this multiply ambiguous expression. We are now in a position to appreciate wherein its primacy lies: it both underlies and explains all of the further marks of the subjective. The secondary conceptions of subjectivity are all generated by the same process of over-generalization: we begin by selecting some characteristic which belongs only to certain specific mental processes and then attribute it, first to the mental as such, and then to all mind-dependent features of the world. Suppose, for example, that we select twinges or after-images as our paradigmatic mental states; we will then think of the subjective as inherently private and perhaps also as incorrigible. In the same manner, if we fasten on tastes or whims the subjective will seem inherently variable and personal; if we are thinking of moods and emotions it will seem vague and unquantifiable; if we have aesthetic judgements in mind it will seem disputable or undecidable. Of course, some regions of subjectivity in the world have some of these characteristics; some may even have all of them. None of these derivative features, however, is implied by subjectivity itself.

The best way to keep this fact firmly in mind is to remember the analogy with perceptual properties. It is, of course, unclear that any subjective analysis of these 'secondary qualities' is correct; objectivism has its defenders in this domain, just as it does for welfare. But suppose that the best theory about the nature of colour or sound or texture turns out to be subjective, as might well be the case. In our ordinary lives these properties of things display a high degree of inter-subjective uniformity, corrigibility by public procedures, discriminability, and measurability. The discovery, or decision, that perceptual properties are mind-dependent could not suddenly make them private or capricious or unstable. Should welfare also turn out to be mind-dependent we need not fear these implications in its case either.

There is one derivative sense of subjectivity which we must take special pains both to identify and to avoid. If we select dreams or hallucinations as our model mental processes, then we will be likely to think of the subjective as the realm of mere appearance. This fallacious implication is encouraged by philosophers who equate the objectivity of a property with its being 'part of the fabric of the world'.[18] What this must mean, if it means anything definite, is that the property in question is one of the aspects of the world which is mind-independent. But it is then perilously easy to conclude that only objective properties really belong to, or in, the world at all. It is this conflation of objectivity with reality which must be resisted. If colour is a subjective property then its existence is dependent on our psychological processes. However, since we have no reason to think that these processes are themselves less real than physical ones, the subjectivity of colour gives us no reason to deny its reality. The same obviously holds for welfare. To claim that welfare is subjective is to claim that it is mind-dependent—that and nothing more. It is not to suggest that it is in any legitimate sense unreal.

The conception of subjectivity which is philosophically primary enables us to divide theories of welfare into two rival camps. The choice of this particular sorting procedure is, of course, not original; indeed, it is virtually a platitude in the philosophical literature on welfare. My explication of the subjective/objective distinction for theories of welfare differs from similar accounts elsewhere chiefly in its reliance on the very plastic notion of an attitude, which makes it possible to generalize over the many varieties of subjective theory.[19] As it stands the line of division is still very rough and crude, but we will be able to add the necessary further refinements as we address particular instances of theories on both sides of it. First, however, we need some reason for thinking that it provides the right grid to be working with.

[18] The phrase is John Mackie's; see Mackie 1977, 15–16.
[19] Brink 1989 draws a very similar distinction: '*Subjective* theories of value claim that the components of a valuable life consist in or depend importantly on certain of an individual's psychological states. . . . By contrast . . . *objective* theories of value claim that what is intrinsically valuable neither consists in nor depends importantly on such psychological states' (220–1; emphasis in original). Like mine, Brink's dichotomy is exhaustive: every theory will be either subjective or objective. However, Brink uses the very broad notion of a psychological state, which includes items (such as perceptual states) lacking the positive/negative polarity typical of values. He also does not differentiate the several dimensions in which a life can be valuable; he thus draws no boundary between, for instance, prudential and perfectionist value.

2.3 THE CASE AGAINST OBJECTIVISM

As it applies to theories of welfare, the salience of the subjective/
objective distinction is certainly open to doubt.[20] Defending the
distinction as a working tool requires an argument showing that
either subjectivity or objectivity is in itself a *sine qua non* in a
theory of welfare. Such an argument, however, is now ready to
hand. It begins by recalling the distinction drawn in the previous
chapter among dimensions of value. There are many ways in which
a life can be a good life; being high in prudential value is only one
of them. What distinguishes welfare from all other modes of value
is its reference to the proprietor of the life in question: although
your life may be going well in many respects, it is prudentially
valuable only if it is going well *for you*.[21] This subject-relativity is
an essential feature of our ordinary concept of welfare. It does not
merely rest on the truism that all welfare is someone's welfare, the
welfare of some particular individual. If lives are the sorts of things
that can have perfectionist value then personal excellence is always
the excellence of some particular person, but the category of
perfectionist value is free of the relativizing indexicals which are
characteristic of well-being. Among the modes of value which can
belong to individual lives, welfare stands out by virtue of incorporating an internal reference to its bearer.

We have already established that no theory about the nature of
welfare can be faithful to our ordinary concept unless it preserves
its subject-relative or perspectival character.[22] It is not difficult to
see how a subjective theory is capable of satisfying this condition
of adequacy. Whatever their internal differences, the defining feature of all subjective theories is that they make your well-being
depend on your own concerns: the things you care about, attach
importance to, regard as mattering, and so on. What is crucial on

[20] Griffin 1986: 'So the distinction between objective and subjective, defined in
the common way that I have defined it, does not mark an especially crucial distinction. It would be better if these terms (at least in this sense) were put into retire-
ment' (33). For a critique of the subjective/objective grid, as it applies to values in
general, see Hare 1981, ch. 12, and 1985.
[21] The subject-relativity of welfare does not entail that a subject is an infallible
authority about the prudential value of her own life. Any descriptively adequate
theory of welfare must preserve the possibility of (at least some) first-person mistakes about welfare.
[22] I take Shelly Kagan to be making the same point in Kagan 1992, 185.

such an account is that you are the proprietor or manager of a set of attitudes, both positive and negative, toward the conditions of your life. It is these attitudes which constitute the standpoint from which these conditions can be assessed as good or bad *for you*. It follows on this sort of account that a welfare subject in the merely grammatical sense—an individual with a distinct welfare—must also be a subject in a more robust sense—the locus of a reasonably unified and continuous mental life. Prudential value is therefore perspectival because it literally takes the point of view of the subject. Welfare is subject-relative because it is subjective.

This connection which subjective theories claim to hold between the subject-relativity of welfare and its subjectivity is neither trivial nor analytic. All we are given by the concept of prudential value is its characteristically positional or perspectival character; the claim that this is rooted in its subjectivity is a substantive thesis, analogous to the equally substantive thesis that causation is a matter of regular succession. To see that perspective need not be ultimately subjective, consider the difference between two of our common systems of spatial ordering. When one thing is described as being to the left of another, the reference is to their relative positions within the perceptual field of an (imagined) observer; the one thing is further to *that subject's* left than the other. The perspective underlying our left/right ordering is therefore subjective. Contrast this with the perspective underlying our use of compass directions. When one thing is described as being to the north of another, the reference is to their positions relative to the earth's poles. Our north/south spatial ordering is perspectival (it makes no sense in spatial regions where the polar reference cannot be supplied), but it is not subjective.

The thesis that welfare is subjective is therefore not merely a reaffirmation of the fact that it is subject-relative; instead, it is a putative interpretation or explanation of this fact. Although this explanation seems initially promising, it could turn out to be mistaken, in which case we would need to look elsewhere for an account of the subject-relativity of welfare. But at least it is clear from the outset what sort of account subjective theories have to offer. Since objective theories exclude all reference to the subject's attitudes or concerns, they will have to supply some alternative account. It is for this reason that the subject-relativity of welfare constitutes a deep problem for any objective theory. Where theories of welfare are concerned, objectivity appears to impede descriptive adequacy.

The fact that it is so easy to construct a general case against objective theories is sufficient to demonstrate the salience of the subjective/objective distinction. It is also sufficient to defend working with a strict dichotomy rather than a continuum. The duality isolates objective theories as a group, since they alone treat welfare as entirely mind-independent. If this is a fatal flaw in them, then the only contenders to survive the first stage of our inquiry will be the various forms of subjective theory. We will then be free in the later stages to seek further salient distinctions among these remaining accounts.

However, it would be premature to count objective theories out at this point. The case raised against them is not a proof of their inadequacy; it is merely a challenge which they must meet. For all we yet know, some version of an objective theory will be capable of meeting the challenge. Although objective theories are, by their very nature, deprived of one promising strategy—reference to the subjective point of view—there may well be others open to them which will suffice to do the job. Since there seems to be no way of compiling an exhaustive catalogue of possible objectivist strategies, a decisive refutation of these theories as a group seems out of the question. However, the presumptive case against them would be considerably strengthened if the main strategies which they have tended to pursue could all be shown to fail. This will be the task of the next chapter.

3

Objective Theories

By their very nature, objective theories of welfare share a common problem: without recourse to the subjective point of view they must somehow account for the perspectival character of prudential value. What remains to be determined is whether any such theory has the resources to meet this challenge. Our next task should therefore be straightforward: we just look at some of the main types of objective account to see how they handle the problem, and decide whether any of their strategies is successful. Alas, matters are not so simple. Although it is easy to find philosophers who count themselves as objectivists about welfare, it is surprising how few of them have anything like a genuine theory to offer. Recall the distinction, set out in the first chapter, between the nature of welfare and its sources. We are seeking an explication of the former, not merely a list or inventory of the latter. Yet such a list is all that most objectivists give us.[1]

A good example of this tendency can be found in the work of John Finnis.[2] Finnis plainly regards himself as an objectivist about welfare (at least about human welfare, which is the only case he considers). In his view, there are seven 'basic aspects of human

---

[1] Which is why Derek Parfit refers to this option as the Objective List Theory (Parfit 1984, 4). But a list of virtues is not a theory of virtue, and a list of (human) goods is not a theory of welfare. At least one objectivist has registered scepticism about the possibility of such a theory; see Scanlon 1993, 190–1.

[2] Finnis 1980, chs. 3–4; 1983, ch. 2; Finnis, Boyle, and Grisez 1987, ch. 10. For another example see Brink 1989, ch. 8, where David Brink, after rejecting the main forms of subjective theory, promises to sketch a plausible objective theory but instead merely goes on to enumerate what he regards as 'the primary components of valuable lives' (231). Since these components ('reflective pursuit and realization of agents' reasonable projects and certain personal and social relationships') are likely to turn up on anyone's roster of the (intrinsic) sources of (human) well-being, including the subjectivist's, we still require a formal account of what it is, on an objective theory, for something to be such a source. At the level of lists, subjective and objective theories are indistinguishable.

well-being' (what we have been calling intrinsic sources of welfare) whose position as such is independent of our desires or inclinations, likes or dislikes.[3] The particular items on Finnis's list do not matter for our present purposes; what does matter is that he has no account to offer of what makes something (anything) a source of our welfare—what gains it a place on the list—if this does not depend on our attitudes or concerns. He therefore provides no formal theory which could stand as an alternative to subjectivism.[4] He also draws no distinction between something's making my life a better specimen of its kind and its making my life better for me, between perfectionist and prudential goods. Therefore, while he obviously thinks that basic ethical values are objective, it is not clear that the items on his list should be counted as sources of welfare at all. In any case, since he does not recognize the special problems faced by an objectivist account of welfare (as opposed to some other dimension of value), he offers no way of dealing with them.

For all we know, objectivists have many strategies available to them in trying to meet the challenge to their descriptive adequacy. However, I am aware of only two, one or the other of which has been resorted to by every objectivist who has constructed a genuine theory and, therefore, acknowledged the problem. The less promising of these options is straightforward and easily comprehended; it will be dealt with in the first section of this chapter. The other, which appears to constitute the objectivist's best hope, requires a little background. We will come to consider it in the final section.

3.1 THE PRIVATE OWNERSHIP THEORY

There is one gambit available to the objectivist, surely tempting in its simplicity, whose principal exponent was G. E. Moore.[5] As

---

[3] Finnis 1980, 72.

[4] What Finnis does say is that the status of each of his goods as a basic aspect of human well-being is self-evident (ibid. 64–9, 92). This seems to imply that we need not determine what welfare is before enumerating its principal intrinsic sources. If so, then Finnis is not merely failing to give us a theory; he is also denying the necessity (and the possibility?) of doing so.

[5] An account similar in many respects is defended by Andrew Moore in Moore 1991, ch. 5.

every philosophy student knows, Moore's primary concern in *Principia Ethica* was not with well-being but with a mode of intrinsic value which he regarded as simple and unanalysable. However, in the course of attempting to refute ethical egoism Moore was led to provide an analysis of the notion of individual welfare:

What, then, is meant by 'my own good'? In what sense can a thing be good *for me*? It is obvious, if we reflect, that the only thing which can belong to me, which can be *mine*, is something which is good, and not the fact that it is good. When, therefore, I talk of anything I get as 'my own good', I must mean either that the thing I get is good, or that my possessing it is good. In both cases it is only the thing or the possession of it which is *mine*, and not *the goodness* of that thing or that possession. . . . In short, when I talk of a thing as 'my own good' all that I can mean is that something which will be exclusively mine, as my own pleasure is mine (whatever be the various senses of this relation denoted by 'possession'), is also *good absolutely*; or rather that my possession of it is *good absolutely*.[6]

Moore's analysis reduces prudential value to two primitive elements: some dimension or other of intrinsic value and the relation of possession or ownership. Moore actually suggests two alternative ways in which these ingredients can be combined. On the first option something is (directly or immediately) good for me just in case (1) it is mine and (2) it is (intrinsically) good. On the second option clause (2) reads instead: the fact that it is mine is (intrinsically) good. Since keeping both of these alternatives in play will greatly complicate our discussion, and since the first is somewhat simpler to work with than the second, I shall henceforth restrict attention to it. As far as I can see, this narrowing of focus is in no way prejudicial to Moore's analysis, since both versions of it suffer from similar defects.[7]

On Moore's account my good consists of my ownership of something which is itself good. The mere fact that this account is reductive does not of course entail that it is also objective, since either of its components might contain a concealed reference to

[6] Moore 1903, 98–9 (emphasis in original).

[7] Similar, but not identical. The second option, but not the first, is vulnerable to a species of counterexample presented in Kagan 1992, 185. Suppose that (as some retributivists may believe) it is intrinsically good that the evil suffer. Further suppose that I am an evildoer who is suffering for my misdeeds. Then (1) this suffering is mine (a state of me), and (2) the fact that it is mine (i.e. the fact that I am suffering) is a good thing. From this it scarcely follows that it is good *for me*.

someone's attitudes or concerns. In order to ensure the objectivity of the private ownership theory, we therefore need to examine both components more closely. Concerning the objectivity of intrinsic value Moore had no doubt: 'to say that any one thing or state of things is *intrinsically good*, or *intrinsically bad*, or that one is *intrinsically better* than another, is . . . not the same thing as to say that any being or set of beings has towards it any mental attitude whatever—either an attitude of feeling, or of desiring, or of thinking something about it.'[8] But which mode of value did he think it was? To say that something is intrinsically valuable is to say that it is valuable in itself or for its own sake; the contrast is with instrumental value, which a thing has by virtue of leading to or bringing about something else which is valuable in its own right. This distinction between the ultimate bearers of value and their causal antecedents cuts across the four evaluative dimensions identified in the previous chapter; there seems every reason to think that prudential, aesthetic, perfectionist, and ethical value can all be possessed by things either intrinsically or instrumentally. Intrinsic value is therefore not itself a distinct dimension of value, which takes us back to our question: which mode of intrinsic value did Moore have in mind? In order to avoid self-defeating circularity, his analysis of well-being obviously cannot appeal to intrinsic prudential value. This then leaves us with three possibilities.

The choice of a unique option is determined by Moore's overall project in *Principia Ethica*. For Moore, an inventory of intrinsically valuable states of affairs is not merely of abstract interest; it is also the basic resource presupposed by the moral appraisal of conduct. The order of inquiry for ethics thus moves from the good to the right. While intrinsic value is (Moore believed) simple and unanalysable, the categories of practical ethics are definable in terms of it; roughly speaking, the right is that which brings about the good. It is clear therefore that the concept of intrinsic value which Moore had in mind is ethical: it is that category of final or ultimate value which we have a moral reason to produce, or whose production lends our actions moral value. His analysis of prudential value thus reduces it to ethical value (plus private ownership).[9]

Turning to the second component in his analysis, Moore clearly

[8] Moore 1947, 138 (emphasis in original).
[9] Moore also reduces aesthetic value to ethical value; see Moore 1903, 201–2. He shows no interest in perfectionist value.

does not intend possession to be thought of as a moral or juridical relation. Instead, he means merely to invoke the ordinary sense in which the attributes of an object belong to it, or in which my mental states or activities belong to me. Moore offers us no explication of this possessive relation, which may indeed be too primitive to be analysable, but it plays a crucial role in his account of individual well-being. For Moore, intrinsic value is an objective property possessed by certain objects or states of affairs. However, from the mere fact that some state of affairs is intrinsically good it plainly does not follow that it is good for me; there may be no connection at all, or no connection of the appropriate sort, between it and me. (Your appreciation of Mozart or the Grateful Dead does not in itself make me better off.) Ownership of the state by me—the fact that it is *mine*—is meant to supply the needed connection. Thus of the two components in Moore's account this is the one intended to capture the subject-relativity of welfare: in order for some intrinsically valuable state of affairs to be good *for* a subject, it must be a state *of* that subject.

The private ownership theory therefore begins by postulating that various states of the world have a special kind of intrinsic ethical value, and then identifies the sources of an individual's well-being with the subset of these valuable states which are in her vicinity or on her territory. The theory obviously owes us some formula for determining when a state of the world is to count as a state of some assignable subject. Although the task of providing such a formula will be far from straightforward,[10] let us assume that this purely technical problem has been solved. Suppose we agree, then, that some particular state belongs to some particular

[10] The danger here is of smuggling in an illicit reference to subjectivity. To use Moore's own example, my pleasure is mine by virtue of being a mental state belonging to the particular subject who is me. If the range of states of me is restricted to mental states then the subject-relativity of prudential value will once again be explained in terms of subjectivity. But if Moore relies instead on our ordinary (and vague) notion of possession then it will be difficult for him to delimit the states of the world which are (also) states of me. It seems intuitively obvious that my age, gender, physical health, place of residence, and so on, are all states of me. But is it a state of me that my children fare well? Is it a state of me that I live in a crime-free neighbourhood? That I am alive when human beings first reach the moon? That the world I inhabit also includes the Rocky Mountains? It is tempting to contain this relentless expansion of my self into the world around me by saying that a state of the world can count as a state of me only if it answers to some concern on my part. But this recourse would also be fatal to the objectivist enterprise.

individual. According to the private ownership theory, the fact that this state has intrinsic ethical value is both necessary and sufficient for it to make that individual better off.

Consider first the claim that it is sufficient. Which states the private ownership theory will lead us to count as ingredients of our welfare will of course depend on the list of intrinsic goods we bring to it. Suppose, as Moore himself once argued, that beauty belongs on that list.[11] In that case, the theory entails that beautiful people are necessarily better off, at least in one respect, than plain or ugly ones.[12] This seems a rather categorical claim even for the case of human beings, since it entirely ignores the importance (if any) which an individual might choose to place on this purely aesthetic feature. But worse is still to come. The private ownership theory will also entail that every beautiful object has its own welfare, since it will be true of each such object that an intrinsically valuable state is a state of it. This would be a spectacular failure of the test of generality; however vague the outer boundary of the class of welfare subjects may be, mountains and sunsets and string quartets do not belong even to its periphery.

Of course, the theory will not generate these destructive results if it is coupled with a more selective menu of intrinsic goods. Although Moore argued in *Principia* that the mere existence of beauty had some intrinsic value, even there he thought its value pretty negligible: 'By far the most valuable things, which we know or can imagine, are certain states of consciousness, which may be roughly described as the pleasures of human intercourse and the enjoyment of beautiful objects.'[13] A few years later, in *Ethics*, he went even further, making consciousness an indispensable ingredient of any intrinsically valuable state.[14] Now if the list of intrinsic goods is restricted to states of consciousness, or to organic wholes which include such states, then it will follow that these goods can belong only to individuals with mental lives. Since it is just these individuals who qualify as paradigmatic welfare subjects, the private ownership theory will thereby be saved from grossly overpopulating the domain of such subjects.

But note how it secures this result. The issue of whether states

[11] Moore 1903, 83–4.
[12] And, I suppose, that equally beautiful people are, in that respect, equally well off.
[13] Moore 1903, 188.   [14] Moore 1947, 153.

of consciousness are the only intrinsic goods is (as we shall later see) a highly contentious one. But it is a contentious *ethical* issue; the opposed parties differ about what we have an ethical reason to bring about for its own sake. It is unclear how the right answer to this question, whatever it might be, could have any bearing on the nature of welfare—how, that is, it could settle what is to count as a source of welfare, or who is to count as having a welfare. What is odd about the private ownership theory is the order of explanation to which it is committed. The theory tells us that prudential value depends on ethical value: certain conditions make our lives go better because we have a moral reason to bring them about. However, if there is an explanatory relation between ethical and prudential value it seems more likely to run in the opposite direction.

Suppose we are wondering whether Moore was right to think that deep personal relationships have a high degree of intrinsic ethical value. One intuitively plausible way of answering this question is to argue that we have a moral reason to preserve or promote these relationships because of the many and profound ways in which they enrich our lives. This dialectical approach makes ethical value depend on prudential value: we have a moral reason to bring about certain conditions because they make our lives go better. And it is easy to see why the approach is intuitively plausible—that is, why the fact that something makes our lives go better might be thought to give us an ethical reason for bringing it about.

The private ownership theory reverses this direction of argument. Suppose we are wondering whether deep personal relationships have any prudential value. The theory reaches an affirmative answer to this question by first establishing that these relationships have ethical value, and then concluding that they must therefore make our lives go better. However, if the ethical value of these relationships is independent of their prudential value, as it must be on the private ownership theory, then it is hard to see how it could establish or guarantee that value. It is believable that intimate connections with others make the world a better place by virtue of enriching our lives, but it is not believable that they enrich our lives by virtue of making the world a better place.

We reach the same destination if we begin by assessing the other claim made by the private ownership theory: that having ethical value is a necessary condition for a state belonging to some individual to contribute to the well-being of that individual. When we reflect on the ingredients of our well-being, all of us will include our participation in activities which we find satisfying or rewarding. Our involvement in some of these activities may be motivated by the conviction that they are ethically valuable quite independently of our commitment to them. This may, for instance, be the right story for joining the peace movement or volunteering to alleviate famine in the sub-Sahara. But we all engage in other pursuits, such as gardening or going for long walks or watching baseball, which seem entirely neutral from the moral point of view. Although we have little doubt that these pastimes make our lives go better, we would be hard-pressed to show that, just considered by themselves, they have the sort of intrinsic ethical value which Moore had in mind. But in that case having this sort of value seems not to be necessary in order for some state or activity of ours to contribute (directly) to our welfare.

This conclusion can be avoided by a move which will by now look familiar. A private ownership theorist could say that, where such ethically indifferent activities are concerned, the intrinsically valuable state of affairs is not the activity considered in isolation but its being found satisfying or rewarding. So it is not gardening or walking or going to the ballpark which has ethical value, but the enjoyment of these things. And each instance of this enjoyment is as much the property of a particular person as is each instance of the activity itself. Now when we switch in this way from the bare pursuits to the quality of our engagement with them, there is admittedly much more plausibility in the idea that this latter is something worth safeguarding or promoting for its own sake. But again the order of explanation seems to run the wrong way for the private ownership theory: we have a moral reason for supporting or promoting these pursuits because they improve the quality of our lives, not the other way round.

The issue of whether ethical value is (wholly or partially) dependent on prudential value is one which will occupy us later, when we come to assess the prospects of welfarism. But if some such dependence does turn out to hold, it will constitute a substantive link between the two modes of value: prudential value will turn out to be one (or perhaps even the only) ground of ethical value. Such a relationship would be entirely consistent with the conceptual autonomy of both modes of value. By contrast, the private ownership theory attempts to reduce the one mode to the other, by analysing prudential value into a compound consisting of ethical value plus the relation of possession. It thereby makes welfare conceptually, and not merely substantively, derivative.

Predictably, the feature of prudential value which the theory is consequently unable to capture is its subject-relativity. Moore's notion of intrinsic ethical value is not subject-relative: if something has this sort of value then it is, as Moore says, good *absolutely*. But in that case it is obvious why there can be no analytic connections between the two modes of value. The fact that some state of affairs is good absolutely cannot entail that it is good for some particular individual, and it cannot entail this even if the individual in question is the owner of the state in question. Subject-relativity is internal to prudential value; it constitutes its peculiar evaluative standpoint. It is not internal to ethical value, at least if we accept Moore's view about the objectivity of the latter. In that case, however, we cannot make the ethical value of a state entail its value for a particular subject merely by adding on some further relation between the state and that subject. Although subject-relativity is internal to the notion of possession, it remains external to the ethical standpoint. Private ownership is incapable of bridging the conceptual gap between ethical and prudential value.

3.2 NEEDS

The private ownership theory is no more than an isolated episode, an idiosyncratic curiosity, in the history of objective accounts. The mainstream of the tradition has tended to rely on one or another conceptual resource which, while appropriately objective, seems intimately connected with well-being. A perennial favourite is the notion of a basic need. In terms of its surface logic, this notion seems particularly well suited to the objectivist's purposes. It has often been remarked, for instance, that needs lack the intentionality which is characteristic of desires. From the fact that I want some water it does not follow that I want some H_2O, since I may not know the chemical composition of water. However, if I need some water then I need some H_2O, whether I realize this or not. Whereas the attribution of a desire for some object forms an opaque context, since its truth value may not survive substitution of a co-referential term, the context formed by the attribution of a need is transparent. Since the opacity of desire contexts reflects (or restates) the intentionality of desire, and since intentionality is one mark of the mental, then an account of well-being in terms of needs looks promisingly objective.

It is clear, however, that not just any needs can provide the materials for constructing a plausible objective theory of welfare. It is also a commonplace that most of our needs are determined by our aims or projects. These transient needs bear no regular relation to our well-being: while I may need a light for my bicycle because I plan to ride it after dark, I may also need a length of strong rope because, in a bout of depression, I have decided to hang myself. Anyway, even if the satisfaction of such needs somehow managed always to make us better off, their role is plainly too instrumental to serve the objectivist's purposes. The real prudential contribution is being made by the aims or projects from which they derive, and these deeper items do not look objective.

What the objectivist (derivatively) needs is a set of needs which are not derivative. By this route accounts which begin by talking of needs in general move quickly to isolate those needs which are basic or fundamental. The inevitable by-product of this shift is a loss of generality. It is certainly true that we are standardly benefited by the satisfaction of basic needs for nourishment, sanitation, security, companionship, and the like. But it is equally true that we can profit by satisfying mere likes or preferences or even whims. The former are, of course, more urgent or important than the latter; that is presumably why we call them basic. It therefore seems likely that any plausible theory of welfare will somehow have to assign a central place to the fulfilment of basic needs. But precisely because they are basic, the needs which seem most hospitable to an objectivist treatment cannot be the whole story about well-being.

Still, they cannot fail to be part of the story. If basic needs are objective through and through then this will be enough to rule out any purely subjective theory.[15] And if the remaining sectors of

---

[15] Some theories appear to be hybrids of subjective and objective elements. For example, Joseph Raz includes the satisfaction of biologically determined needs as one component in his account of welfare (Raz 1986, ch. 12). But not the most important one; this role is reserved for the achievement of goals. In terms of the subjective/objective dichotomy constructed in Ch. 2, a theory can succeed in being objective only by assigning no essential role to subjectivity. It follows that a hybrid theory counts, overall, as subjective. In this sense subjectivity is dominant, objectivity recessive.

well-being can also be accounted for without reference to subjectivity, then the objectivist project will be a going concern. It matters, therefore, whether basic needs really are as objective as they seem.

We need to ask what it is that makes something a basic need. How can we determine which items belong on a list of such needs? Broadly speaking, there seem to be two different ways of answering this question. One approach we may call *constructivist*, by virtue of the fact that the contents of the list are chosen or settled by some favoured group of agents. The other, naturally, is *naturalist*, since it roots basic needs in some aspect(s) of our nature.[16] An intriguing example of the constructivist strategy can be found in the recent work of David Braybrooke.[17] Like most theorists who work with needs, Braybrooke's primary concern is with their role in guiding social policy. His aim is to develop an account of basic needs capable of vindicating the urgency which they are typically accorded in policy deliberations; in our terminology, therefore, his standard of adequacy is normative rather than descriptive. Despite (or perhaps because of) this moral/political preoccupation, Braybrooke's menu of basic needs contains the usual familiar items: nourishment, exercise, rest, companionship, social acceptance, personal security, and the like. It does not seem out of place, therefore, to treat the background story which generates this list as though it also aspired to descriptive adequacy, at least for the special case of human needs.[18]

The first part of this story seems impeccably naturalist: something counts as a basic need if it is 'essential to living or to functioning normally'.[19] This rather open-ended formula is soon given a more determinate rendering: 'The Criterion that I shall settle upon is being indispensable to mind or body in performing the tasks assigned a given person under a combination of basic social roles, namely, the roles of parent, householder, worker, and citizen.'[20] The announcement of this criterion invites a number of questions: Why the relativization to social roles? Why just these roles and not others? Which needs will this criterion accredit as

---

[16] Peter Penz draws a similar distinction between conventionalist and essentialist approaches in Penz 1986, 166–7.

[17] Braybrooke 1987. For a related account see Penz 1986, 170 ff.

[18] In any case, Braybrooke could argue that the notion of a basic need is itself inherently normative, since we determine whether or not someone's need counts as basic by weighing the seriousness of the claim it makes on the rest of us.

[19] Braybrooke 1987, 31.   [20] Ibid. 48.

basic? What is the reference population whose needs are thereby determined? It is in answering these questions that Braybrooke's line of development veers off in a decidedly constructivist direction. All of these matters, including the content of the criterion itself, are to be settled by 'particular self-governing subsets of the linguistic community that has the concept of needs in just the form which I have outlined'.[21] Self-governing linguistic subsets (what Braybrooke calls Selfgovlisets) of the English-speaking community include such anglophone countries as Canada and Australia. Braybrooke therefore imagines a list of basic needs (plus a specification of the minimum standards of provision for each item on the list and a stipulation of the sort of normative priority which needs are to enjoy over mere preferences) being generated by consensus in each of these societies, with no assurance that the resultant lists (or other matters) agreed on in different societies will coincide. Basic needs are thus relative to particular Selfgovlisets, with no independent, natural standard to serve as a higher court of appeal. What counts as a basic need in Canada is whatever would be acknowledged as such by the least generous Canadian.

My purpose is not to assess the adequacy (either normative or descriptive) of Braybrooke's account, which is in any case much richer and more complex than this brief summary suggests. I wish merely to underline the obvious, namely that any constructivist interpretation of needs will be utterly inimical to the objectivist's enterprise. In order for basic needs to be objective their explication must include no reference to people's attitudes, including their preferences or choices. Since Braybrooke's methodology derives needs from the collective decision processes of Selfgovlisets, it treats them as social constructs. If an objective account of needs is possible, it clearly must eschew this entire line of development in favour of the naturalist route.

A naturalist account will ground basic needs, somehow or other, in the nature of their subjects. Naturalism about needs, indeed about welfare in general, seems the generic strategy likeliest to pay off for the objectivist. In the final section of this chapter we will encounter a version of naturalism which appears to constitute the objectivist's last, best hope. Meanwhile, however, it is worth reminding ourselves that choosing the naturalist route does not

[21] Ibid. 62.

guarantee arrival at an objectivist destination. While naturalism requires connecting our needs to some aspect of our nature, it is neutral as to which aspect this is to be. It is therefore compatible with grounding our needs in our attitudes or concerns, which seem as natural as any other feature of us, thus with treating needs as deeply subjective.

A particularly short route from needs to subjectivity can be traced in John Rawls's notion of a primary good.[22] Primary goods have an indispensable normative function in Rawls's version of a social contract theory, in which the contractors are imagined as trying to reach agreement on principles of justice behind a veil of ignorance which deprives them of knowledge of their particular circumstances, abilities, and aims. Since they must have some basis for rational choice in this situation, and since instrumental rationality is a maximizing conception, the veil of ignorance must leave them something to maximize. This residue consists of a stipulated set of primary goods; each agent is then conceived as aiming to maximize her own share of such goods.

Primary goods have an obvious kinship with basic needs, albeit in a special sense of the latter required by a theory of justice:

[I]n regarding the members of society as free and equal moral persons, we ascribe to them certain requirements, or needs, which, given the nature of these requirements and the form of rational plans of life, explain how primary goods can be used to define appropriate claims in questions of justice. In effect, the conception of the person and the notion of primary goods simply characterise a special kind of need for a conception of justice. Needs in any other sense, along with desires and aspirations, play no role.[23]

At the same time, however, Rawls's background theory of welfare is patently subjective: '[A] person's good is determined by what is for him the most rational long-term plan of life given reasonably favorable circumstances. A man is happy when he is more or less successfully in the way of carrying out this plan. To put it briefly, the good is the satisfaction of rational desire.'[24] Primary goods can serve as a surrogate maximand under the special conditions of the veil of ignorance only because they are 'all-purpose means generally necessary for forming and rationally pursuing a conception of

---

[22] See Rawls 1971, 62, 92–3; 1975; 1982.
[23] Rawls 1982, 173; cf. 1975, 554.   [24] Rawls 1971, 92–3.

the good'.[25] Like basic needs, the value of primary goods is not dependent on the pursuit of particular, contingent aims or projects. But they are still tied to aims, albeit more structurally and pervasively, and thus are at bottom subjective.

Subjectivity is implicated less directly, but no less decisively, in the account of needs developed by Garrett Thomson.[26] On Thomson's view a need is basic (and has normative force) if it is for something the lack of which will damage or impair one's life: 'If a man must suffer serious harm so long as he lacks self-respect, then he has need of self-respect. Such a need is non-instrumental in that it relates to the overall quality of a person's life rather than to a particular goal that he happens to have. This kind of non-instrumental need I call "a fundamental need".'[27] So far we are on the same territory as Braybrooke's normality of functioning. In order to understand which needs count as basic (or fundamental) we need to be told what is to count as serious harm (or impairment of functioning). But whereas Braybrooke's story took a constructivist turn at this point, Thomson's stays on the naturalist route. For Thomson the notion of serious harm presupposes a conception of 'the overall quality of a person's life', which in turn is identical to (what we are calling) welfare. It therefore follows, on his account, that in order to explicate the nature of basic needs we must already have on hand a theory about the nature of welfare.[28] This is bad news for the objectivist who aims to work toward such a theory by starting with the special case of needs. But worse is yet to come.

The demands of his own methodology lead Thomson to canvass some candidate theories of welfare. These he divides into two categories, by now at least nominally familiar to us: the subjective and the objective. Rejecting both categories, he then goes on to defend a view which, he claims, belongs to neither. Within the terms of our inquiry, however, this is a misleading way to characterize his result, since his account of subjectivity differs from the one developed in the preceding chapter. (It will be recalled that the

---

[25] Rawls 1982, 169; cf. 1971, 62, 92.   [26] Thomson 1987.   [27] Ibid. 8.
[28] 'For this reason, we should oppose a theory of welfare and harm which attempts to explain these concepts in terms of "need". Because "need" is to be explained in terms of "harm", we require an elucidation of "harm" which does not involve the concept of a need' (ibid. 89). For other accounts which make needs depend conceptually on a prior notion of harm, see Wiggins 1985, 154 ff., and Feinberg 1973, 30, 111.

subjective/objective dichotomy constructed there is jointly exhaustive.) For Thomson a theory is subjective if it equates welfare with the satisfaction of desire. An objective theory then holds that '[w]ell-being is independent of our desires: whether some event is detrimental to a person's well-being depends on whether that event deprives the person of activities and experiences that are truly characterised by certain desirability predicates and does not depend on the person's desires actual or possible.'[29]

Under this construal objective theories are all versions of the discredited private ownership theory, while subjective theories are all versions of the desire theory (which we will explore in due course). It is clear, therefore, why Thomson thinks that there is a third way, since a theory of welfare need affiliate with neither of these families. However, the third way which he himself favours is, in our terminology, plainly subjective. For Thomson our welfare is grounded in our interests or concerns, which he treats as deliberatively and motivationally prior to our desires. It is this notion of an interest which enables him to construct a formal account, first of harm and then of basic needs:

The primary goods we are deprived of when we are harmed (by lacking what we need) are good and worthwhile because they answer our interests, and not because they are desired. The notion of an interest defines the range and type of activities and experiences that partly constitute a meaningful, worthwhile life, and it defines the nature of their worth. These types of activities are primary goods and because they are good something which deprives us of them is bad, and harmful.[30]

In his terminology here Thomson acknowledges the affinities between his account and that of Rawls. It remains to be determined, of course, whether this kind of subjective analysis of welfare, and of needs, is ultimately viable. The point which these accounts illustrate for our present purposes is merely that naturalism and subjectivism appear to make a compatible pair. The notions of an aim or an interest or a concern are all subjective, and if any of these notions turn up at the bottom of an account of the nature of needs then that account is also subjective. While the concept of a need may be superficially objective, and while it may yet turn out to be the objectivist's most valuable resource, its

---

[29] Thomson 1987, 50.
[30] Ibid. 76. For a similar account see Feinberg 1984, ch. 1.

freedom from contamination by subjectivity cannot be taken for granted.

3.3 FUNCTIONINGS AND CAPABILITIES

In several influential works Amartya Sen has sketched a model of well-being which, like accounts which invoke the concept of a need, has a decidedly objective look to it.[31] Sen begins by rejecting two rival theories. The first equates welfare with utility, under one or another of its traditional interpretations—as felt satisfaction, preference, or choice. Any such account, Sen argues, will make an individual's welfare level overly sensitive to such extraneous factors as social conditioning, which can affect personal ambitions and expectations. Furthermore, neither finding something pleasant nor wanting it is the same as valuing it. Since welfare is inherently evaluative—it provides one measure of the value of a life—it cannot be reduced to any non-evaluative activity or state of mind.

The second discarded theory equates welfare with the possession of commodities—either some stipulated list of goods and services or their economic surrogate, namely wealth. Sen's objection to any account of this sort is that it confuses welfare with its standard or all-purpose means.[32] An individual's command over commodities will be a poor indicator of her quality of life, since the factors which affect the conversion of goods or services into welfare vary greatly from person to person. Sen's favourite illustration of the range of these variables is food, whose conversion into nourishment will be influenced by age, sex, metabolic rate, body size, activity level, general state of health, and many other contingencies. He therefore concludes that 'while goods and services are valuable, they are not valuable in themselves. Their value rests on what they can do for people, or rather, on what people can do with these goods and services.'[33]

While Sen faults the first family of theories for their subjectivity, he rejects the second for carrying objectivity too far. His ostensible aim is to construct an account which mediates between these

[31] Sen 1984 (esp. the introduction and chs. 13 and 20), 1985*a*, 1985*b*, 1987*a*, 1987*b*, 1993.
[32] Sen raises the same complaint against the equation of welfare with the possession of Rawlsian primary goods, at least if these are understood as resources or commodities (Sen 1984, 319–20).
[33] Ibid. 510.

extremes. The core notion in this account is that of a *functioning*, which Sen defines as anything which a person manages to do or to be. Functionings are therefore individual achievements or successes; in the food example both being well nourished and giving a dinner party for one's friends would be functionings facilitated by this commodity. The ground floor of Sen's account treats an individual's well-being as a matter of his functionings. But Sen then adds a second level to the analysis. A *capability* is a freedom or opportunity to achieve a certain functioning—the ability to eat well if one chooses, say, rather than actually doing so. Although capabilities may be prudentially valuable chiefly for the functionings which they make available, Sen argues that they also have a certain value in their own right: we are better off for having avenues open to us which we never actually choose to pursue. Our level of well-being is therefore determined both by our set of functionings and by our set of capabilities.

It is easy to see why Sen regards this account as a middle ground between the rejected options. On the one hand, equating welfare with commodity possession ignores the many contingencies which affect the conversion of goods and services into functionings and capabilities. Commodities are too external to our lives, too merely instrumental, to be determinative of well-being. Sen's approach, by contrast, 'builds on the straightforward fact that how well a person is must be a matter of what kind of life he or she is living, and what the person is succeeding in "doing" or "being" '.[34] On the other hand, equating welfare with utility leaves it prey to the many contingencies which affect the conversion of functionings and capabilities into satisfaction or happiness. Utility is too internal to our lives, too shifting and capricious, to serve as the basis of an adequate theory. Functionings and capabilities are the intermediate steps between the commodities over which we have command and their ultimate utility payoff. As such, they are at just the right distance from us to determine the real quality of our lives.

Is Sen's account subjective or objective? At first glance, the answer seems obvious. As noted earlier, he rejects utility accounts of well-being because they are subjective and the commodities account because it is too objective.[35] Furthermore, it certainly appears that

[34] Sen 1985*a*, 28.
[35] Thus Sen complains of 'the fetishism of the commodity focus and the subjectivism of the utility focus' (Sen 1984, 515).

he is aiming at a more moderate and defensible version of an objective theory.[36] The primitive notion in Sen's account is that of a functioning; capabilities, being defined on functionings, are conceptually derivative. His account will therefore be objective if (and only if) functionings are objective. When we ask what Sen has in mind as individual functionings, his list includes such familiar items as healthfulness, longevity, literacy, and the like.[37] For each of these items Sen recognizes a distinction between the functioning itself and its various social indicators. The indicators may be as varied as mortality statistics on the one hand and responses to questionnaires on the other, but what they are all aiming to measure are quite objective features of individuals' lives: whether they are adequately nourished or clothed or sheltered, whether they can read or write or count, and so on. Since all of Sen's functionings appear to be objective, it would seem to follow that his theory of welfare is objective as well.

This conclusion, however, is premature. We need to ask how Sen has arrived at just this list of functionings. According to his definition, a functioning is anything which we manage to do or to be—any activity or state which constitutes an achievement on the part of some agent. My functionings would then seem to include such diverse items as feeding the cat, making polite conversation at boring dinner parties, pursuing a career as a philosopher, reading trashy novels, acting out my mother complex, living in a crime-free neighbourhood, having a good relationship with my children, taking fitness classes, carrying out meaningless administrative chores, and being married to the woman I love. Now these various activities and states have, to say the least, differential implications for my well-being; some of them enrich my life immensely, some have little impact on it either way, and some are just burdens. Furthermore, virtually any item on my personal economy of functionings will have differential implications for the lives of others. How can functionings be ordered in terms of their contribution to the well-being of particular individuals? How do we determine whether some functioning is important or trivial, urgent or dispensable? How can we narrow down the enormous range of functionings achievable by human agents to those that are basic or vital?

[36] Or so I interpret the comments in Sen 1985*b*, 196.
[37] See Sen 1985*a*, 45–8.

In order to answer questions like these Sen adds a further re-source to his account: 'the identification of certain "doings" and "beings" as objects of value is itself a valuational exercise.... The list of functionings reflects a view of what is valuable and what is of no intrinsic value (though possibly quite useful in the pursuit of other things of value).'[38] But then we immediately want to ask: *whose* view of what is valuable does the list reflect? For Sen the answer to this question appears to depend on the unit whose well-being is in question. If it is a collectivity, such as an entire society, then it will be appropriate to appeal to social standards which reflect widely shared values.[39] But where the well-being of an in-dividual is concerned, the decisive ranking will be that of the wel-fare subject herself.[40] This ranking Sen envisages being elicited by means of self-evaluation techniques.[41]

The introduction of personal valuations forces us to rethink the apparently objective character of Sen's account. Initially it seemed as though welfare was constituted by some specified set of function-ings and capabilities, all of which are objective features of an indi-vidual's life. However, it now seems to consist in success at doing or being whatever it is one values. This account closely resembles one of Sen's rejected options, namely the view which equates welfare with the satisfaction of desire. If Sen is correct in thinking that desiring is not an inherently evaluative activity then his account will not actually collapse into the desire model. But in so far as the activity of (individual or social) valuing plays an indispensable constitutive role in the account, it will be no less subjective.

In this respect Sen's theory of welfare resembles the analyses of needs offered by Braybrooke and Thomson; although he places a great deal of weight on objective concerns, and supports expand-ing the range of such concerns from the exclusively economic to the broadly social, his underlying theory about the nature of welfare still comes out looking very subjective. Since Sen began by reject-ing utility accounts on the ground of their subjectivity, this result

---

[38] Sen 1987*b*, 29; cf. 1993, 31–3.   [39] Sen 1985*a*, 55–6; 1987*b*, 30–1.

[40] 'Many functionings are of no great interest to the person.... There is no escape from the problem of evaluation in selecting a class of functionings in the description and appraisal of capabilities. The focus has to be related to the under-lying concerns and values, in terms of which some definable functionings may be important and others quite trivial and negligible' (Sen 1993, 32; cf. 1985*a*, 57; 1987*b*, 30–1).

[41] Sen 1985*a*, 48.

is puzzling. How does the subjective activity of ranking functionings and capabilities come to play such a crucial constitutive role in his theory?

It is easy to see, I think, why the theory cannot get by without this reliance on personal valuation. Recall Sen's criticisms of the commodities account. Welfare cannot literally consist in command over external commodities since (1) commodity possession is only indirectly related to well-being, thus at best an indicator of it, and (2) it is not even a reliable indicator, because the conversion of commodities into well-being is affected by so many extraneous factors. The shift from commodities to functionings (and capabilities) is meant to remedy these defects. To revert to Sen's own example, possession of (or access to) food is a poor indicator of nourishment, since both nutritional needs and consumption patterns vary so greatly from person to person. Going straight to the functioning of *being well nourished* enables Sen to bypass all these contingencies, in order to focus directly on the principal welfare payoff for which food is instrumental. It also facilitates expanding the range of indicators for this functioning to include other signs of adequate nutritional intake, such as freedom from parasites or the ability to work.

Sen's account therefore redirects attention from the mere indicators of well-being to its sources or ingredients. Commodities are mere external means for enhancing functionings (and capabilities); in the latter we find the prudential reason for consuming the former. Although this shift from instrumental to intrinsic benefits is definitely a step in the right direction, we must not lose sight of the fact that no set of functionings can literally constitute individual welfare. Being well nourished is directly beneficial for us, as is being healthy in other respects, being adequately clothed and sheltered, being literate, and so on. But welfare does not (formally) consist in any of these conditions taken separately, nor in their aggregate. To think otherwise is once again to confuse an enumeration of intrinsically beneficial conditions with a theory of what it is for a condition to be intrinsically beneficial; it is to take the sources of well-being for its nature.

A formal theory tells us what welfare is; a list or inventory of sources tells us which conditions will enable us to achieve or maintain it. When a list of sources masquerades as a theory then it will inevitably fail some of the (other) tests of descriptive adequacy. Suppose we simply identify welfare with some catalogue of functionings (and capabilities). We should expect the items in this catalogue to depend on the nature of the welfare subjects in question; being adequately clothed will appear on the list for humans but not for dolphins. We should also expect the list to be socially and culturally variable: being aggressive or ruthless will matter more for Wall Street brokers than for Trappist monks, and even a functioning as basic as literacy may be much less important in undeveloped agrarian communities than in developed industrial societies. Finally, we should expect considerable variation among individuals, even of the same species and society; being well nourished may mean less to an intellectual or an ascetic than to a labourer or a professional athlete. Because of these dependencies on biology, culture, and personal lifestyle, no single list (and no single ordering) of functionings will be appropriate for all welfare subjects. But in that case a formal theory of welfare built around functionings will be hopelessly fragmented and incomplete; it will imply that well-being is different in its nature (rather than merely in its sources) for each distinct group of subjects, or even for each individual.

An account of welfare which simply equates it with some favoured menu of functionings will therefore be vulnerable to objections very like the ones Sen used to discredit the commodities account. Welfare cannot literally consist in functionings (and capabilities) since (1) while functionings are directly related to well-being, they are still only sources or ingredients of it, and (2) they are not even reliable sources, since the conversion of functionings into well-being is affected by so many extraneous factors. We have already seen how Sen's introduction of personal valuations is meant to impose some order on the virtually infinite range of achievable human functionings. Now it should be apparent how profound its impact is: it converts a list of the (standard) sources of (human) well-being into a formal account of its nature. Instead of consisting in some stipulated set of functionings (an account which would vary for different welfare subjects), well-being now comes to consist in achieving whatever functionings an individual most values (an account which is common to all such subjects).[42] If Sen's aim

---

[42] Whether the account will apply to non-human animals will depend on how the activity of valuing is construed. The more cognitive its interpretation, the more exclusive the resultant class of welfare subjects and the less general the resultant theory of welfare.

was to develop a descriptively adequate theory about the nature of well-being then it is easy to see why he assigned a crucial role to individual valuation. But this way of both formalizing and generalizing his theory necessitated also subjectivizing it.

Sen's subjective turn, therefore, seems to have been meant to deflect the sorts of objection he had brought against the commodities account. In accomplishing this, however, it seems to weaken his other flank, by exposing his account to one of the objections he had brought against utility accounts. Welfare cannot consist in utility, Sen argued, because an individual's tastes, ambitions, and aspirations are too malleable by processes of indoctrination, manipulation, and socialization:

A person who has had a life of misfortune, with very little opportunities, and rather little hope, may be more easily reconciled to deprivations than others reared in more fortunate and affluent circumstances. The metric of happiness may, therefore, distort the extent of deprivation, in a specific and biased way. The hopeless beggar, the precarious landless labourer, the dominated housewife, the hardened unemployed or the over-exhausted coolie may all take pleasures in small mercies, and manage to suppress intense suffering for the necessity of continuing survival, but it would be ethically deeply mistaken to attach a correspondingly small value to the loss of their well-being because of this survival strategy. The same problem arises with the other interpretation of utility, namely, desire-fulfilment, since the hopelessly deprived lack the courage to desire much, and their deprivations are muted and deadened in the scale of desire-fulfilment.[43]

This is a powerful challenge; we will need to decide later whether any subjective theory has the resources to meet it. Meanwhile, it will suffice to make an obvious point. Sen regards valuing as a more cognitive and reflective activity than enjoying or desiring. However this may be, personal values are also notoriously subject to influence by accustomed social conditions. If there is a problem here for theories which interpret welfare in terms of felt satisfaction or preference, there is equally a problem for a theory which assigns the same constitutive role to valuation.[44]

This is not, however, the end of the story. The notion of a personal value is, on the face of it, ambiguous between two very

[43] Sen 1987a, 45–6.
[44] This criticism has been made by Nussbaum 1988, 175–6.

different interpretations: (1) assigning a particular functioning a high ranking in one's personal value scheme, and (2) acknowledging or recognizing the functioning's urgency or importance. Thus far I have assumed that Sen's references to (individual or social) valuing are to be understood in the first sense. If this interpretation is correct then personal valuations are constitutive of well-being, which is enough to ensure the subjectivity of the theory. However, Sen's meaning here is far from transparent. For one thing, he holds that personal valuations are open to criticism and correction.[45] He also says that where social standards are concerned it is quite in order to go beyond the brute fact that certain values are widely held, by asking *why* it is so.[46]

Sen has been urged by Martha Nussbaum to move his account away from its apparently subjective orientation by specifying 'an objective valuational procedure that will have the power to criticize the evaluations of functionings that are actually made by people whose upbringing has been hedged round with discrimination and inequity'.[47] Taking this step, in Nussbaum's view, would require 'introducing an objective normative account of human functioning and . . . describing a procedure of objective evaluation by which functionings can be assessed for their contribution to the good human life'.[48] In a recent discussion, Sen has shown himself open in principle to taking this sort of objective direction but unwilling to endorse it as a unique option for his theory.[49] Indeed, he there claims as a virtue of his approach precisely the fact that it is 'incomplete'—i.e. indeterminate on this foundational question.

We are therefore left with two importantly different ways in which Sen's theory of welfare could be completed. Should valuations be understood subjectively, then he will have no objective theory of welfare to offer. On the other hand, should the objective route be pursued, then personal rankings would play a merely evidentiary role in his account. In that case, however, Sen would owe us an 'objective normative account of human functioning' as the foundation of his theory of welfare. The most likely source of such an account (and the one urged by Nussbaum) will be considered in the next section.

---

[45] Sen 1985*a*, 58.   [46] Sen 1987*b*, 32.   [47] Nussbaum 1988, 175.
[48] Ibid. 176. Nussbaum's own preferred 'objective normative account of human functioning' is Aristotelian in nature.
[49] Sen 1993, 46–9.

Before we leave Sen's treatment of well-being there is a question to be raised about its aim or purpose. I have taken for granted that it is intended as a theory about the nature of welfare, and thus have held it accountable to the standards of descriptive adequacy for such theories. This interpretation is encouraged both by the welfare terminology which Sen standardly employs and by his advocacy of his own account as a superior alternative to some of the traditional formal theories.[50] There is, however, room for doubt. In some contexts Sen phrases his account in terms, not of well-being, but of 'the standard of living' or 'the quality of life'.[51] This terminology suggests a somewhat different ambition. If we begin with the descriptive aim of comparing living standards in different societies, or with the normative aim of assessing economic or social policies for their impact on the quality of life, then in order to get on with the job any reasonable inventory of the basic or standard sources of human well-being will suffice; we need not join the philosopher in trying to assemble an adequate formal theory.[52] Sen's intellectual concerns are generally a blend of the economic and the philosophical. As the materials for a normatively attractive account of the standard of living, the basic functionings and capabilities on which he focuses have excellent credentials. Objectivity is no liability in an enumeration of the principal sources of well-being, only in a theory about its nature.

[50] These themes are especially prominent in Sen 1985a, 1985b, and 1987a.

[51] See esp. Sen 1984 and 1987b, but also 1985a, 45–8. Sen distinguishes between well-being and the standard of living in terms of their sources: the former comprehends all sources, including those which impinge on the person from the outside, while the latter is confined to influences rooted in the individual's own life (1987a, 26–9). This seems to make little sense of some of the standard social indicators: whether I live in a crime-free neighbourhood clearly affects my life from the outside but crime rates are commonly included in profiles of the standard of living. The common distinction is more likely policy-driven: the factors which make up the standard of living are those relatively stable features of our lives which are amenable to social influence or control. The objective indicators of my standard of living will therefore include the pollution level in Toronto but exclude its disagreeable winters, despite the fact that both have a significant impact on my well-being.

[52] This may explain why Sen is content with, even proud of, the incompleteness in his account concerning the character of the underlying valuations needed to pick out relevant or important functionings. If both subjective and objective interpretations of this valuational exercise seem likely to yield roughly the same list of functionings, then anyone whose interest lies primarily in social analysis need inquire no further. It is the peculiar burden of the philosopher to remain unsatisfied until the foundational issue has been resolved.

3.4 THE TELEOLOGICAL THEORY

It is now clear what an objective theory of welfare requires: some aspect of the nature of welfare subjects, other than their subjectivity, which can supply the standpoint or perspective characteristic of prudential value. And so we come finally to the secor.d main strategy available to the objectivist, which attempts to supply this vital ingredient. That attempt alone is enough to make it a more promising option than the private ownership theory.

Objective theories of welfare have an impressive pedigree, and the prototype of the account we are now seeking was established early on by Aristotle. As every student of Greek philosophy knows, the concept of *eudaimonia* plays a prominent role in the *Nicomachean Ethics*. Although it is usual to render *eudaimonia* into English as 'happiness', the Greek term actually corresponds much more closely to our notion of welfare: a complete state of being and doing well. Most of the *Ethics* thus consists of an extended inquiry into the ingredients of human well-being. However, it opens by asking not about welfare but about goods as ends of action. 'Every art and every inquiry,' Aristotle begins, 'is thought to aim at some good.'[53] The framing project of the *Ethics* is to identify the highest good, the end we should aim at for its own sake and not for the sake of anything further.

Eudaimonia enters the scene as the consensus candidate for this role: 'Verbally there is very general agreement; for both the general run of men and people of superior refinement say that it is happiness, and identify living well and faring well with being happy; but with regard to what happiness is they differ, and the many do not give the same account as the wise.'[54] In the opening sections of Book 1 of the *Nicomachean Ethics* Aristotle thus distinguishes the two questions which define our own inquiry: What is the value of welfare, and what is its nature? However, his answer to the first question is delivered pretty summarily with little supporting argument: Aristotle seems to find it obvious that well-being is the (sole) ultimate good, the one objective worth pursuing for its own sake. Having reached this result, his attention then shifts to the second question, where he locates the real substantive dispute. From this point the *Ethics* becomes a disquisition on the topic of well-being.

[53] Aristotle 1984, 1094a1–2.   [54] Ibid. 1095a16–21.

The first step in that disquisition, however, determines most of its subsequent course. Arstotle finds that the highest human good consists in 'activity of soul in conformity with excellence [*arete*]', immediately continuing 'and if there are more than one excellence, in conformity with the best and most complete'.[55] Thus the focus shifts here once more, this time from *eudaimonia* to *arete*, from well-being to excellence. Aristotle's principal project, the one for which the *Ethics* is renowned, now becomes the construction of a theory of the virtues, encompassing those of both character and intellect. This road will eventually lead him to locate welfare, and therefore also the ultimate good, above all in theoretical inquiry, or the philosophic life.

Our interest lies not in these further developments, which articulate the pattern of life Aristotle thinks best for us, but in this early step in which he establishes what welfare is. Although Aristotle never quite puts it this way, his final result is that theoretical inquiry is the sole, or at any rate the primary, source of human well-being—a view whose rivals will back other ways of life, such as the pursuit of honour or pleasure. It is not a formal theory about the nature of welfare; instead, it depends on such a theory. The philosophic life turns out to be best for us because of the sort of thing welfare is.

The passages in which Aristotle outlines his theory of welfare (Book 1, chapter 7) are among the most condensed and controversial in the entire *Nicomachean Ethics*. They also constitute his distinctive and enduring contribution to the objectivist cause. Having reaffirmed that the highest good is happiness, Aristotle continues his line of inquiry as follows: 'Presumably, however, to say that happiness is the chief good seems a platitude, and a clearer account of what it is is still desired. This might perhaps be given, if we could first ascertain the function [*ergon*] of man. . . . What then can this be?'[56] Having excluded nutrition and perception, on the (questionable) ground that these are not peculiarly human functions, Aristotle closes in on his conclusion:

There remains, then, an active life of the element that has a rational principle . . . and as this too can be taken in two ways, we must state that life in the sense of activity is what we mean; for this seems to be the more proper sense of the term. Now if the function of man is an activity of soul

[55] Ibid. 1098a16–17.   [56] Ibid. 1097b22–32.

in accordance with, or not without, rational principle, and if we say that a so-and-so and a good so-and-so have a function which is the same in kind, . . . human good turns out to be activity of soul in conformity with excellence.[57]

For Aristotle, therefore, a thing's excellence is conceptually connected to its function and thereby to its welfare. Simplifying somewhat, the argument to his formal theory of welfare contains the following steps: (1) something promotes my well-being just in case it enhances my distinctive function, (2) something enhances my distinctive function just in case it expresses my distinctive excellence, therefore (3) something promotes my well-being just in case it expresses my distinctive excellence.

It is easy to see why the resultant account of the nature of welfare is an attractive option for the objectivist. At least in biological contexts, identifying a thing's function seems to require no reference to its purposes or concerns; the notion, and also the theory of welfare built around it, are therefore nicely objective. At the same time, the proper functioning of a thing seems a promising candidate for the standpoint which underlies the peculiarly perspectival character of prudential value. After all, if I can function either well or badly, then the impact on my functioning of states of the world seems able to explain how these states can be either good or bad *for me*. Finally, the notion of functioning also seems well suited to constructing an objective account of needs, our basic needs being defined as those conditions of mind and body in whose absence we function badly, or not at all.

Ever since Aristotle first articulated it, however, this objectivist strategy has attracted as many critics as supporters. One classic line of resistance attacks the crucial claim that human beings are among the kinds of things which have a characteristic function. And it must be conceded that the idea is a little strange. It is noteworthy that when Aristotle needs clear cases of things with readily identifiable functions he relies either on social roles (craftsmen and artists) or on body parts (organs). It is not at all strange to ask what the function is of a bricklayer or a kidney. But no answer comes readily to mind when we ask what the function is of a human being—or, for that matter, a giraffe or a lichen. In these latter cases of organisms we can, of course, always find

[57] Ibid. 1098a3–17.

functions by referring to the needs or purposes of others, as when one individual serves as the slave of another, or one species as food supply for another. But this gets us no closer to identifying a function which is that of the organism itself.

In the light of this difficulty, it has become fashionable to say that Aristotle's *ergon* argument relies too heavily on his now discredited teleological biology.[58] Perhaps this is so. On the other hand, perhaps there is a lesson to be learned from the fact that many of the contemporary exponents of (some version or other of) the argument can be found in the field of environmental ethics, where one is expected to be thoroughly up to date in one's biology. Robin Attfield, for instance, defends 'the Aristotelian principle that the good life for a living organism turns on the fulfilment of its nature', a principle which he explicates in the following way: 'Let the "essential" capacities of an *x* be capacities in the absence of which from most members of a species that species would not *be* the species of *x*'s, and let "*x*" range over terms for living organisms. Then the flourishing of an *x* entails the development in it of the essential capacities of *x*'s.'[59] This principle 'governing the nature of good and harm' (as Attfield puts it) does not rely in any obvious way on pre-Darwinian assumptions about natural ends or final causes. Instead, it simply seems to presuppose that, while we may indeed be unable to locate the *function* of a particular organism, we generally have little difficulty determining when it is *functioning* well (or badly) by the standards appropriate to its kind.[60]

Paul Taylor has taken a similar view in the course of explicating what he calls 'the biocentric outlook on nature':

Each [individual organism] is seen to be a teleological (goal-oriented) center of life, pursuing its own good in its own unique way. This, of course, does not mean that they all seek their good as a conscious end or purpose, the realization of which is their intended aim. Consciousness may not be present at all, and even when it is present the organism need not be thought of as intentionally taking steps to achieve goals it sets for itself. Rather, a living thing is conceived as a unified system of organized activity, the constant tendency of which is to preserve its existence by protecting and promoting its well-being.[61]

---

[58] This verdict is common even among those generally sympathetic to the Aristotelian enterprise; see, for instance, MacIntyre 1984, 162 ff.

[59] Attfield 1981, 42; cf. 1983, 143 ff.

[60] Martha Nussbaum interprets Aristotle as having intended this sort of account (for the human case) in Nussbaum 1988, 1993.

[61] Taylor 1986, 45.

The philosophical lesson here seems to be that we need not, and should not, expel teleology altogether from our biology.[62] The heartland of teleological explanation is, of course, the behaviour of subjects capable of representing and seeking future states. But where other living things are concerned, functional explanations can still have a legitimate place. After the Darwinian turn that place is no longer foundational; every biological explanation must ultimately invoke mechanistic processes such as random mutation and natural selection. But acceptance of the Darwinian framework does not require us to deny that living things have functions, nor that these functions can figure in legitimate explanations. Indeed, this framework enables us to make the best sense of the notion of a function: the function of a living thing is its tendency to bring about some particular state just in case it is this tendency which figures in a mechanistic explanation of the existence of the thing. To say that teleological notions, like that of a function, are derivative or secondary in biological contexts is not to say that they are inherently suspect.

In the hands of philosophers like Attfield and Taylor notions such as functioning and flourishing are put to work to broaden the class of subjects whose well-being must be taken into account in an adequate environmental ethic.[63] Reacting against the assumption that the notion of a good can be ascribed only to human beings, or (more broadly) only to sentient beings, they wish to apply it across the full range of living organisms. The overall direction of the project emerges very nicely in Taylor's presentation of it. He begins by endorsing what we have called the subject-relativity of welfare:

One way to know whether something belongs to the class of entities that have a good is to see whether it makes sense to speak of what is good or bad *for* the thing in question. If we can say, truly or falsely, that something is good for an entity or bad for it, without reference to any *other* entity, then the entity has a good of its own.[64]

The next step is to argue that having a distinctive evaluative standpoint does not require subjectivity:

There are some entities that have a good of their own but cannot, strictly speaking, be described as having interests. They have a good of their own

[62] See Ayala 1970; Mayr 1988, essay 3.

[63] Essentially the same project, and the same means of executing it, can be found in Goodpaster 1978.

[64] Taylor 1986, 61.

because it makes sense to speak of their being benefited or harmed. Things that happen to them can be judged, from their standpoint, to be favorable or unfavorable to them. Yet they are not beings that consciously aim at ends or take means to achieve such ends. They do not have interests because they are not interested in, do not care about, what happens to them. They can experience neither satisfaction nor dissatisfaction, neither fulfillment nor frustration. Such entities are all those living things that lack consciousness or, if conscious, lack the ability to make choices among alternatives confronting them. They include all forms of plant life and the simpler forms of animal life.[65]

Finally, Taylor draws the inescapable conclusion about the objectivity of welfare:

In order to know whether something is (truly) in X's interests, we do not find out whether X has an interest in it. We inquire whether the thing in question will in fact further X's overall well-being. We ask, 'Does this promote or protect the good of X?' This is an objective matter because it is not determined by the beliefs, desires, feelings, or conscious interests of X.[66]

By now we may seem to have travelled a long way from Aristotle, whose concern, at least in the *Nicomachean Ethics*, was exclusively with the good of human beings. However, the contemporary expansion of focus to encompass all living things merely follows out the logic of the Aristotelian framework. If well-being is given the sort of objective interpretation Aristotle suggested, then the class of welfare subjects will embrace all creatures to whom notions such as functioning or flourishing can be meaningfully applied. And this will certainly include at least all organisms.

It should be clear by now that this teleological form of objective theory cannot be defeated merely by accusing it of biological *naïveté*. Furthermore, once its implications for the class of welfare subjects have been drawn out it surely has a very powerful intuitive appeal. Much of our welfare vocabulary does apply to all living things with no evident strain; thus we speak easily of what is good or bad, harmful or beneficial, for bees and bacteria, trees and toadstools. There is no reason to think that these categories apply meaningfully only to creatures who are conscious or sentient. On the other hand, some of our categories do not generalize so easily, among them the central notions of welfare, well-being, and interest.

[65] Ibid. 63.   [66] Ibid. cf. 65–7.

(There are animal welfare groups but no plant welfare groups.) These (inconclusive) linguistic facts led us earlier to classify all plants and the simpler animals as peripheral rather than core welfare subjects. Our framework of welfare concepts simply does not dictate a definite, unique extension for the class of welfare subjects. It therefore provides us with no unequivocal direction when we are trying to decide whether to include or exclude peripheral subjects. In this domain the best result is the one which follows from the best theory.

However, it is possible to embarrass the teleological theory a little on this issue. What the theory tells us is that something counts as a welfare subject if it has a good of its own. And an entity has a good of its own 'if we can say, truly or falsely, that something is good for [it] or bad for it, without reference to any *other* entity'.[67] What, then, of artefacts? Their good, we are told, is determined by our purposes in making them. Thus rusting is bad for my lawn-mower only because it prevents it from doing what it was designed to do, namely mow my lawn. The evaluative standpoint here is ultimately mine rather than its; it lacks a good of its own.

Suppose we accept this. What are we then to say about natural but inanimate objects, such as mountains or rivers? Can we distinguish a standpoint which is that of the mountain or the river, from which strip mining or damming might be bad *for it* though beneficial to us (or even to all affected organisms)? In Attfield's terms, can it be essential to a mountain not to be reduced to rubble, or to a river not to be dried up or converted into a lake? If so, then will this foothold in the nature of the mountain or the river enable us to talk about its flourishing? And why, in that case, should we accept the restriction which Attfield imposes on his account of flourishing, so that the only essential capacities which count are those of living things? If a thing's flourishing depends on its essence, why is the range of the former not as broad as that of the latter? Perhaps what is necessary in order to speak of flourishing is some inner dynamic, a system of forces which naturally tends toward equilibrium or homeostasis. But a star is such a system, as is a tornado or a geyser. Is it then bad for stars when they die?

On the other hand, what are we to do with organisms which

[67] Ibid. 61; emphasis in original.

have been contaminated by our purposes? What of domestic live-stock who have been selectively bred so as to yield milk or fleece or meat? Do they no longer have a good of their own? What of genetically engineered strains of bacteria which have never existed in nature? Are they both organisms and artefacts? If so, are they to be included by virtue of the former or excluded by virtue of the latter? Suppose, as many people seem to believe, that all living things were created by some deity for some obscure purpose of her own. In that case, do none of us have a good of our own? And if we can still have a good which is ours, in addition to a good which depends on the purposes of another, why cannot the same be true of my lawn-mower or my computer?

Finally, what is this account to do with the fact that notions like functioning or flourishing fit organs at least as well as organisms? Recall that Aristotle's prime examples, meant to soften us up for the notion of the function of a human being, are all either special jobs or body parts. If I have a good which is mine then surely the same is true of my heart and my liver, not to mention all my individual cells. Are we to recognize all these too as welfare sub-jects? Or do we reduce their good to that of the organism as a whole? (Which does not sound right, since what is best for the organism may be, say, to excise or irradiate a particular group of cells.) And if we choose this route, then why do we not also reduce the good of individual organisms to that of the biotic communities or ecosystems of which they are parts? Since ecology now gives us a picture of nature as a system of interconnected and interdependent processes, both organic and inorganic, how can the fixation on individuals as the sole welfare subjects be justified?

These problems about the class of welfare subjects are, as I say, mere embarrassments for the teleological theory. However, they do suggest one motive, albeit a negative one, for preferring a subjective theory. While such theories may be criticized for draw-ing the circle too narrowly, the notion of a subject as a unified centre of experiences does provide a resource which effectively resists expansion of the circle to include machines, works of art, natural objects and phenomena, organic subsystems, and the entire biosphere.[68] In any event, denying peripheral cases the status of

---

[68] Welfarism will have little plausibility if the range of welfare subjects is ex-tended to all these cases. To rely solely on this consideration would obviously amount to choosing a subjective theory about the nature of welfare on the ground

welfare subjects need not result in denying them moral standing. The environmental ethic defended by philosophers like Attfield and Taylor consists of two distinct theses: (1) all and only welfare subjects have moral standing, and (2) all and only living things are welfare subjects. The first thesis is a version of welfarism, while the second is based on the teleological theory about the nature of welfare. If one gives up the latter, by drawing the circle of welfare subjects more narrowly, while continuing to hold the former, then the result will indeed be the denial of moral standing to all of the excluded creatures. For anyone who finds this implication unpalatable, the obvious antidote is to abandon welfarism. This seems a more promising way of expanding the circle than continuing to defend a troublesome theory of welfare.

It is time to turn away from these relatively minor issues, since we have not yet come to terms with the teleological theory's principal asset. We have challenged objective theories to provide an alternative account of the evaluative standpoint of the welfare subject, so as to explain the perspectival nature of prudential value. And this is precisely what the teleological theory claims to be able to do with the notion of functioning, which is why it stands as the objectivist's best option. Has it not, then, mounted a successful response to the challenge? Even if it must answer some awkward questions about the range of welfare subjects, has it not passed the truly crucial test?

It has not, for what seems the theory's greatest strength is really its fatal defect. Recall Attfield's formula, that 'the flourishing of an x entails the development in it of the essential capacities of x's'. Leaving aside any difficulties in the notion of an essential capacity, what this formula ensures is that a living being is flourishing just in case it is a paradigmatic or exemplary specimen of its kind— one which displays to a high degree the capacities characteristic of its species. This result should remind us in turn of the argument Aristotle used to derive his theory about the nature of welfare, to which it is time we returned. That argument contained the following steps: (1) something promotes my well-being just in case it enhances my distinctive function, (2) something enhances my distinctive

of its superior normative adequacy. This normatively driven choice would still be between options left equally open by our descriptive criteria; it would therefore function only as a tie-breaker. In fact, however, the teleological theory is not descriptively adequate, as the remainder of this section will show.

function just in case it expresses my distinctive excellence, there-fore (3) something promotes my well-being just in case it expresses my distinctive excellence. Thus far we have highlighted some of the pitfalls in the notion of a biological function. But the real problem with the teleological theory lies not in the coherence of this notion but in its relevance to the nature of welfare.

The problem is easy to state. Recall the distinction drawn in Chapter 1 between prudential and perfectionist value. A theory of welfare must be a theory about the nature of prudential value. A thing has perfectionist value if it displays the excellences appropri-ate to its kind. Both Attfield's formula and Aristotle's argument equate a creature's welfare with its distinctive excellence. But then both accounts conflate prudential and perfectionist value: they are really theories about the latter rather than the former.

This conflation is concealed somewhat when attention is focused on relatively simple organisms. In the case of a tree we have no way to measure its flourishing save by means of those features which count as excellences in trees: luxuriant foliage, a healthy root system, resistance to disease, and so on. But that is to say that here we do not have two modes of value—prudential and perfectionist —but only one. An account of the functioning or flourishing of a tree does indeed enable us to determine whether states of the world are good or bad for it. But what is good for the tree is whatever promotes its excellence, and what is bad for it is what-ever makes it a worse example of its kind. There is here no point of view which is that of the tree; instead, it is merely the local bearer of a certain kind of generic value determined by the kind to which it belongs.

In the case of a tree the elision of prudential and perfectionist value is facilitated by the ambiguity of phrases such as 'a good of one's own'. 'The good of x' can mean, among other things, either 'the welfare of x' or 'the goodness of x'. Where a thing is capable of having perfectionist value we can certainly speak of its good-ness or excellence. In that sense it undeniably has a good, which is its own by virtue of being grounded in its nature. But it is a fallacy to slip from saying that something can be good or bad of its kind to saying that it therefore has a welfare. It is this fallacy which is committed by the teleological theory. The embarrassing implications of the theory for the class of welfare subjects, while not themselves fatal to it, are the symptoms of this deeper defect.

Tying welfare to the notion of functioning threatens an awkward expansion in its range of application because if functioning tracks any mode of value it is perfectionist rather than prudential.

The two evaluative dimensions come apart when we are dealing with subjects in the strict sense, namely those with a subjective point of view. (Or rather, in these cases prudential value makes its appearance for the first time as a separate and distinct dimension.) And they diverge most clearly for paradigm subjects such as us. Where human agents are concerned, it is a contingent matter whether the possession of some particular excellence makes us better off. There may, of course, be a strong empirical correlation between the excellences of mind and body and the well-being of their owners; it would be surprising if there were not. But as a conceptual matter the inference for any agent from perfectionist to prudential value is never guaranteed; there is always a logically open question. The gap between the two is opened by the agent's own hierarchy of projects and concerns, which is but one manifestation of her subjectivity.

The human case was, of course, the case that interested Aristotle. It is thus hard to understand how he could have committed this fallacy.[69] None the less, it appears that he did in moving from *eudaimonia* to *arete*, from the good (welfare) of a human being to the goodness (perfection) of a human being.[70] Since these are clearly such different matters for us now, it is hard to believe that they were not also for him then. Indeed, the conclusion of Aristotle's argument, the equation of welfare and virtue, has always seemed too good to be true. We simply have too many examples, from our day as from his, of villains and miscreants who seem (as Bernard

[69] The fallacy was clearly identified in Glassen 1957. It is also discussed in Wilkes 1978, although she defends Aristotle against the charge of equivocation. By far the most thorough explication, and defence, of Aristotle's *ergon* argument may be found in Hutchinson 1986, ch. 3. For other interesting recent attempts to defend Aristotle's approach, see Nussbaum 1988, 179 ff.; Whiting 1988; and Sparshott 1994, ch. 1.

[70] The perfectionist nature of Aristotle's account is underlined in Martha Nussbaum's interpretation of it: 'Getting the list of functionings that are constitutive of good living is a matter of asking ourselves what is most important, what is an essential part of any life that is going to be rich enough to count as fully human' (Nussbaum 1988, 175). Again: 'for Aristotle . . . the question as to whether a certain function is or is not a part of our human nature is . . . a question about whether that function is so important that a creature who lacked it would not be judged to be properly human at all' (ibid. 177).

Williams puts it) 'by any ethological standard of the bright eye and the gleaming coat' to be faring very well indeed. With any luck there is a strong tendency for virtue and interest to coincide, but we push our luck if we ask for more than that. Certainly they do not coincide conceptually, nor are they analytically linked in the tight way that Aristotle would have us believe.

In that case, however, the teleological theory is fundamentally misconceived as a theory about the nature of welfare; it is really about something quite different. It bears repeating that this result settles no substantive ethical issues. It is still open to the perfectionist to urge, against the welfarist, that excellence must be included among the basic values in an ethical theory, or even that it is the sole such value. That dispute will be adjudicated later (in Chapter 7). Our result concerns not the value of welfare but its nature. The teleological theory was the objectivist's last, best hope for responding to the challenge posed in the preceding chapter. With its demise goes all prospect of constructing a descriptively adequate objective theory of welfare.

4

Hedonism

THE elimination of objective accounts takes us some distance toward our goal of finding an adequate theory of welfare. But not very far, since nowadays most of the philosophically favoured theories in this domain are subjective, and all of them still remain in contention. We have merely succeeded in narrowing our original question a little: we now wish to know which subjective theory gives us the best account of the nature of welfare. Unluckily, however, not only are there many such theories available, they also differ among themselves in significant ways. We have made progress thus far by utilizing a relatively simple subjective/objective grid; we now need some equally salient way of subdividing the category of subjective accounts.

Without an appropriate principle of division the task of cataloguing the full variety of (actual or possible) subjective theories threatens to be interminable. Recall that a theory of welfare is subjective if it makes your well-being depend (at least in part) on your set of attitudes or concerns. You have an attitude toward, or concern about, something if the thing matters to you, or you mind or care whether it exists or happens. If you have a positive attitude toward the thing then you favour it, if a negative attitude you disfavour it. The range and variety of possible subjective theories is therefore given by the range and variety of possible positive/negative attitudes. Approving of something, valuing it, esteeming it; wanting something, aiming at it, seeking it; liking something, enjoying it, finding it satisfying—these are all types of positive attitude, but both the types themselves and the several varieties of each type are different from one another. An exhaustive array of subjective theories could therefore be assembled only by enumerating all of the many ways in which we can favour or disfavour things. Any such project would be a daunting, and probably fruitless, exercise in philosophical psychology.

Philosophers confronted by this problem have contrived a technique for circumventing it. Instead of trying to catalogue all the possible varieties of subjective account, they distinguish theories which make welfare a *state of mind* from those which make it a *state of the world*.[1] On the face of it, this is an unpromising tactic. After all, we know already that every subjective theory makes welfare depend in some way or other on some state of mind or other. How, then, could a subjective theory fail to be a state-of-mind theory? And how could it ever be a state-of-the-world theory?

When handled with a little care, however, the distinction does turn out to have a point. A theory is subjective if it makes welfare depend *at least in part* on some mental state, but it may make it depend on something else as well. If we draw a boundary around (the subject's own) states of mind and call everything else a state of the world, then we can indeed generate two types of subjective theory: those on which my welfare is *solely* a matter of my states of mind and those on which it is *additionally* a matter of some states of the world. The ground for this distinction, moreover, has been laid in our own account of the subjective, in which we worked outward from states of mind to states of the world.[2] The former category consists of phenomena such as sensations or dreams; because states of the world will play no role in a constitutive account of the nature of such things (as opposed to a causal theory of their origin), we may think of them as purely mind-dependent. The latter category, by contrast, contains those features of the world, such as perceptual properties, an account of whose nature seems to require reference both to subjective processes and to objective properties. Those who regard these features as secondary qualities think of them as partly mind-dependent and partly world-dependent.

On this picture, then, state-of-mind theories treat welfare just as some mental state, or some combination of such states, while state-of-the-world theories bring into the picture some reference to mind-independent reality. While these are all subjective theories, the former are more thoroughly or uncompromisingly subjective than the latter. Of course, it is not enough for our purposes that this line of division among subjective theories is available, nor that

[1] For a paradigmatic use of the distinction, see Griffin 1986, ch. 1.
[2] See s. 2.1, above.

it is now standard, nor even that it coheres with our account of the subjective. It must, additionally, be salient: it must bear directly on the descriptive adequacy of subjective accounts. As with the subjective/objective distinction, there is no way to demonstrate salience in advance; we must simply see how things work out. However, it is a promising sign that this partition of the domain separates the two kinds of subjective theory which have dominated the modern period: hedonistic accounts, identifying welfare with pleasure and the absence of pain, and desire accounts, identifying it with the satisfaction of wants or preferences. These options will preoccupy us over the next two chapters. First, hedonism.

4.1 THE CLASSICAL VIEW

Time and philosophical fashion have not been kind to hedonism. Although hedonistic theories of various sorts flourished for three centuries or so in their congenial empiricist habitat, they have all but disappeared from the scene. Do they now merit even passing attention, for other than nostalgic purposes? Like endangered species, discredited ideas do sometimes manage to make a comeback. Perhaps hedonism is now due for a revival of this sort. Or perhaps not, but even if it is too late to rescue it from extinction we may still learn some valuable lessons by exposing the reasons for its decline.

Orthodoxy has it that hedonism comes in two forms: psychological and ethical. In its psychological version, it is a causal theory of motivation in which all intentional action is ultimately to be explained in terms of seeking pleasure and avoiding pain. In its ethical version, it is a theory of value in which pleasure is the sole good and pain the sole evil. Both theories count as hedonistic by virtue of assigning a foundational (explanatory or justificatory) role to pleasure and pain. Historically, these two varieties of hedonism have been closely associated, the psychological theory being thought to lend support to the ethical.

This picture of the varieties of hedonism is, however, incomplete. A hedonistic theory may also take a third form, distinct from both of the foregoing: it may be a theory about the nature of welfare. Such a theory will begin by taking pleasure and pain to characterize the primitive attitudes, positive and negative respectively, which subjects may have toward objects or states of affairs. Minding something, or caring whether it happens, will ultimately be a matter of finding the experience of it either pleasant or painful. The theory will then go on to assign these attitudes a basic constitutive role in a formal theory of welfare. Such a theory will map the polarity of welfare onto the polarity of pleasure and pain. In order for my life to be going well for me I must be experiencing it, or its principal ingredients, as pleasant or satisfying; conversely, if it is going badly for me then my experience of it must, on balance, be unpleasant or unsatisfying. Likewise, something can benefit me or make me better off only if I find it agreeable, and it can harm me or make me worse off only if I find it disagreeable.

These rather vague formulae will suffice to define the general shape of a hedonistic theory of welfare. However, they need considerable further elaboration in order to yield a specific, determinate version of such a theory. One such version was shared, in most of its essentials, by the principal utilitarians of the eighteenth and nineteenth centuries: Jeremy Bentham, John Stuart Mill, and Henry Sidgwick. Their hedonism about welfare has tended to be somewhat overshadowed by their ethical hedonism.[3] Logically speaking, the two views are quite distinct: the former is an analysis of the nature of prudential value while the latter is a claim about which things have (ultimate) ethical value. However, the utilitarians plainly thought that they were intimately connected.

It is not difficult to find emphatic statements by the utilitarians of hedonism as a theory of the good. One of the best known is J. S. Mill's 'theory of life', on which he takes his moral theory to be grounded: 'pleasure, and freedom from pain, are the only things desirable as ends; and . . . all desirable things . . . are desirable either for the pleasure inherent in themselves, or as means to the promotion of pleasure and the prevention of pain.'[4] However, it

[3] I will pass over the question of psychological hedonism, since it divides the utilitarian camp. Bentham and J. S. Mill both subscribed to it: for their best-known statements of the doctrine, see Bentham 1970, ch. 1, and Mill 1969, ch. 4. Sidgwick, on the other hand, rejected it: see Sidgwick 1962, Book I, ch. 4.

[4] Mill 1969, 210; cf. 214: 'the ultimate end, with reference to and for the sake of which all other things are desirable . . . is an existence exempt as far as possible from pain, and as rich as possible in enjoyments.' Likewise Bentham: 'Now, pleasure is in *itself* a good: nay, even setting aside immunity from pain, the only good: pain is in itself an evil; and, indeed, without exception, the only evil; or else the words good and evil have no meaning. And this is alike true of every sort of pain, and of every sort of pleasure' (1970, 100). Bentham sometimes claimed his ethical hedonism to be true by definition; see 1843, iii. 214, vi. 257 n.

is interesting that Mill himself decomposes this theory of life into two constituent parts. The first of these is a claim about the value, not of pleasure, but of happiness: 'The utilitarian doctrine is, that happiness is desirable, and the only thing desirable, as an end; all other things being only desirable as a means to that end.'[5] The second is an analysis of the nature of happiness: 'By happiness is intended pleasure, and the absence of pain; by unhappiness, pain, and the privation of pleasure.'[6] Mill's line of thought thus appears to be: only happiness is good in itself, happiness is pleasure and the absence of pain, therefore only pleasure and the absence of pain are good in themselves. If we assume that Mill simply identifies happiness and well-being, then he derives ethical hedonism as a conclusion from two premises: welfarism plus a hedonistic theory of welfare.

The equation of well-being with happiness is implicit in the utilitarian tradition—too implicit to count as a developed theory about the nature of welfare.[7] Instead, it is an assumed conceptual identity: for the utilitarians the two notions were indistinguishable. When this identity is kept in mind, counterparts to the two steps in Mill's derivation of ethical hedonism can readily be found in both Bentham and Sidgwick. Consider first their welfarism. Bentham has the following to say about the nature of ethics:

As to the *end* or object of it, if by this be meant the most general end, for this most general end or object it has or ought to have the same end or object which not only every branch of art or science has, but every human thought as well as every human action has—and not only has but ought to have: [namely,] the giving encrease in some shape or other to man's well-being—say in one word the sum of human happiness.[8]

[5] Mill 1969, 234. Note that the passage on p. 210 also begins with a claim about the value of happiness.

[6] Ibid. 210.

[7] Mill nearly always prefers to speak of happiness or utility, as he does throughout Mill 1969. However, he sometimes switches to talk of well-being; see, for instance, Mill 1977, ch. 3. Sidgwick defines egoism in terms of happiness, as opposed to good or well-being, because of its relative freedom from perfectionist overtones (see Sidgwick 1962, ch. 7); it is clear that he is seeking a purely welfarist notion. Bentham sometimes uses well-being and happiness interchangeably (see, for instance, Bentham 1983*b*, 124–5). Where he distinguishes them (Bentham 1983*b*, 130, 135), he treats the former as pointing to an individual's net balance of pleasure over pain, while the latter suggests a run of pleasures of an unusually high degree. See also Bentham 1983*a*, 179–80 n.

[8] Bentham 1983*b*, 124–5. Cf. Bentham's definition of eudaimonics: 'the *art*, which has for the object of its endeavours, to contribute in some way or other to

Whereas it probably never occurred to Bentham that ethics could have to do with anything other than happiness or well-being, for Sidgwick this was a substantive view in need of argument. This argument he attempted to provide in the chapter of his *Methods of Ethics* entitled 'Ultimate Good'.[9] Whether the case he there makes in defence of welfarism is successful is not our present concern, but we should note his conception of the project. Sidgwick begins the chapter by affirming the priority of the good: 'the practical determination of Right Conduct depends on the determination of Ultimate Good.'[10] His next step is to narrow the list of contenders down to goods which include states of consciousness. He then continues: 'If then Ultimate Good can only be conceived as Desirable Consciousness . . . are we to identify this notion with Happiness or Pleasure, and say with the Utilitarians that General Good is general happiness?'[11] As Sidgwick conceives it, the contest at this point is between happiness on the one hand and various (subjective) perfectionist goods, such as knowledge and freedom, on the other. The arguments he then goes on to advance on the side of happiness constitute his case in favour of welfarism and against perfectionism.

That Bentham and Sidgwick both held hedonistic theories about the nature of welfare/happiness is so obvious as to be scarcely worth documenting. Bentham tells us that happiness consists of 'enjoyment of pleasures, security from pains',[12] and elsewhere offers a similar account of well-being as 'enjoyment of the several distinguishable pleasures and exemption from the several distinguishable pains'.[13] For his part, the assumption of a hedonistic account of happiness structures Sidgwick's handling of the substantive issue between welfarism and perfectionism. What distinguishes happiness from the competing perfectionist goods, for Sidgwick, is the

---

the attainment of *well-being*, and the *science* in virtue of which, in so far as it is possessed by him, a man knows in what manner he is to conduct himself in order to exercise that art with effect' (1983*a*, 179–80). There is a striking resemblance between these passages and Mill's views on the relationship between art and science, and on the ultimate end of the 'art of life'; see Mill 1974, 949–52.

[9] Sidgwick 1962, Book III, ch. 14.   [10] Ibid. 391.   [11] Ibid. 398.

[12] Bentham 1970, 74; cf. 1952–4, iii. 308. The empiricist reduction of happiness to pleasure can be traced back at least as far as Locke (1975, Book II, ch. 21, s. 42).

[13] Bentham 1983*b*, 125; cf. 1983*a*, 179–80 n. For a reduction of interest to pleasure and pain, see 1970, 12; 1952–4, i. 207.

fact that it includes no reference to states of the world external to the subject, since it consists entirely in the having of agreeable feelings, i.e. pleasures.[14]

All of this may seem so much belabouring of the obvious. Surely, it will be said, everyone knows that the classical utilitarians were hedonists both in their theory of the good and in their theory of welfare. There is, however, some point to distinguishing the two steps which seem to have led them to their ethical hedonism. The line of thought shared by Bentham, Mill, and Sidgwick yields ethical hedonism (pleasure is the only good) out of welfarism (well-being is the only good) and a view about the nature of welfare (well-being is reducible to pleasure). The exercise of distinguishing these two premises therefore offers the intriguing possibility that, for all their talk about pleasure and pain, what the utilitarians thought ultimately valuable was happiness or well-being. Pleasure and pain came into the picture only because they were believed to be implicated in the nature of well-being. If this hypothesis is correct, then the classical utilitarians were primarily welfarists and only secondarily hedonists.

However this may be, what is important for our present purposes is that the utilitarians all shared the view that welfare consists in happiness and that happiness consists in pleasure and the absence of pain.[15] In order to round out an account of their theory of welfare, it remains to ask only what they meant by pleasure and pain. Different conceptions of pleasure and pain—different accounts of their nature—will generate different versions of a hedonistic theory. Whether a particular version is a mental state theory will depend on whether it conceives pleasure and pain simply as states of mind, with no reference to any states of the world.

A mental state conception is certainly the dominant theme running through the utilitarian tradition. However, the story is slightly complicated by the fact that the classical theorists offered two alternative models of pleasure and pain, one of which appeals to the internal qualities of these feelings while the other invokes their external relations. On both models pleasures and pains each constitute a class of distinctive feelings or experiences whose common properties can be identified by introspection. The *internalist* account

---

[14] See Sidgwick 1962, 92, 95, 398 ff.
[15] Both views still have their defenders; see, for instance, Edwards 1979.

was inherited by Bentham from his immediate predecessors, Hume and Hartley. For Hume pleasures and pains constituted an important category of impressions, along with sense impressions, while Hartley considered them to be one class of 'internal feelings'.[16] In Bentham this basic idea was developed into an elaborate architectonic which began by dividing mental operations into two categories: intellectual (perception, imagination, judgement, etc.) and sensitive (feeling, desire, will, etc.). The basic ingredients for both sorts of operations are what Bentham called experiences or perceptions; in the former case sense impressions, in the latter sensations of pleasure and pain. In each case the perceptions in question are foundational within their domain: all operations are reducible to them, while they admit of no similar reduction. For this reason Bentham regarded sense impressions on the one hand, and pleasurable and painful sensations on the other, as the only classes of real psychological entities.

For Bentham the status of sensations as fundamental real entities precluded any further analysis of their nature. While there is little question that he thought of particular pleasures and pains as discrete mental states or events, he could offer no account of the difference between them, taken collectively, and sense impressions. In his view pleasure and pain are each *sui generis*, readily discriminable in our experience from other perceptions, and from one another, but susceptible of no (non-ostensive) definition.[17] Bentham's inability to provide a reductive account of the nature of pleasure and pain should leave us in no doubt, however, concerning the range of phenomena which he wished to include in these categories. It is abundantly clear that he thought of pleasure, for instance, as embracing not merely bodily pleasures but all forms of gratification, enjoyment, satisfaction, fulfilment, and the like.[18] These various forms of experience differ in their sources or causes— that in which the pleasure is taken. What they have in common, in virtue of which they all count as pleasures, is their positive feeling tone: an intrinsic, unanalysable quality of pleasantness which is present to a greater or lesser degree in all of them.[19] It is this

---

[16] See Hume 1978, Book II, Part I, s. 1; Hartley 1749, Part I, 2.

[17] Cf. Locke 1975, Book II, ch. 20, s. 1.

[18] For Bentham's catalogue of the various kinds of pleasures (and pains), see 1970, ch. 5, and *A Table of the Springs of Action* in 1983b.

[19] Cf. Bentham's remark that pleasure and pain are 'names of homogeneous real entities' (1970, 53 n.).

quality whose intensity supplies one of the two core ingredients (along with duration) in Bentham's celebrated technique for quantifying pleasures.[20] The class of pains, heterogeneous in their sources or objects, would likewise be picked out on the basis of their distinctive negative feeling tone. Pleasures differ from pains, on this view, simply by virtue of feeling pleasant or agreeable rather than unpleasant or disagreeable.

Bentham's identification of pleasure and pain in terms of their purely phenomenal properties was echoed by his utilitarian successors. In his *Analysis of the Phenomena of the Human Mind* James Mill used the term 'sensation' to cover roughly what Bentham called perceptions or experiences. He then introduced pleasure and pain in the following passage:

Some sensations, probably the greater number, are what we call indifferent. They are not considered as either painful, or pleasurable. There are sensations, however, and of frequent recurrence, some of which are painful, some pleasurable. The difference is, that which is felt. A man knows it, by feeling it; and that is the whole account of the phenomenon.[21]

When John Stuart Mill came to edit the second edition of this work, he appended to it quite substantial notes in which he carried on a running commentary on his father's views, often registering dissent from them. Where the account of pleasure and pain was concerned, however, he found little to correct:

In the case of many pleasurable or painful sensations, it is open to question whether the pleasure or pain, especially the pleasure, is not something added to the sensation, and capable of being detached from it, rather than merely a particular aspect or quality of the sensation.... However this may be, the pleasure or pain attending a sensation is ... capable of being mentally abstracted from the sensation, or, in other words, capable of being attended to by itself.[22]

The theme surfaces again in Sidgwick, who treats pleasures as a class of feelings 'so called because they have a common property of pleasantness'.[23]

This internalist view, however, is only part of the official story

[20] Ibid., ch. 4; cf. Goldworth 1979.
[21] Mill 1869, ii. 184; cf. 190 ff., 363 ff.   [22] Ibid. 185 n.
[23] Sidgwick 1962, 94. Sidgwick draws the conclusion that all pleasures must therefore be commensurable in terms of their pleasantness, and all pains in terms of their painfulness (123 ff.).

for the utilitarians. A different model of pleasure and pain can also be traced back at least as far as James Mill. The passage quoted above, in which Mill attempts to characterize the class of pleasurable and painful sensations, continues as follows:

I have one sensation, and then another, and then another. The first is of such a kind, that I care not whether it is long or short; the second is of such a kind that I would put an end to it instantly if I could; the third is of such a kind, that I like it prolonged. To distinguish these feelings, I give them names. I call the first Indifferent; the second, Painful; the third, Pleasurable; very often, for shortness, I call the second, Pain, the third, Pleasure.[24]

On this view, what all pleasures share is not a homogeneous feeling tone but the fact that they are experiences which we like, or enjoy, or seek, or wish to prolong for their own sake—in short, the fact that they are objects of some positive attitude on our part. Likewise, experiences are classified as painful by virtue of provoking a negative, aversive response. This *externalist* account, unlike the uniform sensation model, is capable of recognizing that the great variety of experiences which we find pleasant or agreeable may be heterogeneous, not only in their sources or causes, but also in the way they feel. Pleasures may have nothing in common save the fact that we like them, pains nothing but the (external) property of being disliked.

The younger Mill appears to have presupposed some such model in his well-known emphasis on distinctions of quality among pleasures. Having appealed to the verdict of 'competent judges' to determine degrees of quality, Mill continues:

And there needs be the less hesitation to accept this judgement respecting the quality of pleasures, since there is no other tribunal to be referred to even on the question of quantity. What means are there of determining which is the acutest of two pains, or the intensest of two pleasurable sensations, except the general suffrage of those who are familiar with both? Neither pains nor pleasures are homogeneous, and pain is always heterogeneous with pleasure.[25]

[24] Bentham gives occasional hints of such an account, as when he says that 'Pains and pleasures may be called by one general word, interesting perceptions' (1970, 42), and when he distinguishes pleasures and pains from sensations which are 'indifferent' (1843, vi. 217).

[25] Mill 1969, 213.

However, it was Sidgwick who provided the best statement of the alternative view:

Shall we then say that there is a measurable quality of feeling expressed by the word 'pleasure,' which is independent of its relation to volition, and strictly undefinable from its simplicity?—like the quality of feeling expressed by 'sweet,' of which also we are conscious in varying degrees of intensity. This seems to be the view of some writers: but, for my own part, when I reflect on the notion of pleasure,—using the term in the comprehensive sense I have adopted, to include the most refined and subtle intellectual and emotional gratifications, no less than the coarser and more definite sensual enjoyments,—the only common quality that I can find in the feelings so designated seems to be that relation to desire and volition expressed by the general term 'desirable'. . . . I propose therefore to define Pleasure . . . as a feeling which, when experienced by intelligent beings, is at least implicitly apprehended as desirable or—in cases of comparison—preferable.[26]

For some purposes it would be worth pursuing the differences between these two views of the nature of pleasure and pain—the internalist *sensation* model with its emphasis on a homogeneous (positive or negative) feeling tone and the externalist *attitude* model with its reliance on a uniform (positive or negative) reaction. (We will pursue these differences below, in section 4.3.) However, for the moment what they have in common is more important to us. On both views pleasures and pains are experiences which can be identified as such on the basis of some introspectible feature, whether this is an internal quality (the way they feel) or an external relation (the fact of being liked or disliked). On both views, therefore, pleasures and pains are purely mental states.

A mental state analysis of pleasure and pain is the final component in the theory of welfare shared by the classical utilitarians. As is now evident, this theory was the product of three distinct theses: (1) welfare is identical to happiness, (2) happiness consists of pleasure and the absence of pain, and (3) pleasures and pains are each a class of introspectively discriminable experiences. Any hedonistic

---

[26] Sidgwick 1962, 127; cf. 131: 'Let, then, pleasure be defined as feeling which the sentient individual at the time of feeling it implicitly or explicitly apprehends to be desirable;—desirable, that is, when considered merely as feeling, and not in respect of its objective conditions or consequences, or of any facts that come directly within the cognisance and judgment of others besides the sentient individual.' For the breadth of Sidgwick's notion of pleasure, see also pp. 93, 402.

analysis of welfare will need to endorse some version or other of
(1) and (2). It is the third thesis which is the characteristic marker
of the classical view, and which ensures that it is a mental state
theory of welfare. Our next question is whether any such theory
can be descriptively adequate.

4.2 PROBLEMS WITH THE CLASSICAL VIEW

Classical hedonism yields a mental state theory about the nature
of welfare because it treats pleasure and pain as distinctive states
of mind. The resulting theory tells us that our lives are going well
when we are having pleasurable feelings and badly when we are
having painful ones, that you are better off than me if you are
having more of the former or fewer of the latter, that something
benefits me when it causes the former and harms me when it
causes the latter, and so on.

The two strongest objections to an account of this sort have
been nicely summarized by James Griffin.[27] The first is directed
against the sensation model. Griffin argues that there is no positive
quality of feeling such that having more of it invariably makes us
better off, and no negative quality such that having more of that
must make us worse off. He gives the example of Freud who,
when terminally ill, refused all drugs except aspirin, preferring to
think in torment rather than not to be able to think clearly. As
Griffin asks, 'can we find a single feeling or mental state present
in both of Freud's options in virtue of which he ranked them as
he did?'[28] On Bentham's version of the classical view, Freud seems
plainly to have chosen the option which was worse for him. But
that is a judgement few of us would join in making, and one
which he himself would presumably have rejected. Less dramatic
instances occur in our ordinary lives whenever we choose between
heterogeneous activities or pursuits. There is a recognizable feeling
tone to sexual arousal which is quite different from the relief of
finally completing a long-standing task or the tranquillity of a
walk in the woods. If these are your options for the next hour,
you might have a decided preference for one over the others (on
purely prudential grounds). But it would be difficult for you to

---

[27] Griffin 1986, ch. 1.   [28] Ibid. 8.

locate any particular felt quality, common to all three experiences, which you are thereby aiming to maximize.

Of the classical utilitarians, Bentham was the most clearly committed to the homogeneity of all pleasures, and all pains. Considered as part of a theory of welfare, however, this simple model of pleasure and pain has an ironic implication. The great advantage of a subjective theory is that it makes well-being responsive to an individual's own schedule of concerns. Suppose, then, that all pleasures do share some uniform positive feeling tone, which can be present to a greater or lesser degree. A hedonistic theory will imply that the best choice for you is always the one which maximizes your personal share of this feeling. But what if this does not match your own ranking of the available options? What if, like Freud, you prefer (on prudential grounds) an alternative with a lower hedonic payoff? The theory is then committed to disregarding your own priorities in determining what is best for you. But any result of this sort violates at least the spirit, and probably also the letter, of a subjective theory.

A theory which stipulates that welfare consists in some distinctive feeling, regardless of the place which this feeling is actually assigned in the lives of reflective subjects, is only doubtfully subjective. Its closest kin are those objective theories which find the sources of well-being to consist in such personal goods as knowledge or autonomy or self-realization, regardless of the extent to which individuals seek or value them. What makes a theory of welfare subjective is not what it counts as welfare sources (and therefore not whether these are themselves subjective), but the role it assigns to the subject's concerns in identifying those sources. An objective account does not become more plausible when pleasure, understood as a homogeneous sensation, comes to be substituted for the more common list of perfectionist goods.

As we have seen, however, not all of the utilitarians accepted Bentham's assumption of the homogeneity of all pleasures (and pains). The attitude model is quite capable of acknowledging that the mental states we call pleasures are a mixed bag as far as their phenomenal properties are concerned. What these states have in common is not something about them—their peculiar feeling tone, or whatever—but something about us—the fact that we like them, enjoy them, value them, find them satisfying, seek them, wish to prolong them, and so on. Griffin's first objection to hedonistic theories is therefore not decisive. As long as pleasures are thought of as introspectively discriminable feelings, a hedonistic theory of welfare will necessarily be a mental state theory. But it need not presuppose the homogeneity of all such feelings. When confronted with the case of Freud, the hedonist can say that he chose the option which, despite the greater suffering involved, he found on balance to be the more satisfying or fulfilling. And that seems roughly right.[29]

Against this form of hedonism, however, Griffin brings a second objection:

> The trouble with this eclectic account is that we do seem to desire things other than states of mind, even independently of the states of mind they produce. . . . I prefer, in important areas of my life, bitter truth to comfortable delusion. Even if I were surrounded by consummate actors able to give me sweet simulacra of love and affection, I should prefer the relatively bitter diet of their authentic reactions. And I should prefer it not because it would be morally better, or aesthetically better, or more noble, but because it would make for a better life for me to live.[30]

Robert Nozick has made a similar point by means of a science-fiction hypothesis of a machine capable of synthesizing any experiences we wish, including the belief that they are real and not merely synthetic:

> Superduper neuropsychologists could stimulate your brain so that you would think and feel you were writing a great novel, or making a friend, or reading an interesting book. All the time you would be floating in a tank, with electrodes attached to your brain. Should you plug into this machine for life, preprogramming your life's experiences?[31]

Why not, asks Nozick, if all that matters to us is how our lives feel from the inside?

As striking as Nozick's thought experiment is, it is not clear just what lesson we should draw from it. For one thing, as soon as we start to think realistically about the scenario he sketches then the decision not to plug in quickly seems overdetermined. Once you

---

[29] Griffin says that in Sidgwick's account desire unifies the several mental states which count as pleasures (ibid. 9). This sets up the transition to his own desire theory, once the reference to the states themselves is discarded as redundant. But it is at least as plausible to point to the fact that they are all liked or enjoyed or found fulfilling. This is not the same as saying that they are desired—*au contraire*, it identifies the most obvious reason for desiring them.

[30] Ibid.   [31] Nozick 1974, 42; cf. 1989, 104–8.

have signed on and are floating in the tank you have relinquished all control over how things subsequently go for you; you are in no position to change your mind or demand a refund if the goods are not as promised. We immediately begin to imagine the many ways in which things could go horribly wrong. How do we keep our bodies from atrophying from disuse? How do we know that the technology is foolproof? What happens if there is a power failure? Suppose the operators of the machine are really sadistic thrill-seekers, or the premises are overrun by fundamentalist zealots? In order to isolate the philosophical point which the experience machine is meant to illustrate, we have to control for boundary conditions by supposing that all these risks have somehow been neutralized. But this is very difficult to do, since we know that in real life we cannot eliminate all possible malfunctions and screw-ups. For the thought experiment to yield any results at all we must therefore imagine ourselves in a world quite alien to our own—and who knows what we would choose in a world like that?

We get to Nozick's philosophical point more readily by hypo-thesizing less grand illusions, ones which could be visited from time to time without any commitment to taking up permanent residence. Virtual reality, if it could be made convincing enough, might someday offer us the appropriate sort of temporary escapism. For now, we are dependent on fictional examples: the machine-induced vacation fantasies in Paul Verhoeven's film *Total Recall* (which were also subject to malfunction) or the holodeck in *Star Trek: The Next Generation*. We can more easily imagine having these 'experience machines' available to us, since they are extrapo-lations of technologies currently on offer (movies, television, video games). Because they seem much less risky than Nozick's machine, we can also imagine indulging in them now and again. Suppose you spend a couple of hours some evening wired into a virtual reality console, enjoying the machine-induced experience of exploring a cave in British Columbia or spending an evening with Leonard Cohen. Is this such a bad way to pass your time? Is it worse than watching two hours of *Mission Impossible* reruns, which you could never mistake for reality? Is reality always better for us, as such, than illusion? It seems excessively austere to say so. But then how are our lives supposed to go worse (intrinsically, rather than cir-cumstantially) if we sometimes choose to plug into experience machines?

Nozick asks what matters to us besides the introspectible features of our experiences and answers that we also want to *do* certain things and *be* a certain sort of person. This takes us back to Griffin's point: we care about states of the world as well as our own states of mind. Offered a choice between bitter truth and comfortable delusion, at least sometimes we will opt for truth. Not all the time—that would be too strong a claim. When we find reality hard enough to face, then the comfort afforded by the appropriate delusion may be irresistible. There is, of course, an epistemic problem here: a delusion has no power to comfort unless it is accepted as real, in which case how can we be said to prefer it *as a delusion*? After all, the problem is that *from the inside* delusion and reality may be indistinguishable. However, we do often have an inkling that our carefully safeguarded belief structure is fragile and collude in protecting it against damaging counterevidence; deception shades into self-deception. Furthermore, like Griffin, we can express a standing preference, one way or the other, about specified areas of our lives: 'I don't want to know', 'I would like to be told'.

Our attitudes toward delusion, deception, and fantasy are more complex and ambiguous than the experience machine story allows for. However, we will surely agree with Griffin in preferring reality to illusion over some key sectors of our lives. And we will agree that, in those sectors, being in touch with reality makes for a better life. Since there are many ways in which a life may have value, the question remains open whether, when we get the truth we seek, our lives are *prudentially* better. Griffin claims that he prefers truth to delusion 'not because it would be morally better, or aesthetically better, or more noble, but because it would make for a better life for me to live'. But a life of greater moral or aesthetic or perfectionist value is also, in that respect, a better life for him to live, so we have not yet succeeded in isolating the prudential question. Nor can we easily discount the influence of these other ideals. Could our judgement not sometimes be that a life filled with illusion or deception, while it may be going very nicely for its subject, is none the less unworthy of a human being? If so, then the lesson of the experience machine may be, not that mental state theories are deficient as accounts of the nature of welfare, but that welfare tracks only one dimension of the value of a life.

The internal conflicts possible in this territory are nicely illustrated by an episode in *Asta's Book*, a mystery novel by Ruth

Rendell/Barbara Vine. The central character, Asta, keeps a diary. She has received a letter informing her that her son has been killed in the war and reassuring her that he died quickly, without pain. She records the comfort she has derived from this reassurance: 'You can bear your children dying. What is unbearable is to think of them suffering, to think of that particular person, the child you carried, bleeding and in agony.' Later, she is visited by the sergeant who found her son on the battlefield and carried him back to the lines, and who knows the true circumstances of his death. She writes of that encounter: 'I would have given ten years of my life to have been able not to ask. But bargains like that can't be made. Either you're the sort of person who can hide from things or else you're not. I'd rather be so unhappy I want to die, and see the facts and look them in the face, than delude myself.' She asks the sergeant to tell her the truth. 'So he did. I can't write it. I wanted to know and I got what I thought I wanted.'[32]

Asta's resolve to face the truth can be seen as the choice of a personal ideal—being the sort of person who does not hide from things—even at a terrible cost to her own well-being. After all, it is a commonplace that we care about, and are motivated by, many considerations other than our own interest—considerations to which we are prepared to sacrifice our interest, if necessary. Defenders of mental state theories can try to hold the line here, arguing that every choice of bitter truth over comforting delusion is a case of welfare being trumped by some rival dimension of value.[33] Upon reflection, however, this is difficult to accept. Asta's choice can equally be seen as her way of seeking closure on a matter which cuts right to her heart, facing the truth in order to be able to put it behind her. And that seems to bear directly on how well her life will go, not just from any standpoint, but *for her*.

If what you have accepted as an important constituent of your well-being—your achievements, say, or the feelings of others about you—turns out to have been an elaborate deception, you are likely to feel hurt and betrayed. How else to explain this, except to say that, in this area at least, what mattered to you was not merely how things seemed but how they actually were? Your reaction to the deception certainly looks, and feels, like a reassessment, in the

[32] Vine 1994, 265, 273–4.
[33] This line of response to experience machine objections is pursued by Haslett 1990, 91–3, and Goldsworthy 1992, 18–20.

light of your own priorities, of how well your life has been going. And that seems to place it squarely within the domain of prudential value. Since a subjective theory must be faithful to the full range of our concerns, and since these concerns typically extend beyond appearance to reality, such a theory cannot make welfare consist merely in having agreeable experiences, even of the eclectic variety that the utilitarians were prepared to recognize.

As components of a theory of welfare, the two models of pleasure and pain offered by the classical hedonists fail for the same reason. Each of them overrides the authority of welfare subjects to determine for themselves which goods they will choose to pursue in their lives: the sensation model by stipulating that subjects must always prefer more pleasurable feeling tone to less, the attitude model by dictating that subjects must be indifferent between veridical and illusory experiences, as long as they are equally enjoyable. In the end, therefore, it does not matter which model the classical hedonists plug into their analysis of welfare. In either case the result will fail to preserve the individual autonomy which is the most attractive feature of a subjective theory.

Of Griffin's two objections to the classical view, the second is much the more telling, since it strikes against any hedonistic theory which treats pleasure and pain simply as mental states. Any such theory will entail that the impact on our well-being of some particular experience is entirely determined by features of the experience which are available to introspection—how it feels, how agreeable we find it, how much we wish it to continue, or whatever. We may therefore track how well our lives are going just by attending to how they seem from the inside, bracketing off all questions of their anchoring in the external world. The lesson of the experience machine is that any theory with this implication is too interior and solipsistic to provide a descriptively adequate account of the nature of welfare. Since welfare does not consist merely of states of mind, it does not consist merely of pleasurable states of mind, regardless of how these are characterized.

4.3 THE TRUTH IN HEDONISM

Is this then the end of hedonism as a theory of welfare? Recall that the classical view was a compound of three ingredients: (1) the equation of welfare and happiness, (2) an analysis of happiness in terms of pleasure (and the absence of pain), and (3) a mental state account of pleasure and pain. Since no theory which abandoned the first two components would any longer be hedonistic, the fate of hedonism hangs on whether there is a plausible model of pleasure and pain available on which they are not simply mental states.

We will come at this question by a rather roundabout route, beginning with a closer look at the strengths of the classical view: the areas of our lives in which it seems to tell more or less the right story. Its heartland is the territory of physical pleasure and pain—and especially the latter. One of our most secure convictions about welfare is that the quality of our lives is seriously compromised by extended episodes of physical pain or suffering. Calling (some kinds of) suffering 'physical' in this way does not, of course, commit one to thinking that pain is a merely physical, or neurological, state. Whatever our best understanding of the nature of pain may turn out to be, there is clearly something essentially mental about it. Rather, it points to the fact that some (but not all) pain or suffering has an organic basis or cause, usually (though not always) some threat to tissue integrity. In this sense we can distinguish between pain felt as the result of bodily disease or injury and the suffering occasioned by, say, the loss of a loved one or the collapse of an important project.

To fix our frame of reference, let us focus on pain that is both intense and extended—the sort of chronic suffering associated with such debilitating diseases as cancer or such injuries as serious burns. Few among us would deny that the pain itself—the fact that it hurts so much or makes us feel so bad—is enough to blight our lives, whatever else may also be going on in our bodies. If so, then pain of this sort is one condition which makes us worse off directly or immediately, and not through its connections with any other condition. It may be tempting to deny this. After all, it may be said, physical pain is typically the subjective accompaniment of some bodily injury which impairs functioning, and it is this objective impairment which is the real intrinsic evil, not the subjective feeling which signals it. However, sober second thought will reject this rather austere view. It is true that a serious disease such as cancer impairs bodily functioning, and it seems reasonable to treat this impairment as an important part of the devastation which cancer can wreak on us. But it is also true that cancer accompanied by severe and intractable pain is much worse than the organic impairment alone—otherwise, why would we try to alleviate or control the suffering of terminal patients? Furthermore, some varieties of very intense pain are accompanied by no detectable injury whatever. One of these, trigeminal neuralgia or *tic douloureux*, has been described in the following way: 'This is the quintessential painful disorder, for it is marked by nothing other than sudden bursts of searing, agonizing pain, which appear and disappear for no apparent reason. There is no persistent alteration of sensation, no injury, no signs of disease of any type—just pain.'[34] It would require a pretty heavy commitment to a theory to deny that this kind of suffering makes our lives go badly, just in and by itself.

In the central cases of physical pain, then, it appears that at least part of what is bad about our condition is the way it makes us feel. Here there seem to be no problems with a purely mental state account, no counterpart to the experience machine that could bring us to think that we are being deceived by mere appearances. Classical hedonism thrives on such cases, since they appear to involve no reference beyond ourselves, no beliefs about the world which might turn out to be mistaken. If I am suffering physical pain then I can be quite wrong about the organic cause of my affliction, or even about whether it has one, without that error diminishing in the slightest either the reality of my pain or its impact on the quality of my life. Were the instance of physical pain in every respect typical, then there would be nothing wrong with a mental state theory of welfare.

How are we to understand the nature of something as familiar as physical pain? Is it just a particular kind of sensation to be distinguished phenomenologically from other sensations—pleasure, temperature, touch, taste, kinaesthesia, etc.—by the way it feels? Is it possible to like or enjoy pain, or at least not to be averse to it? Is it possible to seek it, or at least not to shun it? And if so, then in such cases need pain be bad for us? These questions have been sharpened recently by some very interesting data concerning individual responses to pain. Basically, there seem to be two different ways of controlling or managing pain. One is exemplified by analgesia, anaesthesia, and possibly also hypnosis; when these methods are successful, the subject feels no, or at least less, pain.[35]

[34] Kerr 1981, 44–5.
[35] See ibid., chs. 9, 10, 12, 13; Melzack and Wall 1983, ch. 2.

The other way is exemplified by such psychosurgical techniques as lobotomy.[36] In these cases subjects often report that, while they still feel the pain, they no longer mind it.[37] Rather more difficult to classify are the well-known instances, such as the treatment of battlefield wounds, in which individuals endure, with few visible signs of distress, what would ordinarily be agonizing pain. Reflection on these cases, and on the lobotomy patients, has led many analysts to the conclusion that there is an emotional or attitudinal dimension to the perception of pain, in addition to the characteristic pain sensation itself.[38] It has even led some to deny that pain is a sensation at all, giving it instead a purely attitudinal analysis.[39]

Phenomenologically, it seems possible to identify many of the intrinsic properties of pains: their intensity, to be sure, but also many features which enable us to sort pains into different kinds, such as aches, stings, twinges, and so on.[40] The similarity with our linguistic resources for characterizing, say, sensations of taste or touch lends strong support to the idea that there is at least a sensory dimension to pain. At the same time, it also seems possible to distinguish between all of these properties, including intensity, and the extent to which we mind the pain or are bothered by it.[41] In addition to the pathological cases mentioned above, there are quite commonplace instances of our not being averse to, or even relishing, pain. I can deliberately probe a loose tooth with my tongue and find the sharp pang which results quite delicious. In this case I have no difficulty identifying the feeling as painful; indeed, that seems to be part of its appeal. In other cases pain seems to be welcomed because of its contextual meaning. I can remember vividly the shrieking of my leg muscles after I first completed a marathon in my younger days; since the pain was the continuing reminder of my accomplishment, I would have felt

---

[36] Kerr 1981, 146–9; Melzack and Wall 1983, 296.

[37] The cases may be open to different interpretations; see Trigg 1970, ch. 7.

[38] Kerr 1981, 26; Melzack and Wall 1983, 69–71. For an extended treatment of this issue, see Trigg 1970.

[39] Nelkin 1986.

[40] See Melzack and Wall 1983, 56 ff., on the vocabulary available to us for the description of pain.

[41] The distinction is nicely illustrated in a scene in David Lean's film *Lawrence of Arabia* in which Lawrence shows off his ability to extinguish a match with his fingers. When one of his colleagues attempts the same feat, he exclaims that it hurts and asks Lawrence what the trick is. 'The trick', replies Lawrence, 'is not minding that it hurts.'

cheated without it. The same has been said of the pain of child-birth (though I am in no position to verify this), and has also been advanced as part of the explanation of the stoicism of soldiers during the treatment of wounds. For someone on the front lines, what the pain meant was not only that he was still alive but also that he would shortly be going home.

These phenomena remind us that pain is typically, though not necessarily, accompanied by feelings of fear, anxiety, anger, indignity, depression, or despair. These emotional responses, however, are not directed to the physical sensation alone (assuming that this can be isolated from the whole experience), but also to its context, and its meaning in that context. Physical pain generally becomes worse, or harder to bear, when it is experienced as inevitable or intractable, or when it is associated with some permanent impairment or irreversible debilitation. Contrariwise, it is easier to cope with when we feel more in control of it (or at least that it is under someone's control), or when what it promises is healing or recovery of function. The impact on a person's life of an episode of physical suffering cannot be abstracted from her particular history and circumstances, nor from her outlook and expectations.

The seeming (logical and psychological) separability of pain sensations themselves from our emotional or attitudinal responses to them forces a choice on us when we are trying to characterize the nature of pain. One option is to stick with the sensation model: however much it may be affected by its emotional overlay, the pain, properly speaking, is just the characteristic feeling itself.[42] A second possibility is to switch over to the attitude model and identify pain with our aversive response, so that it consists in any feeling, or any mental state, which we dislike for its own sake or find intrinsically disagreeable.[43] If we were simply looking for the best account of the nature of pain, and if these were the only two available options, then there would be much to be said in favour of the former. The attitude model can make no sense at all of the testimony of lobotomized subjects who say that they continue to feel pain but are no longer averse to it. More seriously, it also runs foul of the perfectly obvious fact that pain is not the only physical

[42] In Gilbert Ryle's well-known formulation, 'a pain is a sensation of a special sort, which we ordinarily dislike having' (Ryle 1949, 109). Cf. Hare 1964; 1981; 93; Brandt 1979, 131-2.
[43] See Baier 1958, 268-75; Edwards 1979; Nelkin 1986.

feeling to which we are (normally) averse. Think for a moment of the many physical symptoms which, when persistent, can make our lives miserable: nausea, hiccups, sneezing, dizziness, disorientation, loss of balance, itching, 'pins and needles', 'restless legs', tics, twitching, fatigue, difficulty in breathing, and so on. While none of these is quite the same as physical pain, we experience each as intrinsically disagreeable. The attitude model simply obliterates these categorial boundaries by treating all these states indifferently as pain. While there is something intuitively right about this approach (to which we will return), it is hopeless as a phenomenologically accurate picture of the nature of pain.

Before we leave this issue we should note a third option—a hybrid which combines both models into a complex whole. This is the line taken nowadays by many researchers into the psychology and physiology of pain. For Melzack and Wall, for instance, pain comprises 'those subjective experiences which have both somatosensory and negative-affective components and that elicit behaviour aimed at stopping the conditions that produce them'.[44] However, if this account is to avoid the problem of over-breadth then it must somehow distinguish between pain and other subjective experiences which evoke aversive responses. And how is it to do this, except by saying that pain comprises those experiences which feel painful, or which hurt? And isn't that tantamount to conceding that the sensation model was right all along in identifying the pain proper by means of its purely phenomenal properties?

Reflection on these matters has led Eric Cassell to advance an interesting, and influential, distinction between *pain* and *suffering*.[45] For Cassell, physical pain is merely one possible symptom of disease or injury, whose impact is conditioned by its personal meaning for the subject. Suffering, on the other hand, is a response of the whole person, which takes into account both the subjective experience itself (in the narrow sense) and its meaning or significance. It follows that episodes of pain which are intrinsically indistinguishable (being of the same kind, having the same intensity, and lasting for the same duration) may cause quite different degrees of suffering to different subjects, or to the same subject at different times. It also follows that conditions other than pain may cause

---

[44] Melzack and Wall 1983, 71; cf. Kerr 1981, 26. Trigg 1970 likewise emphasizes the duality of pain.

[45] Cassell 1982, 1991; for a similar distinction see Hare 1981, 93.

suffering. Cassell relates the case of a 35-year-old sculptor with
breast cancer whose symptoms after radiation and chemotherapy
included severe pain, but much else besides. As he observes:

we know why that woman suffered. She was housebound and bedbound,
her face was changed by steroids, she was masculinized by her treatment,
one breast was scarred, and she had almost no hair. The degree of importance attached to these losses—that aspect of their personal meaning
—is determined to a great degree by cultural priorities.

With this in mind, we can also realize how much someone devoid of
physical pain, even devoid of 'symptoms,' may suffer. People suffer from
what they have lost of themselves in relation to the world of objects,
events, and relationships.[46]

In Cassell's conceptual framework, suffering results from 'injuries
to the integrity of the person':

If the injury is sufficient, the person suffers. The only way to learn what
damage is sufficient to cause suffering, or whether suffering is present, is
to ask the sufferer. We all recognize certain injuries that almost invariably
cause suffering: the death or distress of loved ones, powerlessness, help-
lessness, hopelessness, torture, the loss of a life's work, betrayal, physical
agony, isolation, homelessness, memory failure, and fear. Each is both
universal and individual. Each touches features common to all of us, yet
each contains features that must be defined in terms of a specific person
at a specific time.[47]

For our purposes, Cassell's distinction between pain and suffering contains two very important features. For one thing, as the foregoing passages make plain, the range of the latter notion is much
wider than that of the former. While we may (or sometimes may
not) suffer as the result of severe or chronic pain, suffering can be
brought about by any condition which we apprehend as distressing. The possible sources of suffering thus extend well beyond the
organic to include disappointments and setbacks whose roots are
personal or social. Cassell extends the range of suffering by con-
fining that of pain, which is relegated to the level of physical
symptom. In effect, therefore, he accepts the view that pain is
merely a sensation while rejecting the role which the classical
hedonists assigned to it in their analysis of happiness or well-
being. That role is to be played instead by suffering.

---

[46] Cassell 1982, 642.   [47] Ibid. 643–4.

We should note here that Cassell's purpose in drawing this distinction is not metaphysical but normative. He is interested, not in constructing the descriptively best account of the nature of pain, but in the question: To what should medicine be sensitive in the treatment of patients? His answer to this question is: their suffering. This answer, and the normative validity of the pain/suffering dichotomy, can be accepted while thinking that Cassell is mistaken about the nature of pain. Cassell's substantive point is that it is the elimination or reduction of suffering, construed as he does in terms of the individual's aversive reaction to her conditions, which deserves to be the central goal of medicine. We can express this as follows: it is suffering, in Cassell's sense, that is central to an account of happiness and well-being (or, rather, unhappiness and ill-being). In saying this, we need take no stand on the issue of whether pain is really, in its nature, a mere sensation. On the other hand, we have also found no reason for thinking that it is more than this.

This brings us to the second important lesson of Cassell's distinction. No mere sensation is capable of playing the role assigned to pain in the classical hedonists' account of happiness, since sensations which are identical in their internal qualities may evoke very different emotional or attitudinal responses. However, whereas it is (logically and psychologically) possible to be indifferent to painful sensations, or even to enjoy them, this is not possible for suffering.[48] By its very nature, suffering is an experience which we dislike or find disagreeable; but it is just this feature of aversiveness which seems to fit suffering for the role traditionally assigned to pain. It is plausible to say of suffering, as it is not of pain, that its presence necessarily compromises our happiness, and thereby also our well-being. Suffering seems just the sort of condition which, in itself and apart from any further accompaniment, makes our lives go worse.

If we retain the view that pain is just a certain kind of sensation, identifiable as such by the way it feels, then we will have to give up thinking that it is necessarily an intrinsic evil for us. We will also have to give up thinking that the magnitude of the evil, when it is such, is a strict function of the internal qualities of the sensation.

---

[48] Hare 1981, 93: 'it would be self-contradictory to report suffering but claim that one did not mind it, and had no motive for ending or avoiding it, even *ceteris paribus*.'

Instead, we must look to our attitude or reaction to the pain—the extent to which we mind or dislike it, or experience it as unpleasant, disagreeable, discomfiting, or distressing—in plotting its negative impact on our lives. This affective response, in turn, will be conditioned by many factors other than the sensory qualities of the pain itself, factors which are likely to include our expectations, hopes, fears, values, self-image, cultural upbringing, and so on. In short: how physical pain feels to us, how much it hurts, is one thing; how much it matters to us is another.

We began this excursion through the heartland of hedonism by looking at what appeared to be its core case: physical pain. We have now adjusted that initial focus by fastening on the different, and broader, phenomenon of suffering. We are led through essentially the same dialectic if we start instead with physical pleasure. The seeking of pleasure seems a less urgent matter for most of us than the avoidance of pain, which is why the negative side of hedonism has always been the more convincing. However, only ascetics would deny that bodily pleasures make some positive contribution to the quality of our lives, whatever their relative priority in comparison to other goods.

There is a core of physical pleasures which are the counterparts in every respect of physical pains: they have a purely organic basis, they are often localized in one part of the body, they can have a quite specific duration, they vary in intensity, and we employ a similar vocabulary for describing the way they feel. The paradigm instances are the pleasures caused by stimuli such as scratching an itch, being massaged, taking a hot bath, quenching a thirst, using a recreational drug, urinating, defecating, and sexual arousal and orgasm. What these sensations have in common, in virtue of which we distinguish them from physical pain, is just the fact that they feel good. When asked to characterize the peculiar feeling tone of sensory pleasure (or pain) we find, like Bentham, that we have little to say. You either recognize what the intense rush of sexual release has in common with the warm glow induced by a backrub, and what differentiates them both from backache or neuralgia, or you do not.

The feeling tone of pleasure is one which we typically like for its own sake. But just as we need not mind pain, we need not welcome or enjoy physical pleasure. Too much of it can saturate or jade us; while this may result in a more muted sensation from the same stimulus, it can also lead us to care less about new episodes of undiminished intensity. We can also find the experience of embodiment occasioned by physical pleasure uncomfortable or unsettling; we can even regard the accompanying organic functions as vulgar or unclean. The ascetic is the opposite of the masochist: instead of enjoying pain, he shuns and rejects pleasure. Quite apart from the pathological case, the extent to which we prize pleasure itself, considered as an isolated sensation, will be partly a function of its emotional context: an orgasm induced by masturbation may actually be more intense and focused than one with a long-term romantic partner, but that is not to say that it is preferable. (There is more to sex than the physical sensations it engenders.) Besides its strictly phenomenal properties, a sensory pleasure can have a meaning or significance which profoundly affects our attitude toward it, and its attractiveness for us. There is no linear dose-response relationship for pleasures, just as there is none for pains.

It is our ability to distinguish physical pleasures from our emotional responses to them which forces a choice between the two models of the nature of pleasure: shall we identify it with the sensation itself or with our attitude of liking or enjoyment? There is more to be said for the latter option in the case of pleasure than in that of pain, which is why most philosophers have abandoned the view that pleasure is a particular kind of sensation, identified by its peculiar feeling tone, in favour of an account according to which it is any experience liked or enjoyed for its own sake.[49] What chiefly explains this tendency is the fact that our vernacular notion of pleasure covers a broader range of experiences than our notion of pain. While it is commonplace to speak of the pleasure of listening to music or reading, where no particular physical sensation is in question, we strain to extend the notion of pain to all disagreeable experiences.

All things considered, however, the attitude model is not much more satisfactory for pleasure than for pain. For one thing, it conceals the important differences between the special case of physical pleasures and all other sources of enjoyment or satisfaction. Whereas the former are liked just for their phenomenal qualities,

---

[49] See, for instance, Ryle 1949, 107–9; 1954, ch. 4; Gosling 1969, chs. 3 and 10; Edwards 1979; Nozick 1989, 103–4.

the latter depend on our attitudes toward states of the world. The difference is between responding positively to the intrinsic pleasurableness of an experience and finding the experience pleasant because you attach a prior value to its object (walking with your lover, watching horror movies, or whatever). In the one case you like it because it feels good; in the other it feels good because you like it. By labelling all enjoyable experiences indiscriminately as pleasures the attitude model erases this boundary between the intrinsically and extrinsically pleasant. In so doing, it loses sight of the features peculiar to strictly physical pleasures; indeed, it is in danger of forgetting that there are such things. (This amnesia may not be accidental; most analytic philosophers prefer not to dwell on (or in?) the body.) On top of this, the attitude model can make no sense of being indifferent, or even averse, to a physical pleasure. But this phenomenon seems not only a logical and psychological possibility, but a common occurrence.

If we are seeking the model of pleasure which best fits our ordinary experience, then we will probably do best to fly in the face of current philosophical fashion by adopting the sensation model and restricting it to the core cases of physical pleasures. This opens up the possibility of drawing a distinction between *pleasure* and *enjoyment*, which will parallel Cassell's distinction between pain and suffering. Like suffering, enjoyment will consist in a response to a situation as a whole, to which a subject brings her entire hierarchy of values and concerns. Pleasure, in the strict sense, then becomes one thing among others which we are capable of enjoying (though we need not), the difference being that in this case the object of our enjoyment is just a particular kind of feeling. The sources of enjoyment available to us will extend well beyond such feelings, so as to include the objective conditions of our lives.

If we distinguish in this way between pleasure and enjoyment, then it quickly becomes clear that what matters for our well-being is the latter rather than the former. Just as suffering seems the sort of thing which makes our lives go worse, enjoyment seems the sort of thing which makes them go better, just in itself and apart from any extrinsic connections. While the sensation model tells the right story about the nature of both pleasure and pain, what it shows us is that these phenomena have no privileged place in an account of happiness or welfare. (They are sources of well-being, or ill-being, not ingredients in its nature.) On the other hand, while the attitude model tells the wrong story about pleasure and pain, the phenomena to which it properly applies—enjoyment and suffering—seem much more appropriate candidates for this role.

Consider now the question raised at the beginning of this section. Can hedonism be reconstituted so as to be no longer a mental state theory of welfare? Do we have a conception of pleasure and pain available to us on which they are not merely mental states? The straightforward answers to these questions now appear to be negative. On the descriptively most adequate account of the nature of pleasure and pain they are (classes of) sensations, and sensations are paradigmatic mental states. However, this answer is both overly simple and overly negative. To see why, let us return briefly to the classical hedonists.

In entertaining both models of the nature of pleasure and pain, the utilitarians never intended them to apply solely to the core physical cases. They construed pleasure broadly so as to comprehend all kinds of enjoyment, gratification, reward, satisfaction, fulfilment, etc., and pain likewise to include every variety of suffering, distress, discomfort, discontent, and the like. They differed in their analysis of this diverse range of phenomena. Bentham believed that the sensation model could be generalized from the cases of physical pleasure and pain so as to fit all these experiences; in every case, he held, we can find an agreeable or disagreeable sensation whose purely phenomenal qualities will provide an index of the (positive or negative) impact of the experience on our happiness. In this, as we now think, he was mistaken. In favouring the attitude model, on the other hand, Sidgwick and J. S. Mill had a much more promising account of the phenomena, and thus of what matters for our well-being, but they packaged it in a misleading way by continuing to use the labels 'pleasure' and 'pain'. What they called pleasure and pain we now prefer to call enjoyment and suffering. Perhaps this is a reason for abandoning the label 'hedonism', so as to avoid the unfortunate association with (physical) pleasure and pain. But it is not by itself a reason for abandoning the kind of theory which the classical theorists were struggling to articulate.

So far, then, it looks as though it might be possible to rebuild hedonism (or neo-hedonism, or quasi-hedonism) around the notions of enjoyment and suffering. However, we still lack a solution to the most serious difficulty threatening any such enterprise—the problem of solipsism. On the attitude model, as the utilitarians interpreted it, enjoyment and suffering are still mental states. Or are they? What is odd here is that both of the utilitarians' official stories about pleasure/enjoyment seem inadequate to their own implicit understanding of it. Besides the dominant mental state theme it is possible to discern a quite different motif. J. S. Mill, for one, would have rejected the idea of a life spent passively plugged into an experience machine just as scornfully as Nozick or Griffin. The mode of living which Mill consistently commended for human beings was one which develops their powers and exercises their capacities—above all, their intellectual powers and capacities.[50] When Mill spoke of pleasures, therefore, especially 'higher' pleasures, what he chiefly had in mind was the enjoyment of certain kinds of activities or pursuits.[51] Any such pleasure he seemed to think of as a complex whole consisting of the activity in question plus the agent's enjoyment of it.[52] He was not referring to a mental state which was detachable from its accompanying activity and which could therefore, at least in principle, be induced by artificial means in the absence of that activity. (It never seems to have occurred to him that the experience might be synthesized without its usual source; thus does the advance of technology influence the philosophical agenda.) At this working level, therefore, Mill's views about happiness (and welfare) are not vulnerable to the charge of solipsism. The problem is that neither he nor any of the other classical theorists ever seems to have developed a theory of the nature of pleasure/enjoyment which was adequate to their own understanding of it, and their view of its place in our lives.

Since pleasure and pain (strictly speaking) are best construed as sensations, they are best construed as mental states. However, it is not clear that the same is true of enjoyment and suffering. Both notions require intentional objects for their completion: one enjoys, or suffers from, this condition or that. These objects certainly

---

[50] See Mill 1977, ch. 3.

[51] This point is stressed in Brink 1992, 72 ff. Brink draws the conclusion that Mill's conception of happiness is therefore objective rather than subjective. This, however, does not follow: the enjoyment of the activity is still a necessary condition of its prudential value.

[52] This interpretation is offered by Donner (1991, 67 ff.) who, however, continues to treat Mill's theory of welfare as a mental state account.

include (though they are not confined to) states of the world. One option available to the hedonist, which seems to have been implicitly taken up by Mill, is to read enjoyment and suffering extensionally, so that I am not enjoying, or suffering from, some intentional object unless that object actually exists. On this interpretation, in order to be enjoying a game of tennis I must actually be playing tennis (and not floating in a tank), and in order to be suffering from the loss of my job I must actually have lost my job. Construed extensionally in this way, enjoyment and suffering are no longer merely mental states; instead, they are complexes consisting of mental states plus their objects (which will usually, though not always, be states of the world). The same play is available in the notion of experience, which also need not be read purely intentionally. We can say that I have not had experience of Rome until I have been to Rome; the mere illusion of having gone there will not suffice.

If a suitably extensional interpretation of enjoyment and suffering could be developed, and if it were incorporated into the hedonist's framework, the resulting theory of welfare might be immune to experience machine objections. On the other hand, it might also be too immune, having committed itself to the view that an experience has prudential value only when it is reality-based. That conclusion, as we saw earlier, seems objectionably puritanical—surely a good fantasy can contribute something to a life. In any case, subjectivists should want to leave room for individuals to work out their own rates of substitution between illusion and reality. Mill's option, therefore, may be too simple and extreme. However, it is not inconceivable that some other theory working with the materials of enjoyment and suffering might do better at fending off the traditional counterarguments. If so, then the hedonistic project, or something recognizably similar to it, cannot be entirely discounted at this stage of the inquiry. What can be discounted is only the classical version of the theory which treats enjoyment, and therefore also welfare, as a mental state (or a collection of such states).

The prospect of reviving a hedonistic theory of welfare is interesting for more than antiquarian reasons. The idea that welfare is identical to, or consists in, happiness should be attractive to any subjectivist. And a revised account of the nature of enjoyment, one which does not reduce it to a mere mental state, might make a (neo-)hedonistic account of happiness more appealing. Additionally, there are important lessons to be learned from hedonism, insights which are embodied in even the classical form of the theory and which must be preserved in any account of the nature of welfare. For one thing, as we noted earlier, even unrevised hedonism seems to tell the right story for the important cases of physical pleasure and pain. Here it is no defect to treat the sources of our well- and ill-being as mental states, which we (typically) like or dislike just because of the way they feel. Any successful theory must somehow be able to incorporate the hedonist's treatment of these phenomena, which are absolutely central to our welfare.

More importantly, however, hedonism underlines a truth which applies to all goods and ills, whether they consist merely in our feelings or include states of the world. This truth is that nothing can make our lives go better or worse unless it somehow affects the quality of our experience. Whether an adequate theory of welfare will have anything left of hedonism in it remains yet to be seen. But whether hedonistic or not, it will have to be experiential: it will have to connect our well-being in some way or other with our experience of the conditions of our lives. The implications of this lesson are best appreciated by turning attention to a form of theory which has not fully absorbed it.

5

The Desire Theory

EVERY subjective theory makes welfare depend, at least in part, on the subject's attitudes toward the conditions of her life. What all attitudes share is that they are ways of being for or against things, ways of favouring or disfavouring them. Beyond this common defining characteristic, however, attitudes divide into significantly different categories. Hedonists seize on one such category, which they call pleasure and pain, but welfare can also be thought to consist of the satisfaction of wants or preferences. The generic formula of a desire theory is that a condition or state of affairs makes me better off by virtue of satisfying some desire on my part, that my life is going well to the extent that I am succeeding in getting what I want. The role played by desire in this formula ensures that the theory will be subjective, while the requirement that the desire be satisfied (thus that its object actually exist or come about) ensures that it will be a state-of-the-world theory.

Desire theories have come to dominate the welfare landscape in this century in the way that hedonism dominated its own time. However, again like hedonism, these theories come in a variety of forms, some much more promising than others. We begin with the least plausible version of a desire—or preference—account. We then address the theory in its strongest form.

5.1 REVEALED PREFERENCE

The account we are now going to examine is so unpromising that some background is necessary in order to explain its popularity. As we noted in the preceding chapter, the classical utilitarians were ethical welfarists: they held that welfare is the only thing valuable as an end, thus the sole foundational good for an ethical theory. At the same time, welfare was assigned a key explanatory role by the utilitarian economists, the central assumption of whose theory of demand was that in their market choices consumers seek to maximize their own utility.[1] In both of these uses, of course, the utilitarians interpreted welfare in hedonistic terms. Although this interpretation is now firmly out of favour among philosophers, it remained at least respectable in their circles long after it had been decisively rejected by economists. By the end of the nineteenth century the resistance of pleasure and pain to reliable, public measurement was becoming an embarrassment to those who wished to set economics on the sure path of a science. Their remedy was to dissolve the association between welfare and private experience.

At this point our story divides into two distinct but interconnected narrative lines. The first is the invention and subsequent career of 'economic welfare'. The origins of this notion were humble, even quaint. In the early decades of the present century, the utilitarian economist A. C. Pigou still clung to the classical orthodoxy that 'the elements of welfare are states of consciousness and, perhaps, their relations'.[2] However, he also shared the emerging consensus that economic science needed something rather more quantifiable to get its teeth into. 'The one obvious instrument of measurement available in social life is money. Hence, the range of our inquiry becomes restricted to that part of social welfare that can be brought directly or indirectly into relation with the measuring-rod of money. This part of welfare may be called economic welfare.'[3]

But if welfare is a matter of felt satisfaction how can any part of it be brought into relation with the monetary metric? Pigou's answer to this question unfolded in two stages. In the first, intensity of desire was accepted as a surrogate for satisfaction: how much I want something is an index of how satisfied I will be if I get it. Then, in the second stage, income expenditure was accepted as a surrogate for intensity of desire: how much I am willing to pay for something is an index of how much I want it.[4] When these steps are combined we get the result that an individual's market

---

[1] See, for instance, Jevons 1965, 10 ff.; Edgeworth 1881, 15–16; Marshall 1961, Book I, ch. 2.

[2] Pigou 1932, 10.   [3] Ibid. 11.

[4] Interestingly, both of Pigou's shortcuts were anticipated by Bentham. The connection between pleasure and desire was axiomatic for both Bentham and Mill; see, for example, Bentham 1970, ch. 10; Mill 1969, ch. 4. In a number of places Bentham also recognized the difficulties involved in quantifying pleasure and pain, and suggested willingness to pay as a rough surrogate (Bentham 1843, i. 305–6,

choices provide a measure of her economic welfare. The extrapolation to the macro-level is then straightforward. What Pigou called the national dividend, and what we nowadays call national product or income, is the sum total of a society's annual output of goods and services expressed in terms of their monetary value. It was this which Pigou regarded as the 'objective counterpart of economic welfare'.

> Just as economic welfare is that part of total welfare which can be brought directly or indirectly into relation with a money measure, so the national dividend is that part of the objective income of the community . . . which can be measured in money. The two concepts, economic welfare and the national dividend, are thus co-ordinate, in such wise that any description of the content of one of them implies a corresponding description of the content of the other.[5]

We have thus been led, by a series of simple steps, from the classical conception of the welfare of an individual to a macro-economic measure of (one part of) the welfare of a society. Pigou was fully aware that the assumptions behind these various steps were at best rough approximations of the truth. Thus, where individuals are concerned, he explicitly acknowledged that economic welfare is but one part of overall welfare, that an increase in the part may not entail an increase in the whole, that intensity of desire is only a crude indicator of degree of satisfaction, and that the budgeting of income is an index of intensity of desire at best in the special case of market goods.[6] Many of his successors, however, have been somewhat less circumspect, which brings us to our second narrative line.

In the 'new welfare economics', utility, and therefore also welfare, simply came to be redefined in terms of preference, as revealed in choice. The abandonment of the classical conception of utility in favour of revealed preference, and the adoption of a

---

iii. 228–30, iv. 540–1, vii. 568, ix. 14–15; cf. Goldworth 1979). The same theme was repeated by some of the 19th-cent. utilitarian economists; see Jevons 1965, 13; Marshall 1961, Book I, ch. 2, ss. 1–2.

[5] Pigou 1932, 31.

[6] Bentham was also alive to the limitations of economic measures of welfare; see Bentham 1843, i. 371 ff. In particular, he was one of the first to acknowledge that money, like all other sources, makes a diminishing marginal contribution to well-being (Bentham 1843, i. 305–6, iii. 228–9, iv. 540–1, ix. 14–15; Goldworth 1979). Cf. Jevons 1965, ch. 3; Marshall 1961, Book I, ch. 2, s. 2.

suitably idealized model of the market, effectively converted Pigou's rough approximations into necessary truths, with the result that market behaviour came to be treated not as a measure of one part of individual welfare but as constituting the whole of it. The two essential moves were the ones made by Pigou: intensity of desire was first taken to be a surrogate for felt satisfaction and then income expenditure was taken to be a surrogate for intensity of desire. The result was the view that the contribution a thing makes to my well-being is a function of the amount I am willing to pay to get (or keep) it. For Pigou, of course, this behavioural measure was only an indicator of well-being; he continued to believe that in its nature welfare is a matter of felt satisfaction. But it was soon recognized that this residue of hedonism was utterly unnecessary, at least for the purely explanatory theory of consumers' behaviour.[7] All of the central results of general equilibrium theory are derivable as long as the market choices of consumers are assumed to manifest certain basic forms of consistency; it is not necessary to suppose that in these choices consumers are seeking to maximize felt satisfaction, or any other experiential magnitude.[8]

The reconceptualization of utility in terms of revealed preference also seemed to suit the more normative concerns of welfare economics. Since choice is a matter of overt behaviour rather than ineffable feeling, it was thought that under this revised conception individual gains and losses would be suitably verifiable and quantifiable. The resulting dependence of utility on individual choice presented a formidable obstacle to comparing the utilities of different persons. However, despite this liability, or perhaps because of it, the new behavioural notion of utility quickly came to dominate the formal theory of rational choice, both individual and social.

Now at this point the conclusion could have been drawn that the concept of welfare, on any account of its nature, is irrelevant to economics—or at least to positive economic theory. As long as consumers' choices display the consistency required to generate utility functions, who cares what they are motivated by? The assumption of egoism seems to do no useful work here.[9] There may

[7] The evolution of modern utility theory at the hands of economists is outlined in Little 1957, chs. 1–4.
[8] See Samuelson 1938; 1947, ch. 5; 1948.
[9] A weaker assumption, that of non-tuism, may be necessary, since it ensures the independence of utility functions. See Wicksteed 1933, i. 179–81; Gauthier 1986, 87.

(or may not) be interesting empirical connections between market choices and welfare, but the two are logically distinct.[10] If utility is given a technical definition as that which is maximized in consistent choice,[11] then the classical utilitarian equation of utility and welfare has been effectively abandoned. In that case it is utility which is indispensable to demand theory, not welfare.

This is, no doubt, the conclusion that should have been drawn, as a result of which the concept of welfare would have been expelled altogether from positive economics.[12] But that is not what happened. Instead, the metric of individual welfare gains and losses was retained, in locutions such as 'Pareto improvement' and 'Pareto optimality'. These welfarist notions are, strictly speaking, unnecessary to the purely formal results of general equilibrium theory. They appear instead in the interpretation of these results—for instance, when it is said that under conditions of perfect competition no one can be made better off without someone else being made worse off. Strictly speaking, all that 'makes *A* better/worse off' can mean here is 'moves *A* to a higher/lower point in *A*'s preference ranking', but the temptation to equate utility and welfare is seemingly irresistible.[13] By no means, therefore, has the concept of welfare ceased to play an important rhetorical role in positive economic theory. Its continuing presence in normative theory, on the other hand, is attested to by the very label 'welfare economics'. It must be emphasized that none of the (alleged) welfarist results in either domain depends on any assumed empirical

[10] As is suggested in Little 1957, 42 ff.

[11] 'We assume that individuals attempt to maximize utility, and define utility as that which the individual attempts to maximize' (Winch 1971, 25).

[12] Sometimes, it seems, this conclusion is being drawn, as when Paul Samuelson tells us that 'the consumer's market behavior is explained in terms of preferences, which are in turn defined only by behavior. The result can very easily be circular, and in many formulations undoubtedly is. Often nothing more is stated than the conclusion that people behave as they behave, a theorem which has no empirical implications, since it contains no hypotheses and is consistent with all conceivable behavior, while refutable by none' (Samuelson 1947, 91–2; cf. Luce and Raiffa 1957, 50).

[13] '[A]n individual shall be considered better off if he is in a chosen position. This assumption relates the Paretian value judgement directly to the utility function. Since we define utility as that which the individual attempts to maximize, it follows that he will choose more rather than less utility. An increase in his utility can then be regarded as synonymous with his being better off' (Winch 1971, 33). Of course, if one's aim is to recommend the market as a mechanism for promoting social welfare, then it is easy to see why the temptation would be irresistible.

correlation between utility (choice) and welfare. Instead, these results, at least on their standard interpretation, presuppose a logical connection between the two.[14] But in that case economists are (implicitly or explicitly) offering us an account of the nature of welfare, one which takes it to be constituted by 'preference as revealed in choice'.

It is this theory that we wish to assess. In order to make the theory determinate, let us assume that it takes the following form: x makes me better off than y just in case I choose x in a market in which y is also available. As we noted earlier in reading Pigou, this result is reached in two steps: (1) x makes me better off than y just in case I want x more than y, and (2) I want x more than y just in case I choose x when I could have chosen y instead. The first step links welfare and desire, while the second links desire and choice. Because some version or other of the first link is common to all desire theories, we will leave it unexamined here in order to focus on the second link, which is the distinctive mark of revealed preference theories.

The basic idea behind the revealed preference approach is that 'the individual guinea-pig, by his market behaviour, reveals his preference pattern'.[15] Are our preferences revealed by our market choices? It seems clear that they are not revealed *only* by our income expenditures. Even if preference is infallibly manifested in choice, there can be no justification for excluding non-market choices from a general account of welfare. For one thing, some goods which we all value, such as loyalty and friendship, preclude a market by their very nature; any commodities for sale under these labels must be counterfeit. But even in the case of market-able goods, whether there is any actual market for them in our vicinity is a contingent matter. It is difficult to believe that educa-tion or sanitation or health care become less important to us when they are allocated by some non-market mechanism. If there is to

[14] The postulation of this connection is clearly driven by explanatory or norma-tive demands. Since the revealed preference theory is hopelessly inadequate as an account of our ordinary concept of welfare, we have here a clear case of the dominance of theoretical (explanatory and/or normative) over descriptive criteria. Ironically, the theory turns out also to be normatively inadequate, as we shall see later.

[15] Samuelson 1948, 243. Cf. Amartya Sen's statement of 'the fundamental as-sumption of the revealed preference approach, viz., that people do reveal their underlying preferences through their actual choices' (Sen 1982, 60).

be any interesting connection between choice and preference, and therefore between choice and welfare, the restriction to market choices cannot be maintained. Dropping the restriction will, of course, have unfortunate consequences for the measurement of welfare, since decisions about the expenditure of income have (literally) a common currency which is lacking when we bring in such non-market choices as whom to marry or how long to engage in sexual fantasies. But the needs of a theory, even an important theory, cannot be allowed to dictate an account of the nature of welfare.

Dropping the restriction to market choices leaves us with the view that I want x more than y just in case I choose x when y is also available. This formula still restricts us to our actual (market and non-market) choices, a limitation which is imposed by the behaviourism of revealed preference theory: revealed preference, by definition, is preference as actually revealed in choice. But this restriction must also be dropped. If my preference structure is thought of as an ordered set of dispositions to make certain kinds of choices, then it seems clear that this will be revealed only very imperfectly by my actual choices. After all, I am able to reveal my dispositional preferences only if I am presented with the appropriate occasions for choice, but whether these occasions come along is again a contingent matter (I know that I would rather have one great season as a major league pitcher than spend a lifetime as a successful neurosurgeon, but neither will ever be an option for me). Although making an actual choice of one alternative over another presupposes the availability of both, having a preference between them does not. If my preferences are to connect in some important way with my welfare, then it seems reasonable to think that all of them should count, not just those I have had the opportunity to reveal in choice.

Dropping this restriction will involve expanding the account so as to include hypothetical choices.[16] At this point it ceases to be a theory of revealed preference, since it abandons the behaviourist dogma that preferences are verifiable, and measurable, only if they come to be expressed in overt decisions. In order for me to ascertain

---

[16] As is done in the von Neumann–Morgenstern technique for deriving a cardinal utility function, which involves asking individuals to make hypothetical choices among various possible lotteries over ranked goods. See von Neumann and Morgenstern 1953, ch. 3.

your hypothetical choices it will not suffice for me merely to observe your behaviour; at the very least I must also take seriously what you tell me you would choose under specified conditions.[17] But if the result of this expansion is not a revealed preference theory it is none the less a near relation, since it still attempts to explicate welfare in terms of (actual or hypothetical) choice. It does so, furthermore, by employing the same basic strategy of first linking choice to preference and then linking preference to welfare. But is choice a reliable indicator of preference? Will even the fullest set of data concerning my actual and hypothetical choices reveal my preferences?

It may seem so, since if I choose x over y then surely I must have preferred it and, contrariwise, if I prefer x to y then surely I would choose it if I could. However, a little reflection shows that both of these seemingly necessary connections trade on an ambiguity in the vernacular notion of preference.[18] That notion looks simultaneously in two directions: to my *attitudes* on the one hand and to my *choices* on the other. In the first sense, what I (attitudinally) prefer is what I like best (for its own sake) or find most agreeable. This is the interpretation needed by a subjective theory of welfare, since in this sense it is arguable that the satisfaction of my preferences necessarily makes me better off. In the second sense, what I (behaviourally) prefer is just what I choose (for whatever reason). This is the interpretation of preference needed in order to connect it analytically to choice.

Once this ambiguity is recognized, then a choice theory of welfare faces a dilemma. It is only in the attitudinal sense that preference can be plausibly connected with welfare, but in this sense there is no tight connection between preference and choice. The fact that I choose x rather than y (or would choose it if I could) does not show that I expect a higher personal payoff from it, since my choice may be motivated by other considerations, such as altruism or a sense of obligation. Likewise, if I can be motivated by factors other than my intrinsic likes and dislikes, then the fact that I prefer x to y (would rather have it for its own sake) does not show that I would choose it if confronted by these alternatives.[19] On the

---

[17] As Sen argues in 1982, 9, 71–2.

[18] For a similar diagnosis, see Broome 1978, 324; Sen 1982, 69, 94.

[19] Sen makes this point in terms of commitment; see 1982, 93 ff. Another reason that preference does not entail even hypothetical choice is that many states of

attitudinal interpretation, counter-preferential choice is not only possible but common. It is only in the behavioural sense that preference always (trivially) runs with choice. But this is not the notion of preference relevant to a theory of welfare; it is not even a notion on which we can make sense of preferences being satisfied. Only by equivocating on preference, therefore, can a choice theory use it as the middle term between choice and welfare.

There is a parallel ambiguity in our vernacular notion of wanting.[20] Wanting to do something, in the behavioural sense, is just having some reason or other for doing it, with no restriction whatever placed on the range of possible reasons. In this sense, therefore, it is a necessary truth that as long as I am acting voluntarily I always do what I most want. In the attitudinal sense, by contrast, wanting to do something requires finding the prospect of it pleasing or agreeable, or welcoming the opportunity to do it, or looking forward to it with gusto or enthusiasm. If I have this sort of attitude toward some prospective action then I have one particular sort of reason to do it—a reason which is capable of conflicting with others, such as a feeling of obligation or the fear of disapproval. In this sense, therefore, not doing what one most wants to do is depressingly familiar. (The behavioural notion is the one we use when we say, 'Well, he must have wanted to go, since he went.' We switch to the attitudinal notion when we ask ourselves, after the fact, 'Is that what I really wanted to do?')

Like preference, wanting can be linked either with choice or with welfare: the behavioural sense with the former and the attitudinal sense with the latter. But it cannot, except by equivocation, be linked with both at once. Thus it too cannot serve as the middle term between choice and welfare. For all we yet know, our well-being may consist in getting what we want, but not on the interpretation which equates our desires with the full range of our reasons for action. While getting what we relish may make us better off, doing what we feel we ought or must cannot be counted on to deliver the same payoff.

Economists have tended to trade on the ambiguity latent in the

affairs over which we have preferences are not possible matters of choice for us. Think of such items as whether the sun will shine for your picnic, whether your beloved will reciprocate your love, whether your favourite baseball club will win the pennant, etc.

[20] See Gosling 1969, ch. 6.

notion of preference, using the behavioural sense in their explanation of consumer behaviour and then shifting to the attitudinal
sense in their claims about the welfare implications of the market.
Despite its many and obvious deficiencies, the revealed preference
theory of welfare has retained a certain superficial plausibility by
exploiting the same ambiguity. Once the equivocation has been
exposed, the theory can safely be discarded. There is simply no
interesting constitutive connection between welfare and choice.
We are left then with the attitudinal notions of preference and
desire. Do they provide the materials for a theory of welfare?

5.2 INFORMED DESIRE

The basic schema for this kind of account is that something benefits a person (directly or intrinsically) by satisfying some desire on
that person's part. Versions of the desire theory now define the
orthodox view of the nature of welfare, at least in the Anglo-
American philosophical world. In the theory of rational choice the
equation of well-being with utility (preference-satisfaction) has
achieved the status of an unquestioned axiom, while in ethics its
more prominent recent defenders have included Brian Barry, John
Rawls, R. M. Hare, James Griffin, and Joseph Raz.[21]
   It is not difficult to see why the desire theory is so attractive to
subjectivists. It seems a very plausible idea that my life is going
well for me when I am in the way of achieving my aims or goals.
It also seems a plausible hypothesis that the subjective point of
view, from which my welfare is to be assessed, is given by the set
of my preferences, and that the relative importance of the many
goods which enrich my life is determined by their position in the
hierarchical structure of these preferences. The desire theory is
also well placed to satisfy our demand for a unified account of the
nature of welfare, while allowing for the multiplicity and variety
of its sources. Since it can readily acknowledge the importance
of idiosyncratic tastes and interests, the theory has no difficulty
explaining why you who love thrills find the quality of your life
enhanced by sky-diving, while I who value tranquillity realize the

---

[21] See Barry 1965, chs. 10 and 11; Rawls 1971, ch. 7; Hare 1981, ch. 5; Griffin
1986, chs. 1 and 2; Raz 1986, ch. 12.

same gains by reading quietly under a tree. At the same time, however, if there are states of affairs for which everyone strives, or which are the indispensable means for the achievement of any aims, then these will count as (either intrinsic or instrumental) common goods.

The desire theory also circumscribes the class of welfare subjects in an intuitively plausible way. To have a point of view on this sort of account is to have a structure of desires or preferences. The class of primary welfare subjects will therefore include all and only those beings with the capacity to form and order desires. Although the boundaries of this class are indistinct, they clearly include most human beings along with many other animals. They equally clearly exclude plants and inanimate objects. Moreover, the desire theory can also explain how many welfare notions come to be applied in an extended or analogical sense to such entities as simple organisms, artefacts, groups, organizations, and such— all of whom, while lacking desires, can be regarded as teleological systems requiring certain standard conditions in order to function well or properly. In this way the theory can draw a principled, though fuzzy, boundary between the classes of primary and secondary welfare subjects.

In addition to these very considerable merits, the desire theory also seems in tune with the liberal spirit of the modern age, which tends to see human agents as pursuers of autonomously chosen projects.[22] Unlike objective theories, on which the sources of our well-being are dictated by unalterable aspects of our nature, the desire theory offers us the more flattering picture of ourselves as shapers of our own destinies, determiners of our own good. In this way it internalizes within a conception of welfare the paradigmatically liberal virtues of self-direction and self-determination. Once this link has been established it is a simple matter to construct a welfarist defence of political liberty. It is little cause for wonder, therefore, that all of the principal recent advocates of the desire theory have also been political liberals.

Its ease of fit within the framework of liberalism may well count toward the normative adequacy of the desire theory. But is it descriptively adequate? In order to begin answering this question we must make the abstract formula of the theory more determinate.

---

[22] For a recent manifestation of this ethos, see Lomasky 1987, ch. 2.

Remember that within the broad class of what we are calling attitudes we are looking for the particular subclass which is central to a subjective theory of welfare. When we are told that this subclass consists of desires or wants or preferences, we are entitled to ask what distinguishes these particular attitudes from others, such as liking or enjoying. This is not the place to try to construct a full account of the nature of desire. However, any such account will need to incorporate two essential features of wants or desires: they are *intentional* and they are *prospective*.

To say that desires are intentional is to say that they are directed upon objects whose existence they do not logically guarantee. That desires have objects is, of course, scarcely news; this much is ensured by the fact that every desire is *for* something or other. In the surface grammar of desire, these objects are often literally things, as when I want this book or that car. Sometimes, however, they are activities (I want to go to France) or states of affairs (I want the weather to be good for our wedding). It is a simple trick to homogenize all these ostensibly different kinds of object into states of affairs: to want the book is to want to own it or read it, and to want to do something is to want the state of affairs which consists of your doing it. It is then a further simple trick to turn these states of affairs into propositions: to want the state of affairs which consists of my owning the book is to want the proposition 'I own this book' to be true. By this process of transformation, every desire comes to take some proposition as its intentional object. And of course the fact that I want a proposition to be true does not guarantee its truth.

What these transformations highlight is the similarity between desires and beliefs. Like beliefs, desires can be construed as attitudes whose intentional objects are states of affairs or propositions. Just as beliefs can be verified or falsified, desires can be satisfied or frustrated. A belief is verified by the occurrence of the state of affairs (or the truth of the proposition) which constitutes its intentional object. Likewise, a desire is satisfied by the occurrence of the state of affairs (or the truth of the proposition) which constitutes *its* intentional object.[23] Again like beliefs, desires can take as their objects states of the world which are spatially or

---

[23] Griffin offers a different, but equally apt, analogy: 'A desire is "fulfilled" in the sense in which a clause in a contract is fulfilled: namely, what was agreed (desired) comes about' (Griffin 1986, 14).

temporally remote from their holders. This implies that my desire for something can be satisfied without my knowing it (just as my belief about something can be true without my knowing it). All that is required in order for my desire to be satisfied is that whatever I want actually exist or happen. Carl Sagan wants us to establish contact with extraterrestrial beings. Suppose that twenty thousand years from now, some intelligent alien civilization encounters one of our probes in deep space and deciphers the messages which it carries. Sagan's desire will then have been satisfied, though he will know nothing of it. By contrast, I cannot be (occurrently) liking or enjoying something without being aware of this fact. My enjoyments must therefore enter into my experience in a way that need not be true of the satisfaction of my desires.

For a theory of welfare, the intentionality of desire or preference is a very awkward feature.[24] According to the desire theory, something makes me better off when it satisfies some desire on my part. Since my desires can range over spatially and temporally remote states of affairs, it follows that the satisfaction of many of them will occur at times or places too distant from me to have any discernible effect on me. In such cases it is difficult to see how having my desire satisfied could possibly make my life go better.

Sometimes the absence of feedback into my life is due to contingent circumstances. Suppose that my brother suffers from some debilitating disease which I very much want to be cured. Having unsuccessfully sought medical treatment at home, he moves to Papua New Guinea where a promising new treatment is available. After his arrival he breaks off contact with me, and I receive no further news of his fate. Two years later the treatment succeeds and his disorder is completely cured. At this time my desire that he be cured (which I continue to hold) has been satisfied. Because I care deeply about his well-being, if I knew of this I would be greatly cheered. Since I never know of it, how can the cure make me better off?

All of us have many desires which, unbeknownst to us, will come to be satisfied during our lifetime. Like Carl Sagan, we also

[24] For a theory of welfare, it is also an awkward feature of desire that it has no negative counterpart. (Aversion is the opposite not of wanting but of liking.) Desire therefore lacks the positive/negative polarity so characteristic of welfare. This is one of the reasons for casting the desire theory in the comparative language of preference.

have many desires which will be satisfied, if ever, only after we are dead and gone. Sometimes the posthumous satisfaction of a desire is itself due to contingent circumstances, as when I want my daughter eventually to attend university but die before she is able to do so. In this case it is just unlucky for me that my desire is satisfied only after my demise. In other cases this outcome is ensured by the temporal location of the desired state of affairs. Nearly everyone now living wants the ecosystem of the planet to be in a healthy state two centuries from now, but no one now living will be living then. In still other cases, such as your wish to be remembered by your lover after your demise, if the desire is ever satisfied then this must (logically) occur posthumously. In any of these cases, if the desired state of affairs eventually comes about does it make our life go better? If so, *when* does it go better? When our desire is satisfied? But how can the quality of our life be improved after it has ended? Retroactively, at the time we held the desire? But how can what happens *then* affect us for better or worse *now*?

Sometimes it can seem to. James Griffin gives the following example:

It would not have been at all absurd for Bertrand Russell to have thought that if his work for nuclear disarmament had, after his death, actually reduced the risk of nuclear war, his last years would have been more worthwhile, and his life altogether more valuable, than if it all proved futile. True, if Russell had indeed succeeded, his life clearly would have been more valuable to others. But Russell could also have considered it more valuable from the point of view of his own self-interest.

However, when we look closely claims of posthumous benefits always seem to rest on conflating different modes of value. If Russell's work had turned out to contribute to eventual nuclear disarmament then this would of course have shown, retrospectively, that his life had enormous instrumental value; but this, as Griffin recognizes, is not the question at issue. Somewhat closer to the mark, if achievement is a perfectionist value, as it might well be, then posthumous success could make a life a better specimen of its kind. Perfectionist value seems clearly capable of retroactive improvement, and Russell might well have considered his life more valuable from that point of view. But from the standpoint of his own self-interest? That certainly does not follow, and seems much less plausible. It also seems an unlikely interpretation of Russell's own (imagined) evaluation. He can think that a more successful life is a better life, without thinking that he is made better off by it.

The issue of whether posthumously satisfied desires can benefit their erstwhile holders is a hotly debated one. Some people find it just obvious that the dead can be neither benefited nor harmed, while others find it equally obvious that lives are capable of retroactive prudential improvement.[25] I confess that I belong to the former camp. Dying has precious few consolations, but surely one of them is that beyond that threshold we are safe from any further misfortunes. Whatever may befall the living after our demise, nothing can ever again go badly (or, alas, well) for us. That death is the end, prudentially speaking, has always been the principal attraction of suicide for those whose lives appear to have gone into irreversible decline. Where might we seek our comfort if adversity could pursue us even beyond the grave?

Given the division of opinion on this question, the fact that a theory of welfare entails the possibility of posthumous harms and benefits is not sufficient by itself to establish its descriptive inadequacy. However, the posthumous cases are merely the most dramatic instances in which the fulfilment of a desire fails to benefit us because it has no impact, direct or indirect, on our experience. The obvious remedy is to impose on the desire theory what Griffin has called an *experience requirement*.[26] Such a condition would stipulate that a state of affairs can make me better off only if, in one way or another, it enters or affects my experience. A version of the desire theory which incorporated such a requirement might look like this: x makes me better off (directly or intrinsically) just in case (1) I desire x, (2) x occurs, and (3) I am at least aware of x's occurrence.[27]

As his handling of the Russell example suggests, Griffin himself rejects any form of experience requirement.[28] His reason for doing

---

[25] Ernest Partridge defends the first view (Partridge 1981), Joel Feinberg the second (Feinberg 1984, 83–9). With his characteristic judiciousness, Aristotle argues both sides of the question (*Nicomachean Ethics* 1. 10–11), finally settling for the conclusion that, while posthumous events can affect us for better or worse, the effects are relatively minor. Griffin has also felt the pull of both sides; see 1986, 317–19 n.

[26] Griffin 1986, 13.

[27] Need I also be aware that x's occurrence satisfies my desire? Need I still desire x when it occurs? These are further wrinkles for a desire theory to work out.

[28] Griffin 1986, 13–14, 19–20.

so is the same as his reason for rejecting any version of a state-of-mind theory: we desire things other than states of our own experience. But this seems a confusion. A state-of-mind theory treats veridical and illusory experiences which are phenomenologically indistinguishable as equally valuable. Adding an experience requirement to the desire theory has no such implication. Any version of a desire theory is a state-of-the-world theory, since the actual occurrence of the desired state of affairs is one necessary condition in the analysis. An experience requirement makes awareness of this occurrence a further necessary condition. In doing so it does not, and cannot, convert the theory into a mental state theory.[29]

A theory of welfare can be descriptively adequate only if it incorporates some form of experience requirement; this was the important insight in classical hedonism. Only in this way will a desire or preference theory be insulated against highly counterintuitive results flowing from the intentionality of desire, and especially from its capacity to settle on spatially or temporally distant objects.[30] When desire theorists resist such a requirement, this is probably because they suspect that, if an experiential condition is once admitted into their theory, it will eventually make the desire-satisfaction condition redundant. They must therefore hold the line, lest a desire theory with an experiential component mutate into an experiential theory with no desire component. This suspicion is well grounded, as we see when we turn from intentionality to the second essential feature of desire, namely its prospectivity.

In explicating this feature, the analogy between desire and belief will again be instructive. Suppose I now believe that it will snow next Christmas. My belief has two temporal indices, one for the time at which I hold the belief (now) and the other for the intentional object of the belief (next Christmas). Where beliefs are concerned, these two indices can be ordered in any way whatever: I can hold beliefs at a particular time about earlier, contemporaneous, or later times. Likewise, every desire is both held at some particular time and directed upon a temporally indexed state of

---

[29] Contrast the experience requirement imposed in Haslett 1990, which has precisely this effect. For Haslett the only desires which count are those which take experiences as their objects.

[30] Cf. Haslett 1990, 80–2. For a contrary view, see Egonsson 1990, ch. 2. A nicely balanced treatment of the issues at stake here can be found in Kagan 1992, 180–7.

affairs. However, in the case of a desire the two indices must observe a particular order: I can desire now only that something occur later. Desires are always directed on the future, never on the past or present.[31] (I can, of course, want events or activities which I am presently enjoying to continue; but their continuation is still a future state.) In being future-directed in this way, wanting once again contrasts with liking or enjoying. I can (occurrently) enjoy only what I already have, while I can want only what I have not yet got.

Because a desire is always for some future state of affairs, at best it represents our *ex ante* expectation that the state will benefit us. But this expectation may be disappointed by our *ex post* experience of the state. Suppose that I find myself at a career crossroads when I am in college. On the one hand, I am a star pitcher on the baseball team, courted by scouts who assure me that I have an excellent chance of making it to the major leagues. On the other hand, I also have a brilliant record in philosophy, with the prospect of a career in university teaching. Up to now these two career paths have been compatible, but now the former would lead me to the minor leagues while the latter would take me to graduate school. Because I realize that choosing either option will effectively foreclose the other, I investigate both as thoroughly as I can before deciding in favour of the long-range security of a teaching career. I go to graduate school, earn my doctorate, and land a job in a good philosophy department. There I find the demands of teaching and writing to be pretty well as I anticipated. Indeed, as the years pass everything goes more or less as expected, except for the growing realization that this life is just not for me. My dissatisfaction at first manifests itself only in a free-floating irritability, but after a while it deepens into apathy and depression. After staying with the academic life long enough to give it a fair trial, I finally resign, feeling disillusioned and discouraged. Because I am then too old to begin a career in baseball, I become a copy editor at a publishing firm.

In this case I have done what I most wanted to do, realized my

---

[31] I can, of course, wish that past events had been otherwise. I can also have hopes about such events, if I do not know how things turned out. The first time I read Homer I hoped the Trojans would win; now I wish they had. But wishes of this sort cannot be satisfied, and I am assuming that a desire theory of welfare will attach no weight to hopes about the past.

overriding personal ambition, but I have not benefited from doing
so. The problem is not that the state which satisfied my desire
failed to enter into my experience, but that my experience of it
turned out to be negative. Things have not gone as I expected, and
yet I achieved my aim. The problem here is the prospectivity of
desire. My desire to teach philosophy represented my *ex ante*
expectation that I would find this career fulfilling. But in this I was
mistaken. Since our desires always represent our *ex ante* expectations, there is always room for these expectations to be mistaken.
But in that case the satisfaction of our desires does not guarantee
that our lives will go well; only our *ex post* experience will do
that.

Since it is the prospectivity of desire which creates this problem,
it is tempting to try to put matters right by closing the gap between the way things are expected to go and the way they actually
turn out. Thus it is common for desire accounts to stipulate that
the only desires that count are those which are sufficiently rational
or considered or informed, or otherwise 'corrected'.[32] The standard of rationality appealed to may be either minimal, requiring no
more than consistency within one's overall set of preferences, or
rather more stringent, requiring that one's desires be capable of
surviving 'cognitive psychotherapy'.[33] Informational demands likewise may vary, depending on what is counted as relevant information, and on how much of this is reckoned to be sufficient.[34]
Whatever the idealizing conditions adopted, their effect will be to
screen out some of our actual desires.[35] Only the satisfaction of

---

[32] See, for instance, Rawls 1971, ch. 7; Griffin 1986, chs. 1–2.

[33] For the latter requirement see Brandt 1979, ch. 6. Gauthier employs a weaker
standard in 1986, ch. 2. It should be noted, however, that neither Brandt nor
Gauthier identifies welfare with the satisfaction of rational desire.

[34] Griffin's requirement is that the desire be 'formed by an appropriate appreciation of the nature of its object' (1993, 134; cf. 1986, 314–15 n.; 1991, 49). A
conspicuously high informational standard is set by Haslett 1990, 72–4.

[35] Could they also sweep in desires we do not actually have, but would have if
the conditions were satisfied? Rawls's appeal to hypothetical choice seems to entail
this: 'In brief, our good is determined by the plan of life that we would adopt with
full deliberative rationality if the future were accurately foreseen and adequately
realized in the imagination. . . . Here it is worth stressing that a rational plan is one
that would be selected if certain conditions were fulfilled. The criterion of the good
is hypothetical in a way similar to the criterion of justice' (Rawls 1971, 421).
Griffin, on the other hand, requires that a desire be actual when satisfied (1986,
11). It is not clear, however, how this latter requirement is consistent with his
inclusion of posthumously satisfied desires.

the surviving subset of desires will count as enhancing our well-being.

We need not concern ourselves with the precise formulation of these idealizing conditions, since, however they are formulated, their role within a desire theory is inherently puzzling. Consider the requirement that a desire be appropriately informed. This condition is imposed in order to eliminate mistakes about the objects of our desires. But it appears that the condition is either redundant within a desire theory or inconsistent with it. Suppose that the satisfaction of one of my desires has left me worse off. There seem to be two possible explanations of how this could have come about. One is that satisfying the desire made me *to that extent* better off, but it also frustrated other, more important desires, so that on balance I ended up worse off. I take an eagerly anticipated vacation in the Caribbean and find myself in the path of a hurricane; had I known of the danger in advance I would have gone somewhere else instead. My desire not to encounter a hurricane is stronger than my desire to vacation at just that resort; in satisfying the latter I frustrate the former and so end up worse off on the whole than if I had stayed home. The desire theory is perfectly capable of explaining all this without the requirement that my preferences be informed. All it needs to do is bring into play the full structure of those preferences, including my priorities among them. In the light of all my actual desires I have suffered a net loss. Whenever this is the appropriate explanation of my plight, therefore, an information requirement will be redundant.

But there are, in addition, cases in which no further desires are involved and I am still worse off. My choice of philosophy over baseball was such a case. Here we cannot appeal to any additional desires in order to explain how things have gone badly for me. Furthermore, the preference on which I acted was as rational, considered, and informed as I could make it. All of the information I collected in advance about philosophy teaching turned out to be correct; I made no mistakes, except in expecting that I would find a teaching career fulfilling. That mistake resulted from the gap between my *ex ante* expectation and my *ex post* experience. That gap exists by virtue of the prospectivity of desire: my preferences about the future always represent my view *now* of how things will go *then*. Because the gap results from the very nature of desire, it cannot be closed merely by requiring that desires be rational or considered or informed.

The gap could be closed by stipulating that a desire does not count as informed—and thus its satisfaction does not count as making me better off—whenever the desired state of affairs turns out upon later experience to be disappointing or unrewarding. However, to take this step would be to confirm the desire theorist's suspicion that, once our experience of states of the world is admitted as relevant, then whether or not these states satisfy antecedent desires on our part is on the way to becoming irrelevant. For it would be tantamount to conceding that what matters, so far as our well-being is concerned, is *our* satisfaction and not merely the satisfaction of our desires. If an information requirement has any genuine work to do within a desire theory, therefore, it will be inconsistent with the basic rationale of the theory.

The argument to this point has focused on two essential properties of desires—their intentionality and their prospectivity—each of which opens up a logical gap between desire-satisfaction and well-being. All of the difficulties for the desire theory which we have so far canvassed have a common logical form. Desires whose objects prove disappointing in the actual experience of them and desires whose objects never enter our experience at all—these are both cases in which the satisfaction of our desires appears insufficient to make us better off. What they demonstrate is that when a desire is satisfied it is a logically open question whether the welfare of its holder has thereby been enhanced. However, they do not exhaust the problems which the desire theory encounters. If desire-satisfaction is not logically sufficient for well-being, it is not logically necessary either. Once again, the root of the problem lies in the very nature of desire. As we have already noted, because desires are future-directed, at best they represent the anticipation of benefit. But just as we can be disappointed when we get what we expect or have aimed for, so we can be pleasantly surprised when we get what we do not expect and have not aimed for.

There is a distracting side issue here which needs to be disposed of. As we have seen, the expansiveness of desire, its capacity to be directed on a virtually limitless range of (future) states of the world, causes problems for the desire theory. It is tempting, therefore, to narrow the theory by focusing exclusively on those desires which are also aims, by virtue of being incorporated into some hierarchy of intention.[36] If this restriction is introduced then the desire theory essentially equates welfare with success in achieving our aims or goals. But it is obvious that any such account would exclude too much.[37] Broadly speaking, the quality of our lives is enhanced both by what we do and by what happens to us. The fact that some benefits we enjoy are the result of good fortune rather than achievement on our part does not make them any less worthwhile.

Pleasant surprises would be a particularly acute problem for any version of the desire theory which confined attention to the achievement of antecedent aims. But they remain a problem for less restrictive versions as well. The difficulty stems from the fact that the welfare payoff of both achievements and windfalls often exceeds any antecedent expectations on our part. The most striking cases are those in which our expectations are either non-existent or negative. Having never heard bluegrass, I chance on a band playing in the park and find that I like it. Having nursed a long-standing suspicion of the Mediterranean, I am persuaded against my better judgement to holiday there and have a wonderful time. In neither case did I have an antecedent desire for the state of affairs which, as it turns out, enhances my well-being. But then, just as satisfying a desire on my part is not logically sufficient for something to benefit me, it is not logically necessary either.[38]

These problems for the desire theory have all stemmed from (two features of) the nature of desire. But the theory faces another

[36] This seems clearly to be what Rawls has in mind when he speaks of executing a rational plan of life. In his account of well-being, Joseph Raz also focuses on the pursuit of goals, thus on the success or failure of a life (Raz 1986, 288–99). It should be noted, however, that well-being is not the whole story for Raz; what he calls self-interest is a matter of the satisfaction of 'biologically determined needs and desires'.

[37] As Griffin recognizes (1986, 22). An exclusive focus on project pursuit also seems to manifest a masculine bias. It applies only with great strain to close personal relationships, such as friendship and love.

[38] In recognition of these problems, Griffin says that he is working with an 'extended sense of desire': 'The relevant sort of desire does not have to be held antecedently to its fulfilment (a human can enjoy something, want to have it continue or return, that he never knew he would enjoy, or even knew existed)' (1986, 315 n.). Prospectivity, however, is one of the features which distinguishes wanting from other positive attitudes, such as enjoying. If this feature is dropped, so as to include enjoying, then 'wanting' effectively becomes coextensive with 'having a positive attitude toward'. But in that case the desire theory is coextensive with the general category of subjective theories, and is not a particular, determinate instance of that category.

sort of difficulty as well, which has a quite different source. Although some of our desires may be basic, most have *grounds*. The ground of a desire is the reason one has for wanting its object— whatever it is about the object that makes it desirable. The grounds of our desires are to be found in what I am generically calling our concerns: our tastes, interests, ideals, commitments, and so on. Although these concerns will vary from person to person, there are some constants. One item that matters to all of us is our own welfare; self-interest, therefore, is one possible ground of desire. A desire has this ground whenever its object is wanted or valued because of some anticipated payoff for oneself. Call any such desire *interested*. It seems plausible to think that the satisfaction of our interested desires will standardly benefit us;[39] after all, in these cases the expectation of benefit is the ground of the desire. However, not all of our desires are interested in this way. For decades I wanted a democratic, non-racial government to be installed in South Africa, not because I expected to gain from it myself but because it was just. Such a government has now emerged during my lifetime. While I expect South African blacks to be better off for this turn of events, I see no reason to think that it will benefit me, despite satisfying my desire.[40] The reason for this is obvious: my desire was *disinterested*. The desire theory tells us that the satisfaction of any (rational, considered, informed) desire makes one better off, regardless of its ground. But this is not plausible in the case of disinterested desires.

Indeed, the very existence of disinterested desires is awkward for the desire theory. The theory tells us that if I do what I most want to do (in the attitudinal sense) then I necessarily do what is best for me. This is a weaker version of psychological egoism. It does not hold that I always choose to do what I think is best for me, since I may not choose to do what I most want to do. But it does hold that whenever I do choose what I most want then I necessarily maximize my own self-interest. This result, however, threatens to render the very notion of a disinterested desire incoherent.[41]

---

[39] Only standardly, and not necessarily, since the aforementioned logical gaps all apply to the special case of interested desires.

[40] This is not because of either logical gap thus far identified: the desired state is known to me when it occurs and in every respect lives up to my expectations for it.

[41] For an extended argument to this conclusion, see Overvold 1980. Sen makes a similar point when he accuses the revealed preference account of 'definitional egoism' (1982, ch. 4).

To want to do something (on the attitudinal conception) is to find the prospect of doing it positively attractive (in its own right). Since we are not psychological egoists, we are capable of finding enjoyment or satisfaction in doing good to others. Attitudinal desires therefore need not be self-interested; their satisfaction can be sought at considerable personal sacrifice. It is this possibility which the desire theory threatens to erase. No matter how altruistic my aim, no matter how great a personal sacrifice I am willing to make in order to achieve it, if I am successful then I will have made no sacrifice at all, since I will have got what I most wanted. I can represent the desire to myself as disinterested, therefore, only if I do not subscribe to the desire theory of welfare. Acceptance of the theory undercuts the very distinction between self-interested and disinterested desires.

Once again a logical gap opens between desire-satisfaction and well-being, this time in the case of disinterested desires. The only way to close the gap appears to be to exclude this class of desires. The desire theory would then hold that a state of affairs benefits me whenever it satisfies some self-interested desire on my part. But any such qualification of the theory would be patently circular. Our understanding of the nature of prudential value is not advanced by being told that it consists in the satisfaction of just those desires whose ground is prudential.

The desire theory therefore seems simultaneously too broad and too narrow: too broad because it admits desires whose satisfaction produces no benefits, too narrow because it excludes benefits which are not produced by the satisfaction of any antecedent desires. This is not, of course, a proof of the inadequacy of the theory. The problems of scope can be regarded as invitations to qualify the theory so as to contour desire-satisfaction better to well-being,[42] and I can see no way of demonstrating in advance the fruitlessness of this enterprise. Furthermore, since the desire theory is still by far the best-developed account of the nature of welfare, it may well be premature to give up on it without trying out a few possible remedies.

However, I am persuaded that the theory suffers from more than a problem of scope. It also operates at the wrong *level* for an adequate theory of welfare. Among the criteria of adequacy developed in section 1.2 was the requirement that the nature of welfare

---

[42] Which is the way Griffin regards them; see 1986, 16–23.

not be confused with its sources. The sources of our well-being (meaning still those states or conditions which benefit us immediately or directly) can be ordered into categories with different levels of generality. Suppose that one of my aims is to pursue a successful career teaching philosophy. The achievement of that global aim requires a number of more local successes: finding a permanent job, getting something published, getting tenure, etc. In the case of each of these latter states of affairs, their welfare payoff for me depends (in part at least) on their being parts of the larger whole which is success in the profession. They are goods for me because they are all collected together under the rubric of this more inclusive good. That good in turn represents only one of my aims and is therefore a part of the larger good which is success or achievement in my life. We therefore have the ordered sequence: finding a job is a good thing for me because it advances my career, and advancing my career is a good thing because it advances my overall plan of life.

All of this, so far, the desire theory is able to take into account. Indeed, it insists on the structure or hierarchy of our desires or aims, and finds welfare to consist entirely in their satisfaction or achievement. The problems of scope which it encounters, however, cast doubt on this. When the achievement of an aim leaves me feeling hollow or empty, however considered or informed the aim may have been in advance, this suggests that there is more to well-being than getting what I want. When I stumble onto previously unsuspected delights and find myself relishing them, this suggests the same thing. From this wider perspective, desire-satisfaction itself comes to look like one (very abstract and general) source of our well-being: something which standardly, but not necessarily, makes us better off. Furthermore, it seems not to be the only such source; things that happen to us, or that we grow into, or that we only slowly come to appreciate all matter too. The distinctive move of the desire theory is to treat desire-satisfaction not as one welfare source among others, but as the condition which anything must satisfy in order to count as such a source. Thus it purports to be a formal theory about the nature of welfare and not just a (very short) list of its sources.[43] But if getting what we want is

---

[43] See ibid. 31–4. Cf. Griffin 1993: 'Desire fulfilment seems to me best seen not as a substantive value, but as a formal notion of what it is for something to be prudentially valuable: it is for it to be (not entirely trivially) the object of a sufficiently well informed desire' (135).

merely one way in which our good can be advanced then, despite this claim of formality, the desire theory is operating at the wrong logical level.

It is this problem of level which has plagued all of the principal theories which we have so far considered. Each of these theories picks out one important respect in which our lives can be going well: for the teleological theory it is adequate functioning, for classical hedonism it is the having of enjoyable experiences, for the desire theory it is getting what we want. Each is therefore able to give a perspicuous account of its favoured sector of our lives, while being able to make little sense of the sectors covered by its rivals. The mistake made by all these theories is the same: they all attempt to build an account of the nature of welfare around one of its standard generic sources. The symptom of the mistake is also the same in each case: whatever the favoured source may be, its possession is logically neither necessary nor sufficient for our well-being. The logical gaps which have opened up for all these theories can be closed only by a formal theory capable of explaining what it is about all these goods which makes them cardinal ingredients of our welfare.

6

Welfare and Happiness

WELFARE is subjective, but neither of the historically dominant versions of subjectivism is adequate to its nature. Where do we go from here? We know that there is no regressing to objectivism, since even the best objective theory is about something other than welfare. Can either of the principal subjective theories provide us with the materials for a more plausible account? The two rejected theories are mirror images of one another, the strength of each corresponding to the weakness of the other. What hedonism lacks is a reference to the world outside the subject's mental states, while the desire theory, in correcting this problem, loses all connection with the subject's experience of the conditions of his life. Of the two accounts, the latter seems the less promising starting point for building a new and better theory, since the addition of any form of experience requirement is likely to displace desire altogether as the subjective notion central to an understanding of welfare. If we are to work from the established views, therefore, we must return to hedonism.

The classical version of hedonism subscribes to three theses: (1) the equation of welfare and happiness, (2) the reduction of happiness to pleasure (and the absence of pain), and (3) a mental state account of the nature of pleasure (and pain). Since the best theory about the nature of pleasure and pain treats them as sensations, (3) is unexceptionable. However, it is the purely mentalistic nature of pleasure and pain which renders classical hedonism vulnerable to objections from delusion or deception; something must therefore be amiss with either (1) or (2). The idea that there is an interesting connection between well-being and happiness has at least some initial plausibility—much more plausibility than any account of happiness in terms of pleasurable feelings. As a new start, therefore, it seems worthwhile seeking a better (and less hedonistic) theory about the nature of happiness.

By shifting our focus from pleasure or desire to happiness we may also succeed in loosening the grip of the mainline subjective theories. Although there is a sizeable philosophical literature on the nature of happiness, both traditional and contemporary, few believe that it consists either in pleasure and the absence of pain or in the satisfaction of informed desire. Indeed, no simple theory about the nature of happiness enjoys much support among philosophers; there is not even agreement that such a theory is possible. About the only thing everyone agrees on is that happiness is a complex and multi-faceted notion, one not easily reduced to a formula or slogan. This rather messy surface texture will be frustrating for anyone looking for an equally straightforward counterpart to hedonism and the desire theory. But for those open to fresh ideas and willing to tolerate a certain degree of philosophical disorder, it is very fertile ground indeed.

Each of the three previous chapters has been devoted to examining a theory of welfare which has been well developed and articulated in the literature. Our task now is different, since we will be engaged in constructing a theory which does not already enjoy a high profile. In working through the argument of this chapter, it may help to have some sense of its destination. The theory I shall defend does not simply identify well-being with happiness; additionally, it requires that a subject's endorsement of the conditions of her life, or her experience of them as satisfying or fulfilling, be authentic. The conditions for authenticity, in turn, are twofold: information and autonomy. Welfare therefore consists in authentic happiness. This theory is subjective, since it makes a subject's welfare depend on her attitudes, and since the function of the authenticity requirement is to ensure that these attitudes are genuinely hers. It satisfies the experience requirement, since a subject's happiness is a matter of her experience of the conditions of her life. However, it is not a mental state theory since authenticity is a relation between the subject and the world. The happiness theory thus mediates between hedonism and the desire theory, exploiting the strengths of each while avoiding their weaknesses.

That is where we are headed. To get there we need to navigate through some difficult terrain. The first step is to get a better fix on the nature of happiness.

6.1 LIFE SATISFACTION

Happiness, like welfare, is subjective. There is, however, this difference between the two notions: whereas the subjectivity of welfare is disputed and needs to be argued for, the subjectivity of happiness is obvious on the face of it. No objective theory about our ordinary concept of happiness has the slightest plausibility; such theories are taken seriously by philosophers only because of the common, and misleading, translation of *eudaimonia* in Aristotle's *Nicomachean Ethics*. As we saw earlier, we make much better sense of Aristotle's views by rendering *eudaimonia* into English as 'well-being'. Objectivism has at least a superficial plausibility as a theory of welfare; an argument is required to show why it is mistaken. It is completely unintelligible as a view about the nature of happiness.[1]

Classical hedonism, the historically dominant subjective theory, reduces happiness to pleasure (and the absence of pain). The initial plausibility of this view depends on the model of pleasure and pain which it presupposes. In Chapter 4 we distinguished two such models. On the narrower conception pleasure and pain are particular kinds of sensations distinguished by their peculiar (positive or negative) feeling tone. This model treats the characteristics of organic pleasures and pains as paradigmatic: they are usually (though not necessarily) localized in a particular part of the body, they can have a quite definite duration, and they can be compared in terms of intensity. Most importantly, sensations are identified as pleasurable or painful simply by the way they feel, and are typically (though not necessarily) liked or disliked for this feeling quality. Because we can distinguish between the intrinsic phenomenal properties of pleasure and pain, on the one hand, and our attitudes toward them, on the other, it is possible for us to be indifferent to either, or even to dislike the former and like the latter.

---

[1] Richard Kraut has defended the usual translation of *eudaimonia*, and the intelligibility of an objective theory of happiness, in Kraut 1979. However, his (quite justified) insistence that there is a substantive issue at stake between Aristotle and modern-day subjectivists is better supported by the supposition that the two sides hold contrary views about the nature of well-being. His own assessment of the merits of subjective and objective views also makes best sense when read that way. Our ordinary concept of happiness is too thoroughly subjective to be susceptible to an objectivist interpretation. For the same reason, David Brink's contention (Brink 1992) that Mill held an objective conception of happiness is best understood as a claim about Mill's account of welfare.

When pleasure and pain are understood in this way, their connection with happiness becomes very distant and tenuous. As physical sensations, pleasures are discrete episodes in our lives which are certainly capable of contributing to our happiness. A life totally devoid of pleasure is difficult even to imagine; if conceivable, then it seems a great waste of the opportunities available to us as embodied beings. But there is no ground for the dogmatic claim that the ascetic life cannot be a happy one. There are other sources of reward besides the body, and who is to say that they cannot add up to a life which is experienced as rewarding or fulfilling? At the opposite extreme, it seems possible for a life devoted principally (or even exclusively) to sensory pleasure to be a happy one (this may be the happiest life available to most animals). But again the outcome is not guaranteed—these pleasures have a way of cloying when we are glutted, and we may long for deeper or more meaningful sources of satisfaction. In short, the proper place for physical pleasure within a life cannot be dictated by a theory, but needs instead to be fixed by the subject's own priorities. Which is to say that it is not the phenomenal properties of the sensation itself which determine just how much a particular pleasure will contribute to our happiness, but rather the meaning or significance which we attach to it.

With some qualifications, the same holds for physical pain. A life totally devoid of pain is available only to those constitutionally incapable of feeling it, and the lives of such people are filled with injury and constantly threatened by death.[2] When we accept that our lives cannot, must not, be painless, relatively brief episodes even of relatively intense pain need not greatly compromise our happiness. While excruciating in the experience of them, once past they fade rapidly from our memory (are we programmed that way?). If asked to enumerate the experiences which compromise our happiness, we are unlikely to assign an important place to sprained ankles or trips to the dentist; there are far worse evils for us to confront. In most instances of physical pain, we can detach the sensation itself (in all of its phenomenal dimensions) from its meaning for us; the impact of the pain on our happiness is a function of the latter rather than the former. The important exception to this rule is chronic pain, especially if it is intense but also

---

[2] See Melzack and Wall 1983, ch. 1; Kerr 1981, 99–100.

at levels which would be easily bearable for shorter intervals. In these cases indifference to the pain, or assimilation of it into the normal course of our lives, becomes no more than a bare logical possibility. Intense chronic pain is absorbing, exhausting, debilitating, and depressing. It does not merely keep our lives from being happy, it makes them miserable.

It is obvious that if pleasure and pain are interpreted as particular feelings or sensations then they are ill fitted to play a constitutive role in a theory about the nature of happiness. They belong instead in our inventory of the (typical or standard) sources of happiness or misery, and they are not the only items in that inventory, nor necessarily the most important. For the most part, the classical hedonists agreed with this picture. With the exception of Bentham (and possibly also James Mill), they tended to favour the broader conception of pleasure (and pain) which comprehends any and all experiences which we like (dislike) or find agreeable (disagreeable) for their own felt qualities. There is much greater initial plausibility to an analysis of happiness which connects it with the having of agreeable experiences (and the absence of disagreeable ones). But it is misleading to continue to use the labels 'pleasure' and 'pain' to identify these positive and negative attitudes toward the conditions of our lives, especially when our conceptual repertory offers us ready alternatives. We can instead call them enjoyment and suffering, and then raise the question of the relationship between these phenomena and happiness.

At least at first glance, that relationship appears to be a close one. To say that we enjoy a particular experience, whether this be an activity in which we participate or something that happens to us, is not to say that the experience causes us a sensation which we identify, from its intrinsic sensory properties, as pleasurable. Physical sensations do not furnish us with a model which we can generalize to experiences like reading a book, or hiking through the mountains, or spending time with our children. Instead, the enjoyment of these experiences is a matter of receiving or responding to them in a particular (positive) way: liking them as they are happening, finding them rewarding or satisfying, welcoming them, engaging in them with enthusiasm or gusto, and so on. Likewise, to suffer from some condition or event (a disappointment of our expectations, a setback to our plans, the loss of a treasured object or person) is to react to it negatively—by finding it distressing or disagreeable, or regretting it, or enduring it with reluctance or resentment.

Enjoyment and suffering are plausible candidates for a constitutive role in a theory of happiness precisely because they are (positive and negative) attitudes or responses to the experiences which make up our lives. It seems roughly right to say that we are happy when we have a (preponderantly) affirmative attitude toward the conditions of our lives, and unhappy when our attitude tends toward the negative. And, indeed, this *is* roughly right. But only roughly. The appearance of a tight conceptual connection between enjoyment/suffering and happiness/unhappiness is fostered in part by a systematic ambiguity in these latter notions.

This is not the occasion to attempt an exhaustive inventory of the many ways in which we use the terms 'happy' and 'unhappy' (the results would in any case be of limited philosophical interest). However, four kinds or dimensions of happiness are worth distinguishing:[3]

Being happy with or about something. A distinctive feature of this kind of happiness is that it requires completion by an intentional object: there must be something with or about which you are happy (the recent political developments in Europe, the achievements of a friend, your new computer, etc.). Alternatively, we may complete your state of mind with a propositional object: you are happy that the Blue Jays won the World Series, that your daughter is graduating from university, that the solid waste disposal problem is being tackled, etc. As these examples make clear, the objects of your happiness, in this sense, are not confined to your own experiences, or to the conditions of your life. In principle, any state of the world can serve as such an object, as long as you have a positive attitude toward it, or regard it favourably, or like or approve of it. Having such an attitude is, indeed, pretty well all that being happy about something comes to; no affect or occurrent feeling on your part is implied (feeling happy about something is the same as being happy about it). The favourable assessment involved need not be a strong one. Being happy with something is roughly equivalent to being satisfied or content with

---

[3] The distinctions which follow are common ones in the recent philosophical literature on happiness. In one form or another, they can be found in Montague 1966–7; Austin 1968; Lloyd Thomas 1968; Benditt 1974; Tatarkiewicz 1976, ch. 1; Kraut 1979; Telfer 1980, ch. 1; McFall 1989, ch. 2; Nozick 1989, ch. 10.

it, i.e. finding that it measures up reasonably well to some standard. The degree of endorsement in question falls well short of
enthusiasm or delight. Contrariwise, being unhappy with something means regarding it in an unfavourable light, though not as
an absolute disaster.

Feeling happy. This contrasts with the first kind of happiness in
two principal respects: it involves an occurrent feeling and requires no intentional object. Not quite grand enough to count as
an emotion, it is rather a mood of optimism or cheer which colours your outlook on your life and on the world in general, con-
centrating attention on everything that is positive and upbeat. The
feeling in question can range from mere contentment to a state of
intense joy or euphoria accompanying the unshakeable conviction
that the condition of your life is just perfect, that things could not
be going better: the sky is blue, the birds are singing, you whistle
as you walk down the street, everyone smiles at you, and all is
right with the world. Perhaps the most striking feature of this
euphoria is its sense of completeness: right here, right now you
have it all—nothing is lacking, nothing remains to be striven for,
you are utterly at peace. There may be nothing in particular you
feel happy about (except perhaps your life in general); you just feel
happy. As an occurrent feeling, it tends to be short-lived (especially
at the level of bliss or rapture). Feelings of happiness are episodes
(moments, hours, days) in our lives, as fragile as they are wonderful.

The negative counterpart to this mood is feeling unhappy, down,
dejected, or depressed. In the grip of depression nothing seems to
be going right: your friends all hate you, your job is going nowhere, your clothes are boring, and it rains everytime you go out.
The depression may be free-floating, impossible to connect with any
specific object or stimulus; things just generally look black and
hopeless. Like joy or euphoria, bouts of severe depression may be
transitory, though they also have an unfortunate way of overstaying
their welcome, and when persistent may need to be addressed as
a clinical condition.

Elation and depression are the opposite poles of a continuum
which admits of many intermediate stops—you may be up but not
euphoric, down but not suicidal. As long as your mood is positive
we may say that you feel happy, when it is negative you feel unhappy. Whatever its degree, the mood is composed in part of a
certain characteristic feeling: energy, vitality, and buoyancy of spirit

ın the one case, lethargy and sickness of the soul in the other. The feeling component of (this kind of) happiness and unhappiness means that we can find these moods as well in other animals. When I play with the dog next door he bounds in circles, his tail wagging and his eyes bright: he is the very picture of joy. On the other hand, when our cat is sick she displays all the signs of dejection: she mopes, curls up in a corner, refuses to eat, and cries piteously. In human beings, with their greater cognitive capacities, feelings of happiness and unhappiness may also have a judgemental dimension, an assessment of our lives as going well or badly. But even this assessment tends to be tied to the here and now: at this moment everything seems just terrific/awful. Feelings of happiness and unhappiness are frames of mind subject to fluctuation from day to day, rather than settled judgements about the quality of our lives.

Having a happy disposition/personality. While feeling happy is an occurrent episode in your life, you may have a settled tendency toward such positive moods. If so, then we may say that you have a happy (sunny, cheerful, buoyant, upbeat) disposition, or that you are a basically happy person. This is the sense in which animals or infants can be happy, despite being incapable of sizing up their lives as a whole. The opposite, of course, is a personality which tends toward the gloomy, melancholy, grouchy, or misanthropic.

Being happy/having a happy life. We come now to the notion of happiness with which we will be principally concerned, that in which you are (have been) happy or your life is (has been) a happy one. Being happy in this sense means having a certain kind of positive attitude toward your life, which in its fullest form has both a cognitive and an affective component. The cognitive aspect of happiness consists in a positive evaluation of the conditions of your life, a judgement that, at least on balance, it measures up favourably against your standards or expectations. This evaluation may be global, covering all of the important sectors of your life, or it may focus on one in particular (your work, say, or your family). In either case it represents an affirmation or endorsement of (some or all of) the conditions or circumstances of your life, a judgement that, on balance and taking everything into account, your life is going well for you.

Clearly this sort of prudential stocktaking is possible only for creatures capable of assessing their lives as wholes, either at a time or over some extended period of time. The cognitive component of happiness is therefore beyond the range of many subjects-of-a-life, such as small children and non-human animals. However, there is more involved in being happy than being disposed to think that your life is going (or has gone) well. The affective side of happiness consists in what we commonly call a sense of well-being: finding your life enriching or rewarding, or feeling satisfied or fulfilled by it.[4] Because it is less cognitively demanding than a judgement about how one's life is going as a whole, it is what we have in mind when we say that a child or an animal is happy, or is leading a happy life.

The further features of (this kind of) happiness can best be elicited by comparing it with the other three dimensions. Because of the wide range of objects with or about which you can be happy, there is no linear relationship between these attitudes and happiness *tout court*. You may award failing marks to a good many states of affairs (the conduct of politicians, the state of the environment, higher taxes) while still leading a happy life, and you may persist in being unhappy despite thinking that the world in general is not going too badly. The only interesting overlap between the two dimensions occurs when what you are happy with is your life as a whole (or some significant part of it). But even here more is involved in being happy than the bare positive evaluation; you must also experience your life as satisfying or fulfilling.

There is also no straightforward relationship between happiness and feelings of joy or bliss. The latter are related to the former as its contingent sources or ingredients: they will tend to make a life a happier one, but they are not necessary for happiness. Nor is a cheerful or ebullient personality; those of a more stoic or spartan disposition can still affirm the conditions of their lives and find them rewarding. The connections are perhaps stronger when we turn to unhappiness. It is hard to be happy if enough periods of one's life are filled with depression or suffering, or if one is predisposed to be gloomy and sour. But even here the occurrent feelings contribute toward making us unhappy, and they may be counterbalanced by other factors, such as a sense of hope or purpose.

---

[4] Being unhappy is therefore a matter both of evaluating your life (or some part of it) negatively, as failing to meet your standards for it, and of experiencing it as unsatisfying or unfulfilling.

What being happy shares with feeling happy is its affective component—the experience of something (in this case your life as a whole or some important sector of it) as worthwhile or rewarding. There is no sharp distinction between them. Feelings of happiness (especially intense ones) are generally short-lived, but they are capable (at least in principle) of enduring for some time, at which point they become difficult to distinguish from a settled sense of satisfaction with the conditions of one's life.

Our question before we embarked on these distinctions concerned the relationship between enjoyment/suffering and happiness/unhappiness. It should now be clear that the answer will depend on which dimension of happiness we have in mind. The relationship between enjoying something and being happy with/about it is remote. To enjoy something is to find it agreeable or rewarding for its own sake. Since this is possible only for your own experiences, the range of things about which you can be happy is much broader than those you can enjoy. Enjoyment also has an affective component which may be entirely absent from this first kind of happiness. If you are enjoying something then it follows that you are happy with it, but the converse does not hold.

Feeling happy, on the other hand, is much more closely related to enjoyment (as feeling unhappy is to suffering). Like enjoyment, a feeling of happiness is an occurrent (attitudinal and affective) response to (what you perceive as) the conditions of your life—one which is generally episodic, with a fairly definite duration. But there are differences. Whereas enjoyment and suffering always require intentional objects, feelings of happiness and unhappiness can be non-referential. (Though perhaps when you are feeling happy it is always true that you are enjoying yourself.) Furthermore, while the notion of enjoyment may be adequate for capturing many happy feelings, it seems much too tepid for the heights of rapture or bliss. Likewise, only the most extreme cases of feeling unhappy (such as severe bouts of depression) would qualify as genuine suffering.

Since the third kind of (dispositional) happiness reduces to the second, we need not dwell on it. If you are a cheerful or optimistic kind of person then you will be disposed to find your life experiences enjoyable, while if you are given to negativity and gloom then they will tend to seem wearisome or bitter. A much more

interesting question concerns the relationship between enjoyment
and the leading of a happy life. This is the prudentially important
sense of happiness, the sense in which the classical hedonists identified it with well-being. They thought that a happy life was 'an
existence as exempt as far as possible from [suffering], and as rich
as possible in enjoyments'.[5] Were they right?

Enjoyment and suffering are certainly more intimately tied up
with happiness than are pleasure and pain. Once we confine the
latter to certain kinds of sensations, identified by their characteristic feeling tone, then there is no future in the idea that a happy
life must contain a maximum of pleasure or a minimum of pain,
or even a balance of the former over the latter. But enjoyment and
suffering are still too episodic, too tied to experiences of specific
activities or conditions, to be identifiable with happiness and
unhappiness. It is certainly true that, *ceteris paribus*, having more
things you enjoy and fewer you suffer from will make you happier. But there is no algorithm for computing your level of happiness from the intensity or duration of your particular enjoyments
or sufferings. (It was the root mistake of the classical hedonists to
believe there could be such an algorithm.) Like pleasures and pains,
enjoyments and sufferings are typical sources of happiness and
unhappiness. But they are not the only such sources: success or
failure in the pursuit of your aims count as well. The desire theory
went wrong by treating desire-satisfaction not as one important
source of well-being but as constituent of its nature. Hedonism,
even the improved version which takes enjoyment and suffering as
its central notions, likewise confuses an important source of happiness with its nature.

The notions of enjoyment and happiness come closest to con-
verging when the object of the former is one's life as a whole,
either at a given time or over an extended stretch. It makes perfectly good sense to ask whether you are currently enjoying your
life, or whether you enjoyed some particular part of it. And that
is nearly the same thing as asking whether you are, or were, happy
at that time. But not quite. For one thing, enjoyment understates
the judgemental component of being happy, the sense of your life
measuring up well against your prudential standards for it. But it
even fails to capture the full range of the affective dimension of

---

[5] Mill 1969, 214; characteristically, Mill speaks here of pain rather than suffering.

happiness, which can extend from bare contentment to deep fulfilment. Enjoyment is simply too mild to cover the more intense
regions of this scale. (The opposite is true for suffering, which
overstates the blander feelings of discontent or ennui: 'I certainly
wouldn't say that I was suffering at that stage of my life; I just
wasn't very happy.') We will do better at locating the attitudes we
are seeking here if we shift from the notion of enjoyment to something like *satisfaction* or *fulfilment*. The desire theory, of course,
uses these terms in its own way: a desire or preference is satisfied
just in case its object comes to exist. However, as we saw in the
previous chapter there is a logical gap between the fulfilment of
any of your desires and *your* fulfilment, a gap which is fatal to the
desire theory. We are now seeking this latter notion, not desire-
satisfaction but *personal* or *life satisfaction*.

This identification of happiness with life satisfaction is a theme
running through much of the recent philosophical literature on
happiness.[6] It is also the accepted presupposition of most empirical studies carried out by social psychologists, which attempt to
correlate levels of happiness with factors such as age, gender,
work conditions, marital status, and so on. Indeed, over the past
three decades or so a flourishing social-scientific industry has grown
up which is dedicated to the measurement of happiness, especially
on a social scale, and which construes happiness as life satisfaction. In order to understand the motivation behind the emergence
of this industry, we must revisit the notion of economic welfare,
whose history we traced briefly in section 5.1. As we there noted,
this notion led economists to equate the welfare of a society with
the sum total of its goods and services, as measured by national
accounts such as per capita product or income.

It is probably fair to say that this equation of social productivity
and social welfare functioned rather more as an implicit working
assumption, shared by the vast majority of economists, planners,
and politicians, than as an explicit theoretical commitment. Its
most important, and most evident, manifestation was the growth
ethic: the conviction that in the economic sphere more must be
better. After all, since social welfare is a matter of the national product, and since economic growth entailed increased productivity,

---

[6] See Austin 1968, 59–60; Benditt 1974, 8 ff.; Tatarkiewicz 1976, ch. 2; Telfer
1980, ch. 1; McFall 1989, 15 ff.; Nozick 1989, 110–14.

growth could not fail to increase social welfare. This optimistic creed began to be subjected to serious challenge in the 1970s.[7] What united the various sceptics about the growth ethic was the developing suspicion that the quarter-century of continually rising productivity which the developed capitalist societies of the West had experienced since the Second World War had failed to yield a comparable increase in social welfare. The main result of their challenge was to remind economists of some basic truths: (1) for both individuals and societies, economic welfare is not a distinctive kind of welfare but that part of overall welfare which depends on economic activity; (2) personal income or wealth is not constitutive of individual welfare, nor is it a reliable indicator of it; (3) national income or product is not constitutive of social welfare, nor is it a reliable indicator of it.[8]

If the economic growth debate managed to expose the implausibility of merely identifying welfare with income, it did not point to any unique corrective. Social scientists who were concerned to devise indices of social welfare differed in the extent to which they were prepared to deviate from the previous orthodoxy. The smallest adjustment involved moving to a more sophisticated set of national economic accounts, perhaps by incorporating some measure of the distribution of income or allowing for the role of external amenities and disamenities.[9] In principle, the analysis of the economic welfare of entire societies, particular social strata, and even individuals, could become very subtle indeed. But as a profile of social welfare such an analysis continues to be constrained by its employment of a monetary metric. Any source of well-being which cannot be brought into relation with the measuring-rod of money falls through its net.

For departures from the tradition of economic accounting we must look to what has come to be known as the 'social indicators movement'.[10] Broadly speaking, a social indicator is any piece of statistical evidence which can be reliably correlated with the

---

[7] Early doubts were voiced in Galbraith 1958. Thereafter, the critics included Mishan 1967 and 1977, Easterlin 1974, Scitovsky 1976, Hirsch 1977, and Abramovitz 1979.

[8] Cf. Sen's critique of the commodities account in s. 3.3, above.

[9] See, for example, Merriam 1968 and Sametz 1968.

[10] Useful analytic and historical overviews can be found in Carley 1981 and Nissel 1984; see also *Social Indicators Research*, the movement's leading dedicated journal.

welfare of those to whom it applies. Like welfare itself, indicators can be either subjective or objective, the former if they measure people's perceptions of the quality of their lives, the latter if they map external social conditions which standardly affect that quality for better or worse. Since economic indicators are themselves objective, some continuity with the old tradition is preserved if they are merely supplemented by other objective indicators not themselves measurable in monetary terms. This expanded system of national accounts, both economic and non-economic, can then be used to chart the nature and extent of social change.[11]

Programmes of social accounting employing a wide array of objective indicators have been launched by a number of national governments and international organizations.[12] But all of these programmes suffer from the same fundamental weakness: whatever the indicators used, they will correlate only weakly with individuals' perceptions of the quality of their lives. As Richard Easterlin put it, in an influential discussion:

One may attempt to use 'objective' indexes such as consumption, nutrition, or life expectancy to infer happiness. Or one may seek to gauge well-being from various behavioral indicators, for example, measures of the prevalence of social disorganization (delinquency, suicide, and so forth). Ultimately, however, the relevance of such measures rests on an assumed connection between external manifestations and internal states of mind— in effect, on a model of human psychology. And if it is feelings that count, there is a real possibility that subjective reports may contradict the 'objective' evidence. To social scientists, and especially economists, this can be frustrating.[13]

Some social scientists have coped with this frustration by making a virtue of necessity. If objective indicators correlate poorly with people's subjective reports of their own well-being (which they do), then we need better techniques for collecting and quantifying such reports. Enter the survey researchers, with their expertise

[11] This is the aim of the contributions to Sheldon and Moore 1968.
[12] See, for example, Organization for Economic Co-operation and Development 1973, 1982, 1986; a short overview of the OECD programme may be found in Nissel 1984. For its part, the United Nations has devised a Human Development Index (HDI) for its member countries which averages three component indices measuring life expectancy, education, and income. Each of these indices, in turn, can take into account a number of relevant indicators.
[13] Easterlin 1974, 117.

in administering questionnaires and conducting interviews.[14] The subjective indicators of well-being are the responses which can be elicited by these techniques. The indicators are subjective because what they measure are not the external circumstances of people's lives but their own perceptions of how well those lives are going— their 'perceived well-being' or 'assessed quality of life' or what we are calling their life satisfaction. As Angus Campbell puts it:

When individuals themselves evaluate their well-being, they . . . depend on the quality of their own experience, their feeling of being happy and contented, their sense of well-being. In this definition well-being is entirely subjective, known directly to the individual person and known to others only through that person's behavior or verbal report.[15]

To the social scientist who is interested in quantifying welfare, whether individual or social, the subjectivity of the resulting data may be a nuisance:

People are able to describe the quality of their own lives, not as precisely or with as great a degree of interpersonal comparability as one might like, but with a kind of direct validity that more objective measures do not have. Subjective experiences can only be measured subjectively, and we will have to accept the degree of imprecision this requirement implies.[16]

It is that 'direct validity' which makes the nuisance worth tolerating:

we cannot understand the psychological quality of a person's life simply from a knowledge of the circumstances in which that person lives. There are many good reasons for knowing the context of people's lives—their environmental condition, their economic status, their work life—but none of this information gives us more than a partial explanation of why some people find their lives enjoyable and satisfying and some do not.[17]

In one respect the evidential base furnished by subjective indicators is markedly narrower than that of the objective social accounts, since it relies entirely on survey results. But in another respect it is, at least potentially, much richer. At the simplest level, subjects can be asked for a global self-assessment ('How do you

---

[14] Some of the principal advocates of subjective indicators are Campbell and Converse 1972, Strumpel 1974 and 1976, Andrews and Withey 1976, Campbell *et al.* 1976, and Campbell 1981. Overviews of this wing of the social indicators movement may be found in Carley 1981, 34 ff., and Hankiss 1983. For an accessible introduction to the business of researching happiness, see Myers 1992.
[15] Campbell 1981, 14.   [16] Ibid. 12.   [17] Ibid. 1.

feel about your life as a whole?'), the available answers being arrayed on a scale which runs from highly positive ('Delighted') to extremely negative ('Terrible').[18] But survey questions can also be directed at particular sectors or domains of the respondent's life ('How do you feel about your home/marriage/family/neighbourhood/work, etc.'). Subjects can be allowed to determine for themselves which domains of their lives are most important to them, based on their own schedule of concerns; these then figure as the principal sources or ingredients of their well-being. Since their personal priorities need not reflect the demands of public policy, survey results can (and typically do) cover a much broader range than even the most generous set of objective indicators. Furthermore, the priorities reported by a subject can be operationally tested by determining which of the subject's domain assessments actually have the greatest influence on her global assessment of her well-being.

The shift from objective to subjective indicators, as a means of assessing well-being or quality of life, reflects a number of assumptions, implicit or explicit: (1) that welfare is subjective, (2) that it is either identical with or at least closely related to happiness, (3) that happiness consists in life satisfaction, and (4) that people's self-assessments provide the most reliable measure of how satisfied they are with their lives, or with particular sectors of their lives. We have by now ample reason to accept (1), and the earlier part of this section has made a case for (3). What about (4)? Are people generally reliable informants about their own levels of happiness or life satisfaction?

It is easy to think of circumstances in which subjective reports cannot be trusted. For one thing, if subjects misconstrue what is being asked of them then their self-evaluations may be *irrelevant*. Subjects are being invited to report how happy they are, or how well they feel their lives are going *for them*—in other words, to assess the prudential value of their lives. As we know (from section 1.3), lives can be evaluated along a number of different dimensions: prudential, to be sure, but also aesthetic or perfectionist or ethical. Subjects are *not* being asked for self-assessments along any of these other dimensions *except in so far as they affect their level of life satisfaction*. They are therefore not being asked whether

---

[18] This particular (seven-point) scale is used by Andrews and Withey 1976.

they think they are leading *good lives*, as measured by aesthetic, perfectionist, or ethical standards (or any other non-prudential standards, for that matter).

There is no fixed level of correlation among these various evaluative dimensions, even when they are all assessed by the subject himself. Someone may, for instance, think that his life has only a middling value on some or all non-prudential scales, but none the less be highly satisfied with it, perhaps because he cares little about leading a good life, or because his expectations for his own performance are modest, or because he feels he is doing the best he can under unpropitious circumstances. Contrariwise, a subject may rate himself highly in some or all of these non-prudential terms but not feel particularly happy with his life, perhaps because his self-imposed standards for living a good life are too demanding. For most of us, our degree of felt satisfaction with our lives will reflect, to some extent and along with many other things, how artistic or self-realized or virtuous we consider ourselves to be. When asked to rate their level of life satisfaction subjects are not expected to abstract from these further possible dimensions of self-assessment; on the contrary, they are invited to take anything into account which bears on their happiness. But they are expected to report how well they feel their lives are going *for them* and not from some external standpoint.[19]

Even when a subject has got the question right, his report may fail to reflect his true state of mind because it is *insincere*. He may, for instance, be influenced by a (conscious or unconscious) desire to measure up to some self-imposed standard or some (perceived) expectations on the part of others, as a result of which he tells us not how happy he actually is but how happy he thinks (or he thinks we think) he ought to be. There is considerable experimental evidence which suggests that subjects systematically overstate their levels of life satisfaction, so as to represent themselves to others (and perhaps also to themselves) as happier than they actually are.[20] To the extent that this phenomenon is uniform it need

[19] In practice, getting subjects to understand the question, and thus excluding irrelevant responses, does not seem much of a problem. When subjects are asked how they *feel* about their lives as a whole (or some specific domain therein), and when they are offered possible responses which range from 'Delighted' to 'Terrible', they seem to have no difficulty in discerning what would be appropriate by way of a self-assessment.

[20] See Matlin and Stang 1978, chs. 9 and 10.

cause few problems, since the scale on which levels of happiness are measured can be adjusted to compensate for exaggeration. But it is unlikely to be uniform: some subjects will be more candid in their self-evaluations than others. However this may be, self-assessments will be reliable indicators of happiness only when they are frank and honest.

Finally, people's subjective reports about their life satisfaction can be *coloured* by their transitory moods. Recall the distinction drawn earlier in this section between feeling happy and being happy: the former is an occurrent episode in a life while the latter is a relatively stable response to the conditions of that life. When you feel happy everything looks rosy, including your life as a whole; contrariwise, when you feel despondent or depressed then nothing seems to be going right. Clearly an assessment of your happiness will look very different depending on the state of mind in which it is undertaken. The solution to this possible distortion by passing mood is to seek self-assessments which are considered or reflective—that is, consistent over time and representing your settled view of your level of life satisfaction.[21]

In short, people's self-assessments tend to be reliable when they are relevant, sincere, and considered. Of course, it is never possible to eliminate all sources of bias or distortion in self-reporting. But it is also worth keeping in mind that in determining how happy people are we are not solely dependent on what they say. We can also refer to behavioural signs (happy people tend to act happy) as well as second-person assessments by knowledgeable others (happy people tend to look happy to their friends and relations). In the case of very young children, as well as non-human animals, we have nothing but this non-verbal information on which to rely. Despite all of the foregoing epistemic problems, by and large we have a reasonably high level of confidence in our ability to determine how happy (or unhappy) subjects are. There is no reason of principle to think that this confidence is misplaced, any more than our similar confidence in our ability to determine what subjects want or believe on the basis of what they say and do. The real philosophical problems lie elsewhere, not in reliance

[21] Survey researchers try to correct for this kind of distortion by asking subjects for self-assessments at variously spaced intervals. What they have found is that subjective reports tend to show a high level of consistency over time (see Myers 1992, 29).

on subjects as authoritative sources concerning their own happiness but in the bearing of this information on an assessment of their well-being. Those who have taken the subjective turn in the social indicators movement think that their data measure not merely the happiness or life satisfaction of their subjects but their welfare as well (see assumption (2), above). We must now ask whether they are right.

6.2 AUTHENTICITY AND AUTONOMY

So far we know that happiness, or life satisfaction, is a positive cognitive/affective response on the part of a subject to (some or all of) the conditions or circumstances of her life. What remains to be decided is what all of this has to do with well-being. The simplest relationship between happiness and welfare would, of course, be identity—which is the operational assumption of the 'subjective indicators' school. However, there are two serious impediments in the way of accepting this assumption.

The first impediment is the possibility of mistake. However relevant, sincere, and considered a subject's self-assessment, it may still be based on a factual error. Happiness (or unhappiness) is a response by a subject to her life conditions *as she sees them*. It is a matter of whether she is finding the *perceived* conditions of her life satisfying or fulfilling. But what if her perception of important sectors of her life is a misperception? What if she is deceived (by others or by herself) about them? Suppose, for instance, that her happiness depends in part on the loyalty and affection of a partner who in fact is merely using her for his own purposes. When she discovers the truth she will, of course, be miserable. But what are we to say of those months or years during which she was deluded? She was certainly happy then, but was her life going well for her?

We have returned here to the state-of-mind/state-of-the-world issue for subjective theories which we explored in section 4.2. If we identify well-being with happiness, and if we treat happiness solely as a function of a subject's *experience* of her life, then the result will be a mental state theory of welfare.[22] It will not be a

---

[22] Assuming that we interpret 'experience' here intentionally rather than extensionally; see s. 4.3.

version of hedonism, in the strict sense of that term, since we have resisted a reduction of happiness/unhappiness to pleasure/pain. However, it will encounter the same objections as hedonism, since it will still assess a subject's well-being entirely 'from the inside' with no reference to the actual conditions of her life. If those objections are decisive, as we earlier decided they are, then this simple identification of welfare with happiness—of well-being with 'perceived well-being'—must be rejected.

For those who think that there is *some* interesting connection between welfare and happiness, there are two ways to go from here. One is to modify the foregoing account of happiness in such a way as to ensure that it is not a mental state account. This could be done by adding the condition that a person's positive evaluation of her life will count as (real or true) happiness only if it is based on beliefs about the world which are true (or at least justified). Given the implausibility of any such condition, as part of an analysis of happiness, the number of philosophers who have defended it is rather surprising.[23] Consider the woman who for months or years has believed in, and relied on, the devotion of a faithless and self-serving partner. Her belief concerning a crucial condition of her life—a state of the world—was false. Whether it was also unjustified depends on the evidence of the deception which was available to her, whether or not she chose to take it on board. But let us assume, for the sake of the example, that there were sufficient cues for her to pick up, had she not been blinded by love. If you ask her during this period whether she is happy, she will say that she is; if you ask her whether her life is going well for her she will say that it is. If you ask her how she sees the same period after the delusion has been exposed, she will probably say that it now seems to her a cruel hoax and a waste of that part of her life. Clearly she *now* thinks that her life was not going well *then*; she has retrospectively re-evaluated her well-being during that period. But will she now deny that she was *happy* then? To do so would seem a mistake, a rewriting of a piece of her personal history. She may resent the fact that her happiness was bought at the price of an elaborate deception, but happy she was all the same. Wasn't she?

[23] See, for instance, Tatarkiewicz 1976, ch. 2; McFall 1989, chs. 2 and 3; Nozick 1989, ch. 10.

For better or worse, happiness does seem to be a mental state, dependent on how we see our lives and not (necessarily) on how they really are. Where our assumptions about the conditions of our lives turn out to be mistaken, therefore, happiness and well-being may part company. Why then would philosophers be tempted, counterintuitively, to add a truth (or justification) condition to their conception of happiness? Here is one line of thought which could lead them to do so. Begin by being a welfarist—one who thinks that well-being is all that ultimately matters for ethics. Then take the further step of thinking that well-being consists in happiness. You might then be disposed to think that any putative happiness which is based on delusion cannot be the genuine article, since it is not worth pursuing. *Real* or *true* happiness must therefore involve not just a positive assessment of one's life, but also a well-grounded one.[24]

Subscribing to a state-of-the-world analysis of happiness just in order to preserve the identity with welfare is a desperate and ill-fated measure. The better way to go is to accept that happiness is a state of mind and give up the simple identity. Whatever further, epistemic conditions are appropriate will then be part of our conception of welfare, rather than our conception of happiness. But which epistemic conditions *are* appropriate? The strongest candidate would be a *truth* or *reality requirement*, which would stipulate that happiness counts as well-being only when it is based on a view of the conditions of our lives which is free from factual error. As we saw earlier (sections 4.2 and 4.3), this stipulation would be unreasonably puritanical. We do not invariably reassess earlier periods of happiness in this austere manner once we realize the extent to which they depended on false beliefs about states of the world: the intentions of a lover, the integrity of a public figure, the prospects of success at a new enterprise, or whatever. We always have the alternative available of accepting the good times we enjoyed with little or no regret and then moving on with our lives. In my younger days I derived much comfort from the conviction that the course of my life, and of the world as a whole, was being directed by a benevolent deity. When I could no longer sustain this illusion I did not disavow the earlier comfort I derived from it; it got me through a difficult period of my life. When we

---

[24] This line of thought is evident in McFall 1989, 23.

reassess our lives in retrospect, and from a superior epistemic vantage point, *there is no right answer to the question of what our reaction should be*—that is surely up to us. Because a reality requirement stipulates a right answer—any happiness based on illusion can make no intrinsic contribution to our well-being—it must be rejected as presumptuously dogmatic. It seems even more dogmatic from a third-person standpoint: who are we to dictate that the solace someone else finds in a comforting fantasy should count for nothing?

A *justifiability requirement* would be weaker than a reality requirement, since it would not discount the meaning brought to our lives by assumptions which, though false, were at least reasonable under the circumstances. Assuming that we can agree on standards of reasonable belief, a justifiability requirement would have the mild advantage of moving closer to the subject's point of view concerning the conditions of her life, but in reserving wellbeing exclusively for the rational it is not much less arrogant than the stronger demand for truth. Once again it presumes to dictate to individuals how much their deviations from an ideal epistemic standpoint should matter to them. But that is for them to decide.

We can take a somewhat different direction with this issue if we recall a lesson learned from our earlier treatment of the desire theory (section 5.2). In order to bring desire-satisfaction more closely into line with welfare, desire theorists commonly stipulate that our preferences must be *informed*. We had difficulty locating the rationale for this requirement within the context of the desire theory. It is imposed in order to eliminate mistakes about the objects of our desires, thus to avoid outcomes in which getting what I want makes me worse off (or at least fails to make me better off). Whenever this happens, however, it appears that we could just as well say that satisfying the desire in question made me *to that extent* better off, but it also frustrated other, more important desires, so that on balance I ended up worse off. As we said earlier, the desire theory seems perfectly capable of explaining why the satisfaction of misdirected desires may go badly for me without imposing the requirement that my preferences be informed. All it needs to do is bring into play my full hierarchy of preferences.

Now, however, we are talking not about desire-satisfaction but about personal satisfaction, where this is interpreted as an endorsement or affirmation of the conditions of one's life. In this context there is an evident rationale for requiring that the endorsement in question be informed. After all, what we are seeking is an adequate subjective theory of welfare, one on which the subject's point of view on her life is authoritative for determining when that life is going well *for her*. By connecting welfare with happiness we have interpreted that point of view as an endorsement or affirmation of the conditions of her life. When that endorsement is based on a clear view of those conditions, we have no grounds for questioning or challenging its authority: in this respect, the individual is sovereign over her well-being. But when it is based, wholly or partly, on a misreading of those conditions then its authority is open to question, since it is unclear whether or not she is endorsing her life *as it really is*. Where someone is deceived or deluded about her circumstances, in sectors of her life which clearly matter to her, the question is whether the affirmation she professes is *genuine* or *authentic*. In order for a subject's endorsement of her life to accurately reflect her own priorities, her own point of view— in order for it to be truly *hers*—it must be authentic, which in turn requires that it be informed.

At this point an information requirement could be pushed in the direction either of a reality requirement (ideal information) or a justification requirement (reasonable belief given the information available). Since either of these directions would be incompatible with the individual sovereignty which characterizes a subjective theory, we must find some other way of determining how well informed a subject must be in order for her happiness to count also as her well-being. The place to start is with a (slightly) different question: when is (more) information relevant? The obvious answer, on a subjective account, is: whenever it would make a difference to a subject's affective response to her life, given her priorities. Return to the case of the woman who, for a while, lives in ignorant bliss with a faithless partner. Her endorsement of her life lacks information about his character and intentions. Is this information relevant? It is if her possessing it would undermine that endorsement. There are, therefore, two possibilities, which open up once she has been undeceived. One is that she re-evaluates how well her life was going (*not* how happy she was) during the period of deception: 'I thought everything was going so well, but now I can see that it was all a farce.' In that case, the discount rate she now imposes on her earlier assessment of her well-being determines how relevant the information was. The other possibility is that she does not care: 'C'est la vie; at least he was charming and we had a lot of fun.' Here the information turns out to have zero relevance, since that is the status she confers on it.[25]

The problem with reality or justification requirements is that they impose uniform discount rates on everyone alike: happiness has no prudential payoff unless fully informed, or is discounted at a steady rate as it becomes less informed. The relevance of information for a person's well-being is a personal matter to be decided by personal priorities; there is here no authoritative public standard. Still, the problem remains that the self-assessments which individuals report cannot merely be taken at face value; we need to know whether they are authentic. The best way to capture the condition they must satisfy is to say that they are *defeasible*—that is, they are authoritative unless we have some reason to think that they do not reflect the individual's own deepest priorities. Where someone's endorsement of his life is factually uninformed, or misinformed, that gives us one reason for doubting its authority (whether it is a sufficient reason depends on whether the endorsement will, or would, survive the acquisition of the missing information).

Factual error is not, however, the only possible reason for questioning the prudential authority of self-assessments, nor is it the most important. To push the frontiers of our account a little further we will do well to return to some criticisms of subjective theories which have been nicely articulated by Amartya Sen. As we noted earlier (section 3.3), Sen has two main reasons for rejecting all accounts which equate welfare with *utility*: (1) by reducing welfare to pleasure, desire-fulfilment, or any form of felt satisfaction, such theories fail to capture its evaluative dimension, and (2) because of the malleability of personal preferences, they leave individual well-being too sensitive to such extraneous factors as social conditioning. By now, of course, we have left Sen's principal

---

[25] The same options are available in the extreme case of illusion, namely the experience machine (see s. 4.2). A subject who recognizes the illusion, in retrospect, may respond by regretting having passed that period of her life floating in a tank or, alternatively, may embrace the experiences which were artificially induced for her ('Too bad it wasn't real, but it was a gas'). The extent to which the illusoriness of the experiences *matters* for an individual's well-being therefore depends on the extent to which she decides (or would decide) to *make* it matter. By the same token, plugging into the machine for a stretch of time (assuming it is foolproof) may be differentially attractive for different folks.

targets—hedonism and the desire theory—far behind. Furthermore, the account of happiness with which we are currently working insulates it against Sen's first criticism, since it incorporates a cognitive/judgemental element, namely, the subject's endorsement of the conditions of her life in the light of her own standards.[26]

Sen's second criticism, however, remains to be addressed. Its importance cannot be overstated; it is surely the main reason for questioning the adequacy of any subjective theory of welfare, whatever its constituent ingredients, and for favouring more objective accounts. It is worth repeating Sen's own statement of the problem:

A person who has had a life of misfortune, with very little opportunities, and rather little hope, may be more easily reconciled to deprivations than others reared in more fortunate and affluent circumstances. The metric of happiness may, therefore, distort the extent of deprivation, in a specific and biased way. The hopeless beggar, the precarious landless labourer, the dominated housewife, the hardened unemployed or the over-exhausted coolie may all take pleasures in small mercies, and manage to suppress intense suffering for the necessity of continuing survival, but it would be ethically deeply mistaken to attach a correspondingly small value to the loss of their well-being because of this survival strategy.[27]

This problem cannot be met by merely stressing the cognitive/judgemental aspect of happiness, since the extent to which people endorse the conditions of their lives will depend on their expectations for themselves, which are notoriously subject to external manipulation through mechanisms of conditioning, indoctrination, or socialization. Clearly the requirement that endorsement be empirically informed will not suffice to exclude these social influences on the standards by which people judge how well their lives are going; the problem here is rooted not in the adequacy of people's factual information but in the malleability of their personal values. There seems to be nothing in the theory so far which would rule out finding fulfilment in forms of life which are trivial or exploitative or demeaning.

[26] In fact, the account we are in process of constructing is remarkably similar to (some aspects of) Sen's own view. Recall the role which he assigns to (personal or social) valuations in determining the importance of various functionings, and his use of self-assessment as a means of eliciting those valuations.

[27] Sen 1987a, 45–6. As noted in s. 3.3, Sen's own account appears vulnerable to this criticism. See also Jon Elster's analysis of 'adaptive preference formation' in Elster 1982.

Once again those who wish to defend a tight relationship between happiness and welfare could choose to hang tough. They could, for instance, question whether self-assessments made under such conditions can be counted as sincere or considered, thus whether they are reliable indicators of happiness. Or they could question the extent to which such forms of life can be truly satisfying. Can we really say that 'the hopeless beggar, the precarious landless labourer, the dominated housewife, the hardened unemployed or the over-exhausted coolie' are *happy* with the conditions of their lives?[28] Is happiness compatible with a sense of insecurity or hopelessness, with being beaten down or exhausted? There is certainly merit in emphasizing the likelihood that lives conducted under these conditions will manifest signs of stress, anxiety, or depression—all of which are antithetical to life satisfaction. However, these lines of response seem to understate the seriousness of Sen's problem. A subject's ability to recognize a demeaning or dehumanizing life *as such* itself depends partly on the extent to which she has been able to emancipate herself from extraneous influences; effecting that emancipation is one of the purposes of consciousness-raising or psychotherapy. The insidious aspect of social conditioning is precisely that the more thorough it is the less its victims are able to discern its influence on their judgements about their lives.

It is in response to Sen's problem that some philosophers have embraced a kind of hybrid theory, which combines subjective and objective components. After all, if the problem lies with the standards which people use to assess their lives, what remedy could be more straightforward than to stipulate what those standards should be? When cast in terms of happiness, the general form of the hybrid view would be that something can contribute to a subject's well-being (directly or intrinsically) only if (1) the subject finds it satisfying or fulfilling, or endorses it as an ingredient in her life, and (2) it is independently valuable. Given the way in which we have drawn the objective/subjective dichotomy, any such view is still technically subjective, since its first condition preserves the necessity of the subject's positive attitude toward the condition in question.[29] However, the second condition introduces a *value*

---

[28] It is, however, enough for Sen's point if they are happier than they should be.

[29] On the analysis of subjectivity in s. 2.2, a theory is subjective if it treats the subject's favourable attitude toward something as a necessary condition of the

requirement into the analysis of well-being which is reminiscent of objective theories. Hybrid views of this sort are at least as old as Aristotle, who held that the prudential value of pleasure depends on the value of the activity which it accompanies.[30] On one interpretation, J. S. Mill committed himself to a similar view in his celebrated distinction between higher and lower pleasures, the former being those derived from activities given a high rating by a panel of 'competent judges'.[31] More recently, Martha Nussbaum has urged Sen to move his own analysis in an Aristotelian direction, a suggestion to which he has declared himself open in principle.[32] Other versions of a hybrid view have been defended in recent years by Joseph Raz and Ronald Dworkin.[33] Such a view is also hinted at by James Griffin's requirement that desires be 'formed by appreciation of the nature of their object', a requirement he uses to exclude the pursuit of aims whose desirability we find unintelligible.[34]

As a response to the problem of the malleability of people's standards of self-assessment, a value requirement is the counterpart of the reality requirement which we considered earlier as a remedy for factual mistake. Here the subject is presumed to be mistaken not about some state of the world but about the value, from an independent standpoint, of some condition of his life; he takes that condition to be more, or less, valuable than it really is. A value requirement, however, is even more questionable than a reality requirement, since it presupposes that there is an evaluative analogue to empirical truth or reality: a right answer to every question about value. How are we to determine which aims or activities or forms of life *really are* valuable? Can we rank them in terms of value? And who are 'we'? The enlightened élite? Mill's 'competent judges'? Philosopher kings? There is also the question of *which* independent evaluative standpoint is to be brought into play here. Clearly, if circularity is to be avoided, it cannot be

---

thing being beneficial for him. It need not also treat it as a sufficient condition, and most subjective theories will not do so. The hybrid theory differs from other, more orthodox, subjective theories by virtue of adding an independent value condition.

[30] *Nicomachean Ethics*, Book 10, ch. 5.

[31] Mill 1969, ch. 2. For a defence of this interpretation, see Brink 1992; Brink, however, concludes that Mill holds an objective conception of welfare.

[32] Nussbaum 1988; Sen 1993, 46–9.   [33] Raz 1986, ch. 12; Dworkin 1990.

[34] Griffin 1986, chs. 1 and 2; see esp. n. 29, 323–4. Derek Parfit also suggests a hybrid view, without explicitly endorsing it, in Parfit 1984, appendix I.

prudential value. Are ways of life to be compared in terms of their ethical value? That would seem to reverse the order of priority between ethical and prudential value in a way reminiscent of the private ownership theory (section 3.1). Their aesthetic value? That would lead to an unappealing aestheticism which subordinated well-being to artistic accomplishment. Their perfectionist value? This option looks no more appealing in this context than it did as a self-standing account of welfare: it just does not seem true that my life automatically goes better *for me* if the goals I am pursuing rank higher rather than lower from this external standpoint.[35]

Even if all these additional problems could be resolved in some satisfactory way, a value requirement still seems objectionably dogmatic in imposing a standard discount rate on people's self-assessed happiness. Again it helps to think about retrospective assessments of earlier periods of one's life. Suppose that as a young adult you worked for some years on a project—training for the priesthood, let us say—to which you were strongly committed. During that period your happiness, and your well-being *as you then saw it*, fluctuated in part with your success or failure at this project. Now, having achieved (what you regard as) greater maturity, and having revised your values somewhat, you reassess that pursuit as less valuable than you once thought. You do not, and should not, reassess your level of happiness during that earlier stage of your life. What about your level of well-being? Will you automatically conclude that your life was going worse at that time than you then thought it was? Or might you conclude that, while you were engaged in a pursuit which you could not now take seriously, none the less that was not a bad way to spend your life *then*? As in the case of gaining retrospective empirical enlightenment, there seems to be no right answer to the question of how to respond to shifts in personal values or standards: at the extremes you can either write off some earlier part of your life as a complete waste or accept it as an essential component of your past identity ('It's not who I am now, but it's who I was then'). Many

---

[35] Taking up any of these options would, of course, make prudential value dependent on some other value dimension. That would be fatal to the programme of welfarism, which takes prudential value to be the sole foundational category for ethics. However, the implications of a value requirement for welfarism are no reason to reject it as part of a descriptively adequate theory about the nature of welfare.

intermediate options between these extremes are also available; which one you choose to embrace is surely up to you.

When we undertake a retrospective reassessment of our lives we still judge the earlier part from the vantage point of our later standards. Thus from the first-person standpoint the question never arises of the bearing on our well-being of values which, however objectively 'correct', we never accept. To raise this question we need to take a second-person point of view on someone else's life. So suppose that your son decides to train for the priesthood, or join a rock band, or do something else which you, being more mature and enlightened, know to be objectively worthless. Is *his* life going worse *for him* during this period because of *your* knowledge of its lack of independent value? To say so seems incredibly presumptuous; surely that is a judgement which must be left for him (someday) to make.

If a value requirement is too strong, then we could try a justification requirement, again on the analogy with factual mistake. On this approach the prudential value of a subject's life would be discounted, not by the extent to which it lacked independent value, but by the extent to which the subject's belief in its value was unreasonable under the circumstances. But it should be clear by now that all of these reality/value and justification requirements are unacceptably patronizing and puritanical in their implications concerning the quality of people's lives. What we need instead is a counterpart to our earlier information requirement, with the defeasibility it implies for individual self-assessments. And once we begin to reflect on Sen's problem, its solution, within the framework of a subjective theory, seems pretty clear. Why are we reluctant to take at face value the life satisfaction reported by 'the hopeless beggar, the precarious landless labourer, the dominated housewife, the hardened unemployed or the over-exhausted coolie'? Presumably because we suspect that the standards which their self-assessments reflect have been artificially lowered or distorted by processes of indoctrination or exploitation. In that case, the obvious remedy is to correct for the conditions under which their expectations about themselves came to be formed. The problem is not that their values are objectively mistaken but that they have never had the opportunity to form their own values at all. They do not lack enlightenment, or insight into the Platonic form of the good; they lack autonomy.

Let us say, then, that (self-assessed) happiness or life satisfaction counts as well-being only when it is autonomous. But when is that? Luckily we will not need to invent a theory about the nature of autonomy to build into our theory about the nature of welfare. Because of its central role in both the Kantian ethical tradition and the liberal political tradition, autonomy has been the object of much philosophical attention—nearly as much as welfare itself. Developing an adequate theory of autonomy is doubtless just as difficult as developing an adequate theory of welfare, and deserves equally extended treatment. However, we can afford to be brief, since recent work on the nature of autonomy has illuminated the themes appropriate to our needs.

Etymologically, the root idea of autonomy is self-rule or self-direction. In its original use (by the Greeks) it applied not primarily to individuals but to polities such as city-states, where it had more or less the same meaning as our modern notion of sovereignty. Nowadays, however, the concept of primary interest to philosophers is that of *personal* autonomy. What has been carried over from the political to the personal realm is the core notion of managing one's own affairs, of not being subject to the will of others. A person is autonomous when her beliefs, or values, or aims, or decisions, or actions are, in some important sense, *her own*. There is therefore an evident connection between autonomy and what we have been calling authenticity. We have said that a subject's affirmation or endorsement of her life is made from her own point of view, is truly *hers*, only when it is authentic. The demand that self-evaluations be authentic flows from the logic of a subjective theory, which grounds an individual's well-being on *her* (positive and negative) attitudes. One side of this demand is the requirement that subjects be informed about the conditions of their lives. The other is the requirement that they be autonomous.[36]

Authenticity is a core element in the concept of autonomy, just as subject-relativity is a core element in the concept of welfare. But it is not sufficient to yield a theory about the nature of autonomy, since it is the common property of all rival theories.[37] Where these

---

[36] Scoccia 1987 also argues that well-being requires autonomy; however, he does so within the framework of a desire theory of welfare. Scoccia's account of autonomy incorporates the requirement that desires be informed.

[37] See, for example, Dworkin 1988, 12–13: 'There is then a natural extension to persons as being autonomous when their decisions and actions are their own;

theories part company is on how this core element is to be explicated, just as competing theories of welfare offer divergent interpretations of subject-relativity. Two main types of theory have predominated in the recent philosophical literature on autonomy. On one approach a person's values count as her own if she has identified with them, or acknowledged them as her own, or endorsed them as *her* standards for the conduct and assessment of her life. This process of identification requires the capacity for critical reflection on one's aims or goals. This capacity is often expressed in terms of a hierarchy of desires or preferences.[38] First-order desires take as their objects actions of the agent or states of the world; second-order desires take as *their* objects first-order desires. On this hierarchical view to endorse or accept a first-order desire is to make it the object of a second-order desire.

The model of a hierarchy of desires has come under justified attack as a way of explicating the process of an agent's critical reflection on, and identification with, her goals or values.[39] Critics have pointed out that a second-order desire not to have a certain first-order desire is, on the face of it, just a conflict of desires. There seems, so far, no reason to assume that the former is more critical or reflective than the latter, nor that the subject identifies more with it.[40] This problem with the hierarchical model could presumably be rectified by stipulating that the higher-order process includes an element of critical reflection on lower-order aims. It will then be appropriate to say that it can issue in an endorsement or acknowledgement of these aims, and not merely a desire for their perpetuation. But a deeper problem remains. Whatever the specification of the second-order reflective process, the question can be raised whether the values or standards under which it is conducted have themselves been accepted autonomously. After

when they are self-determining.' Compare Christman 1991, 1: 'Virtually any appraisal of a person's welfare, integrity, or moral status, as well as the moral and political theories built on such appraisals, will rely crucially on the presumption that her preferences and values are in some important sense her own.'

[38] As in Dworkin 1988, ch. 1; Haworth 1986, chs. 2 and 3; Young 1986, chs. 4 and 5. The hierarchical model of desires is derived from Frankfurt 1971, who used it, however, to explicate not autonomy but free will.

[39] See, for example, Thalberg 1978, Friedman 1986, Scoccia 1987, and Christman 1991.

[40] This criticism is reminiscent of Sen's rejection of the desire theory on the ground that it fails to capture the evaluative dimension of welfare (see s. 3.3).

all, if a system of indoctrination is sufficiently thorough then it will be capable of structuring not only an individual's life goals but also the values to which she appeals in reflecting on these goals. Thus the 'dominated housewife' may accept her subordinate status as the appropriate social role for a woman.

At this stage an infinite regress threatens. The higher-order process of critical reflection was introduced in order to distinguish autonomous from heteronomous aims or goals. Now that the same distinction is needed for values or standards, do we move to a yet higher level (about which the same questions can be raised)? The analysis of autonomy which highlights the psychological process of identification, and which therefore requires the capacity to step back from and assess one's goals or values, seems to be on the right track as far as it goes. But it cannot tell the whole story about autonomy. For the rest of that story we need another approach.

The rival theory looks not to whether an agent has identified with a particular life goal but to the process by which that goal was adopted in the first place. As John Christman has put it, 'what is crucial in the determination of the autonomy of a desire is the manner in which the desire was *formed*—the conditions and factors that were relevant during the (perhaps lengthy) process of coming to have the value or desire'. As a result, 'the central focus for autonomy must make particular reference to the processes of preference formation, in particular what makes them "manipulative" in a way crucially different from "normal" processes of self-development'.[41] Christman contrasts this historical approach with (what he calls) 'time-slice' theories which confine attention to the attitude the subject *now* has to the value or desire in question. Explicating autonomous aims or goals in terms of the history of their formation seems an apposite response to Sen's problem. After all, the reason we are reluctant to take at face value the level of life satisfaction reported by Sen's beggars, labourers, and housewives is that we are suspicious of the socialization processes by means of which they have internalized the standards they use in assessing their lives. Why not then just stipulate what these processes must be?

---

[41] Christman 1991, 10 (emphasis in original). Cf. Elster 1982, who argues 'the need for an analysis of the *genesis* of wants' (237, emphasis in original), and Scoccia 1987: 'desires are autonomous in virtue of their formation, not content' (594).

The solution cannot, however, be quite as simple as that. As Christman himself acknowledges, the historical approach is not complete until it has offered some means of distinguishing between 'manipulative' and 'normal' processes of the formation of desires or values. How is this distinction to be drawn? We must keep in mind here that *all* of our aims, values, and ideals will have been influenced *to some extent* by our peculiar personal histories and the socialization processes which have shaped us; none of us developed in a social vacuum. This, presumably, is what Christman means by 'normal' processes of self-development. How, then, are we to identify the processes which depart from the norm? Intuitively, a socialization process seems manipulative when it compromises or fails to respect the autonomy of its subject, by denying the subject the opportunity for critical reflection on the process itself and its outcome. But if this is the right answer then the historical approach to autonomy needs to be supplemented by the kinds of resources offered by the hierarchical model. Roughly speaking, an autonomy-preserving socialization process will be one which does not erode the individual's capacity for critical assessment of his values, including the very values promoted by that process itself.

The incompleteness of the historical approach is also shown by people's ability to come to accept autonomously values which were initially formed by non-autonomous means. Imagine a young man raised in a religious community which strictly limits information about other ways of life and points of view (let us say that it forbids the teaching of modern physics or biology). Since this looks like a paradigm instance of indoctrination, his acceptance of his community's values would be paradigmatically non-autonomous. Suppose, however, that he then gains access to the outside world for an extended time (he is accepted at a large urban university), during which he fully confronts the modern world's challenges to his community's way of life. After a period of doubt and indecision he decides to reaffirm his commitment to that way of life. Despite the fact that his values have a tainted history, we would not wish to exclude the possibility that his present endorsement of them counts as autonomous. In that case, the history of the initial formation of a value or goal cannot tell the whole story about its autonomy.

It appears, therefore, that neither of the currently dominant theories about the nature of autonomy is self-sufficient. Theories which emphasize the importance of identification must provide some reassurance that the agent's values or standards have themselves been autonomously adopted, while theories which look backward to this formation process must require preservation of the capacity for critical distance and reflective assessment.[42] However the details of a fully adequate view are worked out in the end, the implications for our theory of welfare are clear. Self-assessments of happiness or life satisfaction are suspect (as measures of well-being) when there is good reason to suspect that they have been influenced by autonomy-subverting mechanisms of social conditioning, such as indoctrination, programming, brainwashing, role scripting, and the like. Since these are all socialization processes, and since we are all historically embedded selves, the practical question becomes how much emancipation from her background and social conditions a subject must exhibit in order for her self-assessment to be taken at face value. As in the case of the information requirement, the best strategy here is to treat subjects' reports of their level of life satisfaction as defeasible— that is, as authoritative unless there is evidence that they are non-autonomous.

On a subjective theory, individuals are the ultimate authorities concerning their own welfare. Their self-assessments are therefore determinative of their well-being unless they can be shown to be inauthentic, i.e. not truly theirs. The requirements that these assessments be informed and autonomous spell out the conditions of authenticity. A person's own view of her life satisfaction carries an initial presumption of authenticity, and thus of authority. It can be mistaken, even deeply distorted. But it must be shown to be so before we can have any ground for discounting it.

6.3 A THEORY OF WELFARE

Our remaining task is to pull together the threads of the theory we have developed and to integrate it into the themes of earlier

---

[42] The mutual dependence of the two approaches has been at least partially recognized by their advocates. On the one hand, the hierarchical analysis in Dworkin 1988 includes a condition of 'procedural independence', which means roughly that identification must not have been influenced by conditions which subvert or impair the agent's critical and reflective capacities. On the other hand, the historical account developed in Christman 1991 requires that the formation process for a value or desire be free of factors which inhibit self-reflection.

chapters. First, a recapitulation of the ground covered in this chapter. We have been exploring the linkages between welfare and happiness. The latter notion, we have found, can be equated with life satisfaction, which has both an affective component (experiencing the conditions of your life as fulfilling or rewarding) and a cognitive component (judging that your life is going well for you, by your standards for it). The best way of determining people's happiness levels is to ask them, and a sophisticated methodology for eliciting self-assessments of life satisfaction has been developed by social scientists. However, an individual's report will accurately reflect his perceived happiness only if it is relevant (focused on the prudential dimension of the value of his life), sincere (uninfluenced by the desire to maintain a particular social image), and considered (uncoloured by transitory feelings of elation or depression). The question then is whether happiness, as so measured, is identical to well-being. We have found two reasons for thinking that it is not: a person's self-evaluation may not be informed and it may not be autonomous. In either case it is inauthentic, in that it does not accurately reflect the subject's own point of view. Welfare therefore consists in authentic happiness, the happiness of an informed and autonomous subject.

This theory of welfare as authentic happiness[43] is clearly subjective, since it makes a subject's well-being dependent on his (positive or negative) attitudes. In section 2.2 we laid out the four variables to be specified in any subjective analysis of welfare: (1) the objective features of things by virtue of which they evoke (2) some attitude on the part of (3) some reference group of subjects under (4) some set of normal conditions. Because we are here dealing with prudential value, there is only one plausible candidate for slot (3): the welfare subject himself. Different subjective theories then diverge in their instantiations of variables (2) and (4), thereby determining different contents for (1). The happiness theory interprets the relevant attitude (2) as the subject's endorsement of the conditions of his life, or his finding them satisfying or fulfilling, and specifies authenticity as its normalizing condition (4). The result is an analysis on which some condition of a subject's life is (directly or intrinsically) beneficial for him just in case

---

[43] To avoid needless repetition, in what follows I will drop the qualifier that happiness must be authentic except where it is demanded by the context. It is, however, to be understood as applying throughout.

he authentically endorses it, or experiences it as satisfying, for its own sake. The intrinsic sources of welfare will be whatever conditions of subjects' lives elicit this response.

Like all subjective theories of welfare, the happiness theory preserves the analogy between welfare and perceptual properties. A subjective analysis of any perceptual property must also furnish values for four distinct variables: (1) the objective features of things by virtue of which they evoke (2) some characteristic mode of experience on the part of (3) some reference group of subjects under (4) some set of normal conditions. To say that colour, for instance, is a secondary quality is therefore to say that it consists in a power or disposition on the part of objects with certain primary qualities to evoke certain visual experiences under certain circumstances on the part of creatures with a certain perceptual apparatus. Whether colours, or any other perceptual properties, really are secondary qualities in this sense remains, of course, to be determined. However this may be, we now have good reason to think that welfare (or, more accurately, the property of being intrinsically beneficial) *is* a secondary quality: a power or disposition on the part of some conditions of our lives to evoke the appropriate positive attitude on our part. This dispositional analysis of prudential value also connects it with similar accounts which have been offered of other evaluative dimensions, including ethical value.[44] (It is, of course, completely agnostic on the question of whether such an analysis is appropriate in any of these other cases.)

Preserving the analogy between welfare and secondary qualities may not be thought to be a happy result for a subjective theory. Subjective analyses of perceptual properties have frequently been criticized on the ground that the values for variables (3) and (4) cannot be supplied without covertly presupposing the objectivity of the property in question. Consider, for example, a typical dispositional analysis of colour according to which an object *is red* just in case it *looks red* to standard observers under normal conditions. Who are to count as standard observers? Those who are not colour blind, i.e. to whom things look (under normal conditions) to have the colour they really have. What are to count as normal conditions? Those under which things look (to standard

---

[44] See, for instance, McDowell 1985, Railton 1986, and Brower 1993.

observers) to have the colour they really have. Specifying the reference group of perceivers and the conditions of perception for a subjective analysis of redness thus appears to presuppose the logical priority of *being red* to *looking red*, so that the dispositional formula really analyses the latter in terms of the former.[45]

The same objection can be raised against a subjective account of welfare.[46] On the account we have developed, welfare consists not merely in happiness but in happiness as experienced by informed and autonomous subjects. When does a subject count as informed and autonomous? When what she experiences as satisfying, or endorses as a part of her life, really is prudentially valuable for her. But then *being valuable* is logically prior to *being endorsed as valuable*, in which case the latter cannot provide an explication of the former.

Whether subjective accounts of perceptual properties can be defended against this circularity objection is a matter which need not be decided here. However, the form which such a defence will take in the case of a subjective analysis of welfare is by now clear. The aim of such an analysis is to ground an individual's well-being in her attitudinal point of view on the world. This has been accomplished only when a subject's responses to the conditions of her life are authentic, i.e. truly hers. The requirements that her responses be informed and autonomous flow from this basic demand of authenticity. If a subject's endorsement of some particular (perceived) condition depends on a factual mistake, or results from illusion or deception, then it is not an accurate reflection of her own underlying values. And if those values have been engineered or manipulated by others then they are not truly *hers*. The specifications of who is to count as a 'standard observer' and what is to count as 'normal conditions' are therefore entailed in this case by the nature of subjectivity itself. The happiness theory therefore has the resources to rebut accusations of circularity, or of the covert presupposition of some objective account of welfare.

In Chapter 4 we followed standard practice by distinguishing two types of subjective theory: those on which welfare is *solely* a matter of the subject's states of mind and those on which it is

---

[45] For an influential version of this argument, see Sellars 1956, s. III.

[46] It has been raised by Ripstein 1993 against preference-based accounts of practical rationality; his critique would apply with equal force against a subjective account of any dimension of value, including welfare.

additionally a matter of some states of the world. Classical hedonism is a mental state theory, vulnerable to objections from illusion or deception for this very reason. The desire theory is a state-of-the-world theory, since whether or not a desire is satisfied is a matter of how the world goes. In some important respects the happiness theory resembles hedonism, most obviously in its endorsement of an experience requirement: according to the theory, it is a necessary condition of a state of affairs making me better off (directly or intrinsically) that it enter into my experience. It was the absence of an experience requirement which was fatal to the desire theory. However, in an equally important way the happiness theory sides with the desire theory against classical hedonism. Since it also incorporates an information requirement (as part of its condition of authenticity), it is a state-of-the-world theory. That I experience a state of affairs is necessary in order for it to benefit me, but (since the experience may be illusory or deceptive) it is not sufficient.

The happiness theory is therefore 'something in between' hedonism and the desire theory, avoiding both the former's solipsism and the latter's disengagement from our lived experience. Is it therefore superior, as an account of welfare, to both of its rivals? To answer this question we must revisit the acceptance criteria which we laid out in section 1.2. Since we are seeking a descriptively adequate theory, the basic requirement is that of fidelity to our ordinary concept of well-being and our experience of it in our everyday lives. Since the happiness theory is subjective, it easily passes one important part of the fidelity test. As we have repeatedly stressed, the prudential value of a life is its value *for the individual whose life it is*. A descriptively adequate theory must at least preserve the subject-relativity of welfare, but it should also do more. It should provide an interpretation of this subject-relativity, by explaining what it means for a life to be going well not just in itself or from some other standpoint but *for its subject*. This is, of course, the demand that objective theories of welfare are unable to meet. Subjective theories satisfy it by referring to the subject's attitudinal point of view; in the case of the happiness theory, that point of view is made up of the values or standards which the subject uses in determining whether her life is satisfying or fulfilling. The authenticity requirement, which is an essential part of the happiness theory, guarantees that the operative point of view in a subject's self-assessments of her happiness is genuinely hers.

Determining just how well the happiness theory fits our many preanalytic judgements about welfare would be a complex, and probably endless, task. However, it is possible to point to the ways in which its fit is superior to that of its subjective rivals. We found classical hedonism to be deficient both in its preoccupation with the episodic feelings of pleasure and pain (or enjoyment and suffering) and in its mental statism. The happiness theory avoids these pitfalls by shifting attention to the more global attitude of happiness or life satisfaction and by introducing an information requirement which is capable of overriding subjective reports of happiness. On the other hand, the desire theory failed because of its rejection of an experience requirement, which opened up a logical gap between the satisfaction of a person's desires and *her* satisfaction. By incorporating an experience requirement, and shifting to the notion of personal satisfaction, the happiness theory is able to distinguish between those desires which, when satisfied, make a subject's life go better and those which do not. Being 'something in between' hedonism and the desire theory— more reality-based than the former and more experience-based than the latter—thus enables the happiness theory to make better sense of at least many of our judgements about well-being.

A further component of fidelity was adequate fit with the role which welfare plays in our common-sense psychology, and especially rejection of the thesis of psychological egoism. Since our own well-being is just one possible end of action for us, a theory of welfare must not imply that all intentional action is, or must be, self-interested. Avoiding this implication is a potential problem for both hedonism and the desire theory, the former because it can be tempting to try to derive prudential (or ethical) conclusions from a hedonistic psychology, and the latter because every rational action (which maximizes preference-satisfaction) threatens to be self-interested by definition. At first glance, it might appear to be a problem for the happiness theory as well, since it makes a person's well-being depend on her autonomously adopted values or standards. On this view, how could an autonomous agent fail to be acting in her own interest whenever she pursues her own ends or goals, whatever these may be? The answer to this question is given by the relevance condition for subjects' reports of their own happiness. Subjects are being asked to reveal how well they feel their lives are going *for them*, not for self-assessments in any other value dimensions (except in so far as their self-rating in these dimensions affects their level of life satisfaction). The personal values which are pertinent to an individual's happiness are prudential ones. An autonomous agent is therefore free also to embrace aesthetic, perfectionist, or ethical ideals whose pursuit may conflict with her well-being.

Besides the basic test of fidelity, we developed three more specific criteria of descriptive adequacy for theories of welfare: generality, formality, and neutrality. Taking these in order, a theory of welfare must first be general or complete, by virtue of covering all of the different sorts of welfare assessments we make. We earlier sorted these assessments into two categories: those which situate a subject at some particular welfare level and those which chart a subject's gains or losses (movement from level to level). Both types of assessment may be either positive or negative: someone's life may be going well or badly, and a change may be for the better or worse. There seems no reason to think that the happiness theory will have any problem with any of these types of judgement: in general, people seem capable of determining both how satisfied they are with their lives and whether some particular development has made them more or less so. In explicating the happiness theory we have focused almost exclusively on welfare rather than illfare, happiness rather than unhappiness. But the analogous treatment of these latter notions is straightforward, resting as it does on the negative counterparts of personal satisfaction and endorsement. A life is therefore going badly for someone when she (authentically) experiences its conditions as unsatisfying or unfulfilling, or disclaims or disowns them.

Our everyday welfare assessments also include interpersonal comparisons, both of levels of well-being and of gains and losses: I am doing better/worse than you, benefited more/less than you from the recent budget provisions, and so on. How these various kinds of comparisons are to be interpreted and supported is too large a topic to be dealt with adequately here. This is an area in which subjective theories are commonly considered to be at a disadvantage *vis-à-vis* their objective counterparts; when the preference theory was riding high in the social sciences it was even thought to entail that interpersonal comparisons were impossible. Such comparisons are now commonplace in the research into happiness or life satisfaction carried out by the 'subjective indicators' school. Ordinary people always seem to have managed them easily on a daily basis. What we rely on in the straightforward cases is a rich vein of information, both verbal and non-verbal, about the way other people's lives are going for them. The hard cases are ones in which, for one reason or another, our information base is thin. This sometimes happens because we find the other relatively opaque, as when we attempt to compare ourselves with members of very different cultures or with people who have serious mental or physical disabilities. Where we are unable to represent to ourselves how the life of the other is for him, from the inside, then we may be at a loss to decide whether that life is better or worse, for him, than ours is for us.

The problem of opacity is exacerbated when we move beyond the realm of human subjects. The final dimension of generality is that a theory provide some plausible rationale for delimiting the class of core welfare subjects, plus some illuminating explanation of what makes other subjects peripheral. For the happiness theory, the minimal wherewithal for having a welfare is being a subject who is capable of being satisfied or unsatisfied by the conditions of one's life. In the case of paradigm human subjects with complex cognitive capacities, more is necessary as well: their judgements about the quality of their lives must be authentic. Where these more sophisticated skills are absent, the *sine qua non* is the baseline ability to experience one's life, in the living of it, as agreeable or disagreeable.[47] The most primitive form of this ability is the capacity for enjoyment and suffering, or for pleasure and pain. If we call this capacity *sentience* then we may say that on the happiness theory the class of core welfare subjects is populated by all sentient creatures.

This leaves some important kinds of creature on the periphery: all non-sentient animal species (as well as plants), human embryos and fetuses up to a certain stage of prenatal development, and persons who have permanently lost the capacity for conscious

---

[47] If a creature is incapable of acting inauthentically, then the authenticity requirement is trivially satisfied. Can non-human animals respond inauthentically to the conditions of their lives? Can this be true, for instance, in the case of domesticated animals whose affective responses have been deliberately engineered, for our convenience, so as to lead them to be satisfied by ways of life which are unnatural to them? If so, then the authenticity requirement will apply (non-trivially) in those cases as well, and it may not be safe to conclude that an animal is faring well just because it is happy.

awareness. The happiness theory entails that none of these creatures has a welfare of its own; no change in their condition could make them either better or worse off. Yet in each case it is easy to see why the class of beings in question is only a short (but crucial) step away from counting as a welfare subject. The primitive capacity for experiencing pleasure and pain appears to be the exclusive property of vertebrate animals.[48] Although this means that neither invertebrates nor plants can have an affective point of view, as living beings they do have natural tendencies which can be either enhanced or frustrated, which is why we can speak of them as either flourishing or languishing, and of conditions as being either good or bad for them. Strictly speaking, however, what is at stake for non-sentient organisms, and what we are capable of affecting for better or worse, is not their well-being but their excellence or perfection as specimens of their kind (see section 3.4).

The earliest stage of fetal development at which sensitivity to pain is possible seems to be just beyond the midpoint of pregnancy, more or less at what currently counts as the stage of viability.[49] Before they reach the threshold of sentience, and therefore count as core welfare subjects in their own right, human embryos and fetuses also have natural developmental tendencies which can be furthered or retarded and which make it possible for us to speak of their good (though not their well-being). Where they differ from non-sentient animals is in their potential for developing into core welfare subjects. While this potential gives them a particularly intimate relationship to such subjects, it does not make them subjects in their own right.

Finally, in contrast to the desire theory, the happiness theory implies that the dead, no longer having lives to experience as either satisfying or unsatisfying, can have no welfare of their own. For our purposes 'the dead' includes not only all those whom we would unreflectively classify as such but also those who satisfy contemporary criteria for brain death, though their respiration and circulation may continue to be artificially supported, and persons in a persistent vegetative state who have irreversibly lost the capacity for consciousness, including the most basic sensations

[48] Rose and Adams 1989; Smith and Boyd 1991, ch. 4. The latter make a tentative case for including cephalopods as well.
[49] See Anand and Hickey 1987.

of pleasure and pain.[50] Pre-sentient fetuses and the dead are both temporally connected to core welfare subjects, but in opposite directions: while the former may have subjectivity in their future, the latter have it in their past.

The happiness theory also renders a decision on the question of the status of collectivities as welfare subjects. In company with other subjective theories, this account has located well-being firmly within the lives of individuals with the appropriate affective and/ or cognitive capacities. Any talk, therefore, of the welfare of groups, if it is not merely metaphorical, must be interpreted as referring to the aggregate or collective well-being of their members. Collectivities have no interests to be promoted beyond those of individuals.

The criterion of formality requires that a theory not confuse the nature of well-being with its (direct or intrinsic) sources; a theory must offer us, not (merely) a list of welfare sources, but an account of what it is for something (anything) to be such a source. Clearly the happiness theory offers such an account: a condition of someone's life counts as an intrinsic source of well-being for her just in case she authentically endorses it, or finds it satisfying, for its own sake. The subject-relativity of prudential value requires the reference to the subject's own endorsement. However, it does not prevent us from generalizing over the conditions which will standardly be experienced as intrinsically rewarding or fulfilling by creatures who share a common nature (such as us). The happiness theory is therefore capable of generating a set of *standard human goods*: such items as health, mental and physical functioning, enjoyment, personal achievement, knowledge or understanding, close personal relationships, personal liberty or autonomy, a sense of self-worth, meaningful work, and leisure or play. These items should look familiar, since they commonly turn up on the lists of human goods invoked by objectivists. Each of these goods has enormous instrumental value for us, since each is the condition of realizing many other goods in our lives (for one thing, the items on the list are mutually interdependent). And each is something whose relative value in our lives may vary considerably from person to person: you may place much greater store on achievement or success and less on maintaining close personal relationships than

---

[50] For the criteria of brain death, see Ad Hoc Committee 1968 and Consultants 1981. A description of persistent vegetative state, and a distinction between this condition and brain death, can be found in Cranford 1988.

I do. But for each item on the list it is plausible to say that everyone cares about it *to some extent* for its own sake, thus that its presence in a life makes that life *to some extent* more satisfying or fulfilling, quite apart from its instrumental value. If asked why it should be that just these goods achieve the status of intrinsic sources or constituents of our well-being, the only intelligible answer is: because that is the kind of creatures we are.[51]

Because subjective theories of welfare are formal, they have the advantage over objective theories of being able to explain why the list of standard prudential goods contains just these items and not others. They are also able to explain why the relative importance of these goods can vary so much across individuals as well as cultures. But the happiness theory has a further advantage over its principal rivals, each of which focuses on one of these generic goods to the exclusion of the others. For the teleological theory the highlighted item is mental and physical functioning, for classical hedonism it is enjoyment, for the desire theory it is personal achievement. The root problem with all of these theories is the same: they all attempt to build a formal theory about the nature of welfare around one of its standard intrinsic sources. Only the happiness theory provides a general rubric capable of explaining the prudential significance of all of these goods, as well as many others.

Finally, neutrality requires that a theory not exhibit any bias in favour of some particular list of goods or some favoured way of life. Objective theories have difficulty with this requirement, since they typically stipulate a pattern of the good life for all members of a particular natural kind (such as us). For subjective theories neutrality is generally not an issue, unless they incorporate some objective elements, either overtly or covertly. The kind of hybrid theory considered, and rejected, in the previous section makes explicit room for a ranking of forms of life on some independent (non-prudential) scale, thereby threatening to violate neutrality. But subjective theories can be non-neutral in subtler ways, by rigging their normalizing conditions so as to ensure selection of some predetermined set of goods. The happiness theory avoids this trap by deriving its information and autonomy conditions from an

---

[51] The analogous list of intrinsic prudential goods for members of other species will likewise be determined by their nature.

authenticity requirement, which is in turn entailed by subjectivity itself. It will therefore endorse as prudentially valuable whatever ways of life are found to be fulfilling by informed and autonomous subjects. No independent restrictions of content are imposed.[52]

One implication of a neutral theory of welfare is that ways of life which we regard as trivial or demeaning or depraved can, in principle at least, be prudentially valuable for their subjects. Where the happiness theory is concerned, there is no way of excluding the possibility, for any such way of life, that it can be endorsed by an informed and autonomous subject. However, we can have pretty good empirical reasons for thinking that, say, a life of servility or subservience is rarely embraced under conditions of full information and autonomy; in fact, the ways in which the conditions of such a life compromise and subvert autonomy form our principal objection against it. In other cases, such as a life devoted to watching daytime talk shows or pursuing a career in the sex trade, we may have to discipline ourselves not to make *a priori* assumptions about the degree of autonomy manifested by those who make choices which we find personally distasteful. At any rate, an open mind and a willingness to attend to the specifics of people's particular circumstances seems less patronizing than simply assuming that the lifestyle in which they are engaged, besides failing to measure up on some other value dimension, is also necessarily bad for them.[53]

In summarizing the criteria of descriptive adequacy in section 1.2, we constructed the following profile of the ideal theory of welfare: it will be faithful to our ordinary assessments of well-being, including the role they play in our common-sense psychology, it will cover all core cases and provide a principled resolution of peripheral cases, it will not confuse welfare with its sources or ingredients, and it will be free of distorting bias. We also noted the obvious implication that any comparison of candidate theories will be multidimensional, leaving open the possibility that a theory may satisfy some criteria better than others, thus that there may

---

[52] The neutrality of the happiness theory is guaranteed in part by the 'content neutrality' of the conception of autonomy which it incorporates; see Scoccia 1987, 594; Dworkin 1988, ch. 2; and Christman 1991, 22–3.

[53] Scarre 1992 argues that at least some disreputable lifestyles—those which involve the enjoyment of others' suffering—are bad for us because they erode the basis of our self-respect. I am less sanguine.

be no theory which fully satisfies them all. Having reviewed all of the principal contenders, we are now in a position to exclude this possibility. The happiness theory scores no worse than any rival theory on any criterion and better than all of its rivals on most. It therefore provides us with the best picture of the nature of welfare.

7

Welfarism

WE began our inquiry with two questions: What is welfare? And how much does it matter for ethics? Answering the first question has taken us down a long and winding road which finally led to the happiness theory developed in the previous chapter. The time has now come to put this theory to work, by turning from the nature of welfare to its ethical value.

Welfarism is the view that nothing but welfare matters, basically or ultimately, for ethics; it is therefore a normative theory about the foundations of morality. Nowadays it is decidedly a minority view: most philosophers reject it, either implicitly or explicitly, in favour of other foundationalist (or anti-foundationalist) options. Perhaps it deserves its fate; we shall see. But I venture to suggest that, latterly at least, it has not had a fair hearing, since the case against it has typically presupposed a distorted and misleading picture of what welfare is. The currently dominant theories of welfare are the ones we considered earlier—objective theories, hedonism, the desire theory—and found to be inadequate. Since one or another of these same theories tends to be assumed when the merits of welfarism are debated, it is not surprising that the view has recently won few friends—if *that* is what welfare is, then it could not possibly represent the fundamental point of ethics.

Welfarism deserves to be tested on the basis of the best available theory about the nature of welfare. Having that theory in hand will greatly facilitate the rest of our inquiry, since it will enable us to isolate the real issues at stake between welfarists and their opponents. But who are the opponents? To answer that question we first need to take a closer look at what is involved in being a welfarist.

Ethical realism. Welfarists believe that there are right answers to questions in ethics, answers which can, at least in principle, be discovered and defended by means of evidence and argument. This form of ethical realism is epistemological rather than metaphysical; epistemological realists are free to be agnostic as to the ontological status of values or other ethical entities or properties.

Ethical theory. The function of an ethical theory is to reveal the deep structure underlying and unifying the surface diversity of our moral thinking—the set of aims or principles which constitutes the overall point or rationale of it all. Welfarists believe that the project of theory-building in ethics is not futile or misguided.

Foundationalism. The concepts we employ in our moral thinking can be sorted into a few general categories: the axiological (good and bad, better and worse), the practical (ought and should), the deontological (duties, rights, justice), the aretaic (virtues and vices), and so on. Welfarists believe that the structure of the best moral theory will assign priority to just one of these categories by using it to derive and justify all of the others.

The priority of the good. One possible foundationalist structure for an ethical theory will install axiological principles on the ground floor and use them to support a deontological and/or aretaic superstructure. On this picture the ultimate point of ethics is to bring about intrinsically valuable states of affairs, or to make the world go well. Welfarists affirm the priority of the good.

Agent-neutrality. A value is agent-neutral if everyone has a reason to promote it, or at least to want it to come about; it is agent-relative if that reason is restricted to those specially connected to the value in some way (e.g. because it is theirs).[1] Welfarists believe that the foundational values in an ethical theory are agent-neutral in this sense.

Each of these methodological assumptions is controversial, indeed quite unfashionable these days. However, they will serve nicely to sharpen our characterization of welfarism. Someone who shares them all thinks that the foundation of ethics consists in a *theory of the good*: a list of foundational agent-neutral values whose pursuit and promotion is the point of the whole ethical enterprise. Welfarism is a theory of the good whose list of foundational values contains a single item: well-being. Since being a welfarist requires subscribing to all of the foregoing points, it is

---

[1] For an explication of agent-neutrality (and agent-relativity), see Parfit 1984, 27, and Nagel 1986, 152–3, 158–63.

easy to be an anti-welfarist: one need only reject any one of them. There are therefore many possible varieties of anti-welfarist: anti-realists, anti-theorists, anti-foundationalists, deontologists who affirm the priority of the right, virtue theorists who affirm the priority of virtue, axiological dualists who hold that some foundational values are agent-relative, and so on. Dealing with all of these opponents would require us to settle some of the deepest and most persistent problems in the metaphysics and epistemology of morals. To simplify the issues at stake, we will concern ourselves with only one class of anti-welfarists: those who share all of the welfarist's assumptions about ethics but support a rival theory of the good. This very narrow focus will of course limit the appeal of our discussion, since advocates of many popular contemporary views about ethics will think that we are wasting our time asking the wrong question. On the other hand, if we are able to make a strong case for welfarism then that may suggest that their dismissal of the question has been a little premature.

A theory of the good can take two possible forms: it is *monistic*, if it includes only one item on its list of foundational values, or *pluralistic*, if it makes room for more. Welfarism is monistic; its rivals are therefore both other monisms and any form of pluralism. The first two sections of this chapter consider these rivals in that order. Before we proceed any further, however, a cautionary note is in order. In the history of ethics, at least in its modern period, welfarism has been defended most insistently by utilitarians. Some may fear, therefore, that to accept welfarism is to become a utilitarian. This fear is misplaced: although utilitarians are necessarily welfarists, welfarists are not necessarily utilitarians. In order to be a card-carrying utilitarian you must accept two further commitments, in addition to welfarism. The first commitment is to *consequentialism*: the idea that the right consists in maximizing some measure of overall or collective welfare.[2] The second commitment is to *aggregation*: the idea that collective welfare consists in the sum total of individual welfares. It is possible to be a welfarist without being either a consequentialist or an aggregationist; the view that well-being is the foundational value for ethics can therefore be shared by both deontologists and virtue theorists.[3]

---

[2] For a fuller characterization of consequentialism, see Sumner 1987, s. 6.1.

[3] For an example of a welfarist deontology, see Finnis 1980, chs. 3–5. Aristotle defended a welfarist virtue theory (at least in his own view of it).

Deontologists are free to reject the maximization of aggregate welfare as the root of all evil, while still maintaining that the underlying rationale of duties and rights is the protection of (individual) interests. Likewise, virtue theorists can hold that dispositions are ethically meritorious in proportion to their tendency to promote well-being, whether that of the agent or others. If utilitarianism happens to be your favourite moral theory then you are certainly welcome to keep its particular structure in mind as we proceed. But we will be working at a deeper level of ethical theory-building.

7.1 THE CASE FOR WELFARISM

On such a fundamental question in ethical theory we cannot expect proof but only, as J. S. Mill famously put it, 'considerations . . . capable of determining the intellect either to give or withhold its assent to the doctrine'.[4] The theory of the good which we are trying to establish here bears more than a passing resemblance to the 'theory of life' that Mill undertook to defend in chapter 4 of *Utilitarianism*: 'that happiness is desirable, and the only thing desirable, as an end; all other things being only desirable as means to that end.'[5] However, the route taken by Mill, in his notorious 'proof' of this theory, is closed to us. Mill argued that happiness is the only thing people desire as an end, and derived this conclusion from a hedonistic analysis first of happiness and then of desire: 'desiring a thing and finding it pleasant, aversion to it and thinking of it as painful, are phenomena entirely inseparable, or rather two parts of the same phenomenon; in strictness of language, two different ways of naming the same psychological fact.'[6] Mill's case for his ethical hedonism thus rested on his psychological hedonism. But he was doubly mistaken since, as should be clear by now, neither happiness nor desire can be given a hedonistic analysis. Furthermore, it is a commonplace that people are psychologically capable of valuing and pursuing ends other than happiness (either their own or that of others).

If welfarism cannot be supported by psychology, it is tempting to turn to practical reason. The argument might run as follows: while welfare is not the only thing people are capable of seeking for its own sake, it is the only thing which it is rational for them

---

[4] Mill 1969, 208.   [5] Ibid. 234.   [6] Ibid. 237.

to seek, and therefore it is the only rational basis for ethics. The problem is that the premiss of this argument is blatantly false, since it confuses the *self-interest* theory of practical rationality, which requires individuals to maximize their own welfare, with the *instrumental* theory, which requires them to maximize the satisfaction of their desires or preferences. The confusion usually arises because of the identification of preference-satisfaction with welfare, which is especially common among economists (see section 5.1). As we know by now, however, the two are quite distinct, as a result of which the self-interest theory and the instrumental theory are in reality mutually incompatible: the former holds that each individual has one uniquely rational ultimate end, namely his own well-being, while the latter holds that rationality applies to means only and not to ends.[7] That the self-interest theory is in any case false is easy to see from our response to someone who knowingly makes himself worse off in pursuit of some rival category of value: the ethical, perhaps, or aesthetic, or perfectionist. We do not normally regard such persons as irrational, or even unreasonable, unless their degree of self-sacrifice is carried to the extreme that they become a danger to themselves.

There is therefore no carryover here from practical reason to ethics: the unique status of welfare in the latter domain cannot be derived from its similar status in the former. Welfarism affirms the foundational unity of ethics, its resolvability into the promotion of just one kind of value. But as an ethical theory it is not committed to the foundational unity of practical reason. Nor does any such unity appear to be defensible: reasons can emanate from distinct, independent, and possibly incommensurable points of view, of which ethics is but one. Besides ethical value we can be called on to protect or promote other dimensions of value. When one such dimension conflicts with another, practical reason appears to furnish no higher court capable of adjudicating the conflict, and no higher mode of value capable of subsuming these particular standpoints. Pluralism therefore seems to be the right story about practical rationality.

So why is it then not also the right story for ethics? Perhaps the rational and the ethical *should* be symmetrical. If there are a variety of (basic and irreducible) values which it can be rational

---

[7] For an extended analysis of the self-interest theory, see Parfit 1984, chs. 1, 6–9.

to pursue, why is there not a similar variety which it can be ethical to pursue? Why the asymmetry? Why should ethics have a more restricted domain? Suppose that with eyes wide open you choose a plan of life which you expect to be worse prudentially—worse *for you*—but better from some other evaluative standpoint. So that we might leave ethics out of the picture for a moment, let this standpoint be aesthetic. In order to dedicate yourself exclusively to the pursuit of your artistic vision, and bequeath your immortal works to posterity, you sacrifice family, fortune, and health. Welfarists concede that this choice may be rational, but they also claim that it is appropriate for ethics to protect your well-being rather than your artistry *even though this is not your own highest priority*. Is this not an objectionable form of paternalism, a meddlesome denial of your autonomy?

By way of reply, we may begin by noting that sacrificing your well-being for the sake of some other end, though possible and possibly rational, is not quite as easy as it may seem from this example. Your welfare, we have said, is a matter of how satisfying or fulfilling you authentically find your life. If you are driven by aesthetic passion then the form of life in which you sacrifice all *other* prudential goods (family, fortune, health, etc.) may, all things considered, be the most rewarding *for you*. The subjectivity of welfare is a crucial factor here. Since your welfare already incorporates and reflects your authentic point of view, a welfarist ethics will not entirely disregard or override your own priorities for your life. However, the point must not be overstated. Since you can have ends other than your own well-being (we are not psychological egoists), your welfare cannot simply be identified with the achievement of whatever you choose to aim for. In order to locate genuine self-sacrifice we have to suppose that in the relentless service of posterity you adopt a life goal which actually makes you miserable, or at least leaves you cold. (One begins to wonder what kind of artist you would then be.) But in that case, it is not at all clear why ethics should be concerned with the (assumed) gain in aesthetic value which compensates for the loss of your well-being. Aesthetic value is the concern of, well, aesthetics. This is ethics; why should it take aesthetic value on board?

Furthermore, we should not suppose that the rules of a welfarist morality will forbid individuals to make non-welfarist choices. Any reasonable set of arrangements will protect autonomy, among other values, as an intrinsic prudential good—the kind of thing which enriches our lives by its very presence. They will therefore ensure that individuals have sufficient space in which to set their own priorities for their lives, imposing limits only at the margin (when others will be adversely affected, when you become a danger to yourself, when you are not competent to make such choices, etc.). Indeed, securing that discretionary space is one of the principal functions of a theory of rights.[8] A welfarist ethics—an ethics with a welfarist ultimate justification—should be flexible enough to make room for idiosyncrasy, eccentricity, even a little craziness.

If we can argue to welfarism from neither psychology nor rationality, how can we get there? Suppose we try a different tack. Welfarism, we have said, is a monistic theory of the good. Even if you accept the priority of the good, the monistic story may seem particularly implausible. Is it really possible that all of the complex structure of ethics has as its point the furthering of just one particular kind of value? After all, the world throws a bewildering array of values at us; how could it be that just one of these constitutes the ground floor of ethics? Well, we can at least specify what a value would have to be like in order to be capable of occupying this theoretical niche. First, it would have to be *intrinsic* —that is, worth having or pursuing for its own sake, not merely by virtue of some further good with which it is connected or associated. This condition will eliminate anything whose value is merely instrumental or contributory. Second, it must be *abstract* or *generic*. Our ethical deliberations and evaluations cover a wide range of contexts from the larger issues of law or politics through questions of community and personal relations to our own individual aspirations and actions. In these different realms we pursue or promote many goods: liberty, autonomy, equality, sociality, loyalty, intimacy, security, health, achievement, enjoyment, and so on. It is not believable that any one of these could somehow turn out to be the point of the whole enterprise or the deep justification of the rest; they are all too parochial for that. If there is a single foundational value then it must be broad enough to encompass all of these local goods and to explain their appeal. Nothing short of an abstract category or mode of value will have the requisite degree of generality.

[8] See Sumner 1987, ch. 2.

Third, the value in question must be *important*. What is characteristic of morality, across most of its domains, is its peremptory or insistent tone. Moral considerations are advanced as constraints on our wishes or desires, as demands we must heed even when we would prefer not to. If these constraints and demands are all in the service of some category of the good, then the case for promoting this good had better be pretty compelling. Finally, the good we are seeking must be *ethically salient*. We are not merely asking for an inventory of intrinsic values. We also want to know which of these values might count as foundational *for an ethical theory*. Now an ethical theory has a certain distinctive content and function, dealing as it does with such matters as the distribution of rights and duties, the assessment of motives and dispositions, the assignment of responsibility, the allocation of blame and punishment, the appropriateness of guilt and shame, and so on. If there is a foundational value for ethics, then it must be not only worth pursuing for its own sake but also capable of supporting this characteristic structure of judgements and practices. Not all values, however central they may be to their own domain, can bear this particular weight. Aesthetic value, for example, is (arguably) instrinsic, abstract, and important, but it can provide at best the materials for building an aesthetic theory; it seems out of the question as a foundation for ethics.

Welfare possesses all four of these features. Its value certainly seems to be intrinsic; we normally regard benefits and harms as mattering in their own right and not merely as means to further ends. It is generic, since it embraces a wide variety of more specific goods as standard sources of well-being. It is important, since it tracks the way in which individuals' lives go well or badly, in their own eyes or from their point of view. Finally, it is ethically salient: the fact that a course of action would make someone better off counts in favour of it, and the fact that it would make someone worse off counts against it. The central thesis of welfarism is that *ethics has ultimately to do with ensuring that lives go well, or at least that they not go badly*. Whenever we are told that we have a moral reason to do something we are therefore entitled to ask: 'Where is the good in it? Whose life will go better as a result? Who will be benefited (or saved from being harmed)?' And likewise, when we are told that we have a moral reason not to do something we may rightfully ask: 'Where is the harm in it? Who will be made worse off as a result?'[9] Where there is no answer to this question, no linkage to benefits or harms, however remote or indirect, then the alleged reasons may be rejected as so many fictions. Now I find this an enormously attractive picture of the ultimate point of the whole ethical enterprise. If something will improve the conditions of no one's life, make no one better off, then what ethical reason could be given for recommending it? And conversely if something will harm no one, make no one worse off, what reason could be given for condemning it?

Welfarism also gives a credible account of what we may call the circumstances of ethics: the conditions under which it is both possible and necessary. These conditions are twofold: (1) a set of *moral agents* who possess the requisite rationality and autonomy to recognize and act on moral reasons, thus to regulate their lives by means of ethical standards, and (2) a set of *moral patients* who must be taken into account in the deliberations of moral agents. Welfarism has no special theory to offer of moral agency, but it does give us a *criterion of moral standing* for determining who qualifies as a moral patient. To have moral standing is to count or matter morally in one's own right or for one's own sake.[10] Welfarism entails that moral standing is shared by all creatures with a welfare, thus (on the happiness theory) all sentient creatures. This is, I suggest, an intuitively plausible account of the limits of our moral consideration; it explains why it is a morally trivial matter for me to pull the weeds in my garden but not for me to poison my neighbour's cat.[11] But welfarism also tells us that the existence of rational agents is not sufficient by itself to make moral thinking possible. It is conceivable that such agents might be utterly lacking in affect (they might be superintelligent computers, for instance), thus quite incapable of finding their lives (if that is the appropriate term for them) either satisfying or unsatisfying. If that were the case, then nothing could go either well or badly

---

[9] In phrasing the questions in this manner, I do not mean to suggest that for a welfarist something morally significant happens only when someone is made better or worse off than she would otherwise have been. For a critique of this boundary condition for welfarism, see Parfit 1984, ch. 16. It is enough that, as a result of one's action, lives will go better or worse.

[10] See Sumner 1981, ss. 5, 16, and 23.

[11] For an extended defence of a welfarist criterion of moral standing, see Sumner 1981, s. 16. We will consider, in s. 7.2, the objection that welfarism defines the limits of moral standing too narrowly.

for them. If the world were lacking in any other sentient creatures then, whatever intellectual abilities these rational beings might have, ethics would lie beyond their range: there would be nothing for moral thinking to be *about*. The preconditions of ethics include not merely agency but also sentience.

Since welfarism is a theory about the foundations of ethics, it is difficult to know how to go about defending it. On what does one support the foundations? The best way to make a positive case for welfarism is to explain as clearly as possible what the view entails, and what welfare is, and then to say: 'There now, don't you find *that* attractive?' Alternatively, we can try to show that welfarism makes good sense of some of our other intuitive ethical commitments, such as our view about the boundaries of moral standing. But at a certain (disappointingly early) point these positive considerations run out, and the case for welfarism moves into a decidedly negative mode. As a monistic theory of the good, welfarism claims that (1) welfare matters (ultimately and for its own sake), and (2) nothing else does. It is the second claim that is the sticking point for most critics of welfarism. They do not find it difficult to acknowledge the intrinsic ethical value of welfare, but they find the exclusion of all other goods arrogant and dogmatic. Their preferred theory is pluralistic, admitting welfare alongside some of these other goods. Against this pluralistic alternative, welfarists are forced onto the defensive, arguing for each such additional good that it does not deserve a foundational role in ethics.

The merits of pluralism will be debated in the next section. Meanwhile, we should pause to note that the argumentative gains to this point have not been trivial. If the intrinsic value of welfare is conceded, then that is sufficient to rule out every competing version of monism. To appreciate what this means, let us look at one such competitor. We outlined above four desiderata for any value capable of serving in a monistic theory of the good: it must be intrinsic, generic, important, and ethically salient. These prerequisites serve to screen potential candidates, thus to narrow our search down to a short list of genuine contenders. I suggest that this short list contains only two items which merit serious consideration, namely welfare and perfection. It seems to me that throughout the long history of ethics virtually all theorists who have accepted a monistic theory of the good have grounded their moral structure on one or the other of these categories. I conclude that welfarism's only serious monistic rival is perfectionism.

To say that something has perfectionist value is to say that it is a good instance or specimen of its kind, or that it exemplifies the excellences characteristic of its particular nature. Whereas welfare is subjective, perfection is objective; the criteria which determine the perfectionist value of a life are derived entirely from the natural kind to which the subject of the life belongs, and not at all from her own attitudes or values. Therefore, while happiness is constitutive of welfare, it is peripheral or contingent where perfection is concerned. We have already seen (in section 3.4) how the teleological theory is really a theory about perfection rather than welfare. We there noted that this conclusion settles no substantive ethical issues, since it remains open to the perfectionist to urge, against the welfarist, that perfection must be included among the basic values in an ethical theory, or even that it is the sole such value. This is the serious claim that can be made on behalf of perfectionism: not that it can help us understand the nature of welfare but that it can serve instead as the axiological foundation of ethics. Like welfare, perfection seems initially well suited to playing this role. It appears to be intrinsically valuable, it is a broad, abstract category of value which embraces and supports many more specific goods, it is seemingly important, and it is plausible to think of it as ethically salient. Could a case then be made for perfectionism as a monistic theory of the good?

Some have thought so, most recently Thomas Hurka in his admirably thorough articulation and defence of perfectionism.[12] Hurka shares the assumptions which are structuring our present inquiry; indeed, he goes further by endorsing a maximizing consequentialism. He also distinguishes clearly between perfection and welfare. His question then is which value should be maximized in ethics, and his answer is: perfection. Actually, he is somewhat ambivalent as between two answers: (1) perfection alone, and (2) perfection along with other foundational values.[13] The former option, which Hurka calls *pure perfectionism*, is monistic; the latter is pluralistic. We will consider perfection as one constituent of a value pluralism in the next section; for the moment we are interested only in the question whether it can stand alone as a foundational good for ethics.

---

[12] Hurka 1993.   [13] Ibid. 6, 27–8, 101, 190.

Like welfarism, perfectionism is most interesting in its strongest and purest form. Hurka is clearly tempted by it in this form:

The narrow perfectionist idea—that the human good consists in the development of human nature—is not only attractive but also makes a peremptory claim. It is of sufficient depth and power to present itself as not one moral idea among others but the foundation for all morality, and it therefore dismisses concerns that cannot be connected to it. If a proposed moral idea has no connection to properties constitutive of human nature, it has no moral weight.[14]

On balance, however, he draws back from endorsing this uncompromising version of the theory: 'I am not sure whether the most plausible moral theory is a pure perfectionism based on the narrow ideal of human nature or a pluralist view that also gives weight to other moral concerns.'[15] One of these moral concerns is welfare. A monistic perfectionism attributes no value to happiness or satisfaction or enjoyment (however authentic), except in so far as these conditions are indicators or accompaniments of proper (mental or physical) functioning. This seems, to say the least, a trifle austere. Worse, as Hurka recognizes, pure perfectionism cannot recognize pain or suffering as intrinsic evils; indeed, it has no room for the very concept of an intrinsic evil.[16] It therefore can make no sense of the idea that a life might be scarred by great tragedies (losing one's family in the Holocaust, being raped or tortured, suffering from chronic depression) and might even, under extreme conditions, be no longer worth living. Since these conditions seem to make sense, indeed are discouragingly common, their omission is a serious defect in a monistic perfectionism. No theory which fails to find a place for well-being (and ill-being) could possibly tell the whole story about the good.

Perfectionism is most credible not when it purports to provide the entire foundation for ethics, but when it insists on being accorded a place in a pluralistic theory of the good. Before we move on to examine pluralism more closely, however, we have one item of unfinished business to which we should attend. Welfarism, we have said, is the view that only welfare matters, ultimately and in its own right, for ethics. Does this imply that *all* welfare has agent-neutral value, regardless of its source? In an influential discussion, Thomas Nagel has argued against this inclusive view.[17] Nagel

[14] Ibid. 190.   [15] Ibid. 190–1.   [16] Ibid. 100–1, 190.
[17] Nagel 1986, chs. 8 and 9.

distinguishes two generic categories of prudential goods—physical pleasure or comfort and the achievement of aims or goals—and argues that while the value of the former is agent-neutral, the value of the latter is only agent-relative. He takes the same view of their negative counterparts: the disvalue of physical pain or discomfort is agent-neutral, that of the frustration of our projects is agent-relative.

In assessing the weight of this distinction, let us remind ourselves what is at stake. A thing has agent-neutral value if it provides everyone with a reason at least to want it to happen, and possibly (in the appropriate situation) to take steps to bring it about; it has agent-relative value if the reason it generates applies only to those connected to the thing in some special way. The value of pleasure, for instance, is agent-neutral if everyone has a reason to want it *for anyone*, and agent-relative if everyone has a reason only to want it *for themselves*. Likewise, pain has agent-neutral disvalue if everyone has a reason to want *anyone's* pain to stop, and agent-relative disvalue if this reason applies only to *their own* pain. The hypothesis of welfarism is that welfare, regardless of its source, is agent-neutrally valuable. If this claim cannot be made out for some intrinsic prudential goods then welfarism is defeated.

Nagel accepts the claim for the case of physical pleasure and pain; here he believes that the most plausible story concerning their value (or disvalue) will treat it as agent-neutral. This is clearest in the case of pain or suffering, which seems to have the strongest ethical grip on us. If the badness of pain is only agent-relative then I have no reason to want your pain to stop, or to do anything to alleviate it, unless I happen to care about it or it bothers me in some way. Likewise, I will have to believe of my own pain that while I have a reason to relieve it, you have no reason to care whether it is relieved, or to help in any way. Nagel argues, correctly I think, that this is not the way we normally think about the badness of pain, whether our own or that of others. On the contrary, we take the view that there is a reason for relieving anyone's pain which is rooted in the intrinsic nature of the experience itself: the fact that it feels so awful.

Where the achievement of aims or projects is concerned, however, Nagel switches to an agent-relative account. If you have taken on the project of training to run a marathon then, while that gives you a reason to want to succeed and thus to do what is necessary for this end, it gives me no reason to want you to succeed, let alone aid you in any way. Now I find the disparity in Nagel's treatment of these two kinds of case strange. If I have a reason to want your headache to go away, or to help you to relieve it, why don't I also have a reason to want you to achieve your aim of running a marathon, or to help you do so? The asymmetry seems especially odd when we reflect that success at your project may be more important *to you* than relief from your headache. Why should we think that agent-neutral value is confined to pleasure or enjoyment, and denied to equally important prudential goods such as achievement?

Nagel's reasons for affirming the asymmetry appear to be two-fold. First, he says, we can assign particular pleasures and pains to a more general category—*having experiences which we find intrinsically agreeable or disagreeable*—which is a plausible candidate for agent-neutral value/disvalue. But we cannot do this for success at our aims or projects, since the only available general category is *getting what we want or prefer*, which has no such value. Nagel is right, I believe, to deny that desire- or preference-satisfaction has agent-neutral value as such. But the reason he is right tells against, rather than for, his denial of such value to the achievement of our aims. Desire-satisfaction has no agent-neutral value as such *because it does not reliably correlate with welfare* (it was the mistake of the desire theory to think that it does). I have no reason to aid you with your project, or even to hope that you succeed, if success will make you no better off. But suppose that it will make you better off, that it will be a prudential good for you. Then I have the same generic reason for wishing that you not fail as I have for wishing that you not suffer, namely, that *your life will go better that way*. The general category of pleasure or enjoyment has agent-neutral value because it is a generic (and intrinsic) source of well-being. But achievement has the same value for the same reason. The ultimate category within which both kinds of prudential good can be located, and which supports their claim to agent-neutral value or disvalue, is welfare itself. That is why it seems so strange to drive a wedge between them.[18]

The other difference Nagel notes between the cases of pleasure/

---

[18] Nagel seems to offer a similar analysis ibid. 171–2.

pain and success/failure is that the latter, but not the former, are in a certain sense optional for us. By this he means that while we cannot help liking pleasure and disliking pain, we can choose which projects to take on and thus which states of the world will be sources of satisfaction or frustration for us. Now one could reply to this that we have no more (or less) control over liking success and disliking failure than we have over our attitudes to pleasure and pain, but that would be to miss Nagel's point. What he is worried about, I think, is the kind of ethical claim that our projects will have on others if they are acknowledged to generate agent-neutral reasons. Nagel invokes in support of his view an influential argument by T. M. Scanlon which concludes: 'The fact that someone would be willing to forgo a decent diet in order to build a monument to his god does not mean that his claim on others for aid in his project has the same strength as a claim for aid in obtaining enough to eat.'[19] Scanlon's argument, and therefore Nagel's as well, is based on the foreseeable implications of an ethical theory: according agent-neutral value to the achievement of aims (where this has prudential value) will result in unreasonable burdens being imposed on others. But whether or not this is so will depend on how one chooses to generate a theory of the right (in particular, a theory of justice) out of a welfarist theory of the good. (The normative context of Scanlon's argument is that of distributive justice.) This will play out in very different ways for different ethical theories and seems a matter to be determined at the interface between the good and the right.[20] Welfarism works at a prior stage: the formulation of a theory of the good. It seems premature to contour this theory just so as to forestall unwanted deontological implications, especially if doing so seems to rely on what, from the point of view of the good, is an arbitrary distinction between equally important generic sources of welfare.

If we reject that distinction, there can still be further reasons for questioning whether all prudential goods have positive ethical value. What about happiness or satisfaction derived from a lifestyle which is trivial or demeaning or degrading? Does this count too? We must be careful here to specify the kind of case we have in mind. On the happiness theory a lifestyle genuinely enhances a person's

---

[19] Scanlon 1975, 659–60; quoted at Nagel 1986, 167.
[20] I return to this issue in s. 7.3.

well-being only when it has been endorsed by her under conditions of adequate information and by means of values or standards which she has autonomously adopted. These authenticity conditions are themselves sufficient to exclude many cases of repugnant lifestyles, since they will not count as prudentially valuable for their subjects. But not all: as we noted in the previous chapter, people are capable in principle of adopting such ways of life authentically, however unlikely this may be in practice. Where the authenticity requirements are satisfied we have no reason to think that the choice in question is bad for the person who has made it. However distasteful we may find her choice, for all we know it is the lifestyle which will be most fulfilling for that person in her full particularity. In that case, what reason could we have for denying ethical value to her well-being?

A step further takes us to forms of satisfaction which are morally repugnant. Does welfarism assign positive ethical value to *schadenfreude*—the enjoyment of others' misfortune? Worse, what about the sadistic pleasures of rapists or torturers? Is it a morally better state of affairs that they should take pleasure in their evil practices, since at least then there is something of positive value to balance against the harm they do to their victims? The authenticity conditions may also suffice to screen out many of these unpalatable desires as sources of well-being; in particular, we may doubt the extent to which they can be autonomous.[21] However, it seems to me unlikely that they can be excluded *by their very nature* without smuggling in illicit forms of non-prudential value. If so, then we must face the fact that people are also capable in principle of deriving authentic enjoyment both from their own nastiness and from the suffering it inflicts on others.

These kinds of satisfaction stretch welfarism's toleration to its limit: if our aim is to build a welfarist moral theory, how can we admit such tainted sources of welfare onto its ground floor? The solution to this problem, I think, lies once more in reminding ourselves how little welfarism determines of the structure of a moral theory: while it tells us wherein the good consists, it does not dictate how the right is to be derived from it. One possibility, of course, is consequentialist or, more narrowly, utilitarian, where all welfare gains and losses are counted in calculating the optimal

---

[21] For some such doubts, see Scarre 1992.

overall balance. Utilitarians have tended to include even sadistic enjoyments, relying on the injury that sadists inflict on their victims to ensure that their practices will be condemned.[22] Whether or not that is the way to go is a question we need not here decide, since welfarism leaves other directions open as well, including the option of ruling the deliberate infliction of harm on others impermissible in principle, whatever its overall welfare payoff. An ethical framework with this deontological structure is still welfarist, since it admits nothing but welfare to its theory of the good. It simply addresses the moral problem raised by evil appetites elsewhere, in its account of the right. In general, this seems the appropriate way to deal with it, rather than by launching a pre-emptive strike at the deeper level of the good.[23]

7.2 PLURALISM

Pluralists maintain that there are many foundational goods, each irreducible to any of the others and each worth furthering for its own sake. In ethics nowadays, as in politics, this view is in the ascendant: in recent years versions of it have been defended by philosophers otherwise as disparate as Isaiah Berlin, Thomas Nagel, Bernard Williams, John Finnis, Charles Taylor, Stuart Hampshire, Peter Railton, Amartya Sen, Joseph Raz, Michael Stocker, and John Kekes.[24] Much of the popularity of pluralism, I surmise, derives from the fact that it mirrors the temper of our times. In its respect for diversity, its acknowledgement of individual and cultural differences, it is ideally suited to the ethos of toleration which distinguishes the modern multicultural liberal state: pluralism is the theory, liberal neutrality the practice. It is also tailored to fit the modest ambitions of recent moral and political philosophy which, chastened by feminist and communitarian critiques, has

---

[22] See, for example, Smart 1973, 25–7. Bentham included the 'pleasures of malevolence or ill-will' in his catalogue of kinds of pleasures (Bentham 1970, ch. 5) and did not exclude them from his 'felicific calculus'. However, utilitarians have not been unanimous on this issue; for the contrary view, see Narveson 1967, ch. 6; Harsanyi 1977, s. 8; and Scarre 1992.

[23] I interpret James Griffin to be taking a similar approach to these problems in Griffin 1986, 24–6, 72. But see Powers 1994 and Griffin 1994.

[24] Berlin 1969; Nagel 1979; Williams 1979; Finnis 1980; Taylor 1982; Hampshire 1983; Railton 1984; Sen 1985*b*; Raz 1986; Stocker 1990; Kekes 1993.

turned its back on grand, comprehensive, reductive, universalistic theories. By contrast, pluralism need offend, silence, or exclude no one: if the values of community seem important in their own right, they can find their place alongside more individual goods; if traditional theories have ignored the distinctive virtues of personal relationships then there is a place for them as well. Pluralism has the potential to accommodate or adjust to any shifts in the prevailing social or philosophical winds; it is the low church of ethics and politics.

Defending welfarism against competing monistic theories of the good is relatively easy; it involves only arguing that *if you are going to restrict yourself to one foundational good* then welfare is your best choice. Contending with pluralist views is much harder. The cutting edge of welfarism is not the claim that welfare matters, in its own right, which most of us would grant and which is enough by itself to defeat rival monisms; it is the denial of equal foundational status to all other values. The welfarist must be prepared to argue that every non-welfarist item on the pluralist's list has no intrinsic ethical value. And that seems just as arrogant and intolerant as the claim made by some religions to provide the only path to eternal bliss. Welfarism may therefore be top of the monistic class, but the whole class may be made up of slow learners.

Checking the foundational credentials of every non-welfarist good would be a tedious, and endless, task. In an effort to economize on argumentative resources, I will divide rival goods into two categories. The first consists of *personal goods*: valuable states or activities realized within the lives of individual persons (or, more broadly, sentient beings). Items which fall into this category include health, pleasure or enjoyment, achievement or success, rationality, knowledge or understanding, close personal relationships, safety or security, risk or adventure, liberty, autonomy, a sense of self-worth, meaningful work, and leisure or play. The second category consists, naturally enough, of *impersonal goods*, which belong to entities other than persons. These include goods which can be manifested in the lives of non-sentient organisms (such as functioning or flourishing), values realized by social groups or communities (such as collective achievement or self-determination), and environmental values inhering in still broader collectivities (including the survival of species and the integrity and stability of biotic communities). For each of these rival values, personal and impersonal alike, the welfarist is committed to adopting one of two strategies: either co-opting it as a welfarist good or denying that its pursuit as an end has any place in ethics.

For personal goods the co-option strategy is the most promising. For consider: any personal value which could plausibly be advanced as basic or foundational for ethics will also be a standard intrinsic source of well-being. Recall how this goes. Since welfare consists in (authentic) happiness or life satisfaction, something (anything) can make our lives go better only if it contributes, directly or indirectly, to making our lived experience more rewarding or fulfilling. When the contribution something makes to our lives is direct—when, that is, we find its presence in our lives enriching in itself, independently of any further good to which it leads—then that counts as an intrinsic source of our well-being. The intrinsic sources of our well-being are therefore intrinsic prudential goods for us; aspects of our lives which we care about or prize for their own sake. Despite our individual differences, it is not difficult to compile a list of generic goods whose prudential payoff for us is, *inter alia*, intrinsic—the items on the foregoing list of personal goods will serve very nicely. (An analogous list could be compiled for non-human welfare subjects.)

The resources of welfarism serve to sharpen somewhat the question about a pluralism of the good. The pluralist wishes to include some (or all) personal goods as basic ethical values, alongside welfare. She therefore believes that they are worth promoting *for their own sake and independently of the extent to which they make our lives go well*. Is this a plausible view? Here, I think, we have reached one of those bedrock questions in ethics which can be answered only by sitting down in a cool hour and thinking it over as clearly and carefully as possible. For my own part, I can find no ethical value in promoting achievement or knowledge or liberty, or any other personal good, if *no one at all* will be better off for it: neither the person whose good it is nor anyone else. To my mind, the value of these states of affairs is adequately captured by the role they play in enriching our lives; there is no remainder which requires independent acknowledgement beyond this prudential payoff. I can offer here no proof that installing these items as separate, non-welfarist basic goods is redundant, but I do think that at this point it is fair to shift the argumentative burden to the pluralist. Since welfarists can already make sense of the ethical point of promoting and protecting these personal goods, and since foundational values should not be multiplied beyond necessity, some reason is needed for according them an independent status. This anti-pluralist argument is very general and abstract; its force may be easier to assess if we focus on a test case. Amartya Sen has articulated a version of pluralism which finds room for two co-equal foundational values: well-being and agency.[25] We have already examined his analysis of the former in terms of functionings and capabilities (section 3.3). By agency Sen means 'what the person is free to do and achieve in pursuit of whatever goals or values he or she regards as important'.[26] Agency is thus a broad kind of freedom or autonomy, which Sen thinks matters as much for ethics as welfare: 'Persons must enter the moral accounting by others not only as people whose well-being demands concern, but also as people whose responsible agency must be recognized.'[27] 'Although the agency aspect and the well-being aspect both are important, they are important for quite different reasons. In one perspective, a person is seen as a doer and a judge, whereas in the other the same person is seen as a beneficiary whose interests and advantages have to be considered. There is no way of reducing this plural-information base into a monist one without losing something of importance.'[28]

Sen's case for pluralism depends in part on the possibility of conflict between the two goods. He gives the following case:

> Your friend is injured in an accident and is unconscious. The doctor says that either treatment *A* or treatment *B* can be used and one would be just as effective as the other, but that your friend would suffer less from *A* because of its smaller side effects. However, you happen to know that your friend would have chosen treatment *B*, since treatment *A* is associated with some experiments on live animals of which your friend disapproves totally. He would, in fact, agree that treatment *A* would have been better for his well-being, but as a free agent he would have nevertheless chosen treatment *B*, if he were given the choice.[29]

If you authorize treatment *B*, Sen says, then you are attaching an independent value to your friend's agency, in competition with his well-being. And that seems a reasonable thing to do.

---

[25] His theory of the good is set out most fully in Sen 1985*b*. Sen is also a pluralist about well-being; see Sen 1980–1.
[26] Sen 1985*b*, 203.   [27] Ibid. 204.
[28] Ibid. 208 (footnotes omitted).   [29] Ibid. 209–10.

We have already noted, in the previous section, that a rational agent can decide to sacrifice his own well-being for the sake of some competing value. Sen interprets the foregoing case as just such a sacrifice, where the competing value is a (presumably autonomous) ethical commitment. As Sen sees it, you are in the position of choosing to side either with your friend's welfare or with his agency. However, it is not clear that your friend himself will subsequently see your choice in this light. He might, for instance, regard himself as having been tainted or corrupted by a form of treatment which is associated with animal suffering. Furthermore, we are to suppose that since he values fidelity to his ethical commitments, and cares deeply about being able to manage his affairs according to his own conscience, he would regard a life in which his agency has been seriously compromised as the poorer for that reason. He may well feel, therefore, that his life goes better, on balance, when his agency has been preserved, even at the cost of some additional suffering. In that case the conflict will seem to him to be, not between his well-being and some competing value, but between different prudential goods. Sen seems to be assuming that the only potential welfare cost for your friend is the additional suffering which would result from choosing treatment *B*. This would be true, however, only on a narrowly hedonistic theory of welfare. On a more robust theory, choosing treatment *A* for your friend can have serious costs for him as well.

Sen's case is therefore not an unambiguous one of conflict between welfare and agency. In order for agency to function here as a strictly non-welfarist good, we need to suppose that your friend would not regard his life as going worse for him *in any way* were he to discover subsequently that his agency had been overridden or compromised. I am not certain that this supposition is psychologically coherent, since it invites us to imagine that your friend attaches a high value to his own agency but does not regard his life as going better when that agency is secured. But if it is coherent then it seriously weakens your reason for choosing treatment *B* for him. Now you must think that this choice will not just be worse for him on balance (as it would be if the additional suffering were great enough to outweigh the benefits of preserving his agency) but a dead prudential loss. It is one thing for your friend to choose to sacrifice his own interest in this way for an ethical cause, and quite another for you to make this choice on his behalf.

Your friend has two commitments: to his own well-being and to the cause. You have only your commitment to him; the ethical cause matters to you only to the extent that it matters to him. If protecting what matters to him does not make his life go better, then you have no further reason to care about it. Being dedicated to doing what is best for your friend, all things considered, will normally require you to take his commitments seriously, just because they are his. But that is because doing so will normally make him better off. Where this condition fails, where honouring his commitments will not be a good for him, you have only the remaining aspects of his well-being to take into account.

Agency has value, therefore, in so far as it enriches the lives of agents. It is worth noting that there is an especially intimate relationship between welfare and this particular personal good. On Sen's construal, agency seems to have primarily to do with freedom, but he would probably not resist deepening the notion to include autonomy as well. Autonomy is an intrinsic prudential good: something whose presence in our lives makes them go better in itself. But it is also one of the conditions of anything having prudential value, since it is embedded in the nature of welfare. A person's endorsement of the conditions of her life is determinative of her well-being only when that endorsement is authentic, and it is authentic only when it is autonomous. In the absence of autonomy, a person's welfare is indeterminate or unknowable. Fostering autonomy is therefore necessary, not only as one particular way of enhancing people's welfare, but also as a condition of knowing wherein their welfare consists.

Working through the issues posed by Sen's notion of agency serves to remind us that arguments in support of value pluralism often point to the possibility, or inevitability, of conflicts among goods.[30] Goods conflict whenever, whether necessarily or contingently, they cannot all be realized or brought about. Conflicts among goods are a familiar feature in the landscape of practical reason. For our purposes, they can be sorted into two types: (1) conflicts across different dimensions of value, and (2) conflicts within a single dimension. The former are not at issue here: as a monistic theory of value for ethics, welfarism has no problem in acknowledging that ethical values may compete for rational attention with

[30] See, for example, Stocker 1990, ch. 8; Kekes 1993, chs. 2 and 4.

aesthetic or perfectionist ones. It does license us to ignore these competing dimensions of value *when we are doing ethics*, except to the extent that they affect well-being; in themselves, they are irrelevant to the ethical enterprise. They can, of course, conflict with ethical values, but such conflicts must (somehow or other) be settled in the higher court of practical reason. They are not internal to ethics.

But what of conflicts within the ethical domain, among intrinsic goods? Surely they too are commonplace: achievement, for instance, may be bought at the price of enjoyment, or leisure, or play. Do these conflicts presuppose that the goods at stake are many rather than one? Is welfarism then committed to denying the existence of ethical conflict? It may seem so, if we assume an account of welfare in which it consists of some homogeneous mental state such as pleasure. For then any two bits of it must be commensurable (since they are bits of the same generic sort of stuff) and we can always, at least in principle, figure out which is more worth having. Even in this limiting case welfarism would still allow the reality of conflict, since not all the pleasures we would like to have, or bring about, are compossible. But at least we could be reassured that a foregone good was always being compensated by a larger good of the same kind.

We know by now, however, that this Benthamite calculus distorts the nature of welfare. (It even distorts the nature of pleasure —or, rather, of enjoyment.) Welfare does not consist in pleasure or enjoyment; rather, these latter constitute an important kind of personal good alongside others (such as achievement). It is conflicts among these various personal goods which pluralists are fond of celebrating. And they are right: within a single life pursuit of some goods limits or forecloses entirely the pursuit of others. As agents we must face these conflicts continually, *and they do not get any easier if we think of these goods as so many components of our well-being.* Welfare is not some overriding or higher-order value to which we can appeal in order to resolve conflicts among more local goods; rather, it is the outcome when we have settled our priorities among such goods. Welfarism feeds information about individuals' interests into an ethical decision-making procedure (whatever it may be), but since welfare is subjective the determination of those interests is left (within limits defined by the requirement of authenticity) to those individuals. This is surely the way it ought to be: no one can presume to dictate to others the balance they ought to seek among the possibilities open to them. As welfarists all we can, and should, say is that the choices a subject makes should be as informed and autonomous as possible—that is, that they should genuinely reflect the subject's own priorities. But that is what pluralists say. In which case, the acknowledgement and preservation of conflict among personal goods cannot be a uniquely pluralist accomplishment. Were welfarists somehow to erase conflict they would be correctly accused of simplifying and distorting our lives as agents. For the welfarist in this case, failure is success, less is more.

It might be thought that welfarists *must* provide the resources for resolving prudential conflicts, for do they not believe that all prudential goods—all sources of well-being—are commensurable? And if they are commensurable, is it not always possible, in principle at least, to determine which competing good will provide the greater prudential payoff? Sadly, the answer in each case is: no. For one thing, commensurability is no guarantee of conflict resolution. The more similar things are, the more commensurable they are. So we might think that commensurability holds within particular categories of prudential goods (such as enjoyment or achievement) but not across different categories. However, choices among generically similar goods may still be hard ones (think of deliberating among different leisure activities, or how to divide your time and energy among your various friends). In any case, welfarism provides no assurance that all prudential goods *are* commensurable.[31] Some incommensurabilities are no obstacle to conflict resolution; *au contraire*, they trivialize it. This will occur whenever one good is lexically prior to another, so that no amount of the former, however small, is worth sacrificing for any amount of the latter, however large. The worrisome kind of incommensurability is not this but incomparability, where no prudential ranking can be made of the goods among which we must choose. Can personal goods be incommensurable in this way? They can be if there is sometimes no answer at all to the question of which will be more satisfying or fulfilling for us. If this is possible, then there will be gaps in prudential evaluations, and therefore, for welfarism, gaps

---

[31] An excellent discussion of the various dimensions of commensurability can be found in Griffin 1986, ch. 5.

in ethical evaluations as well. Where such gaps occur, all we can say is 'C'est la vie'. Welfarism cannot introduce more certainty into ethics than the subject matter allows.

In the end, thinking of personal goods as so many intrinsic sources of welfare probably makes little practical difference to the resolution of conflicts among them. The adoption of welfarism as a theory of the good seems to me pretty well to leave value conflicts of this sort neither more nor less tractable than they already are. What it does is to focus our attention on one particular way of thinking about these conflicts, which highlights the need for individuals to engage in thoughtful (and authentic) deliberations about what will most enrich their lives. But welfarism need not take on the task of resolving, or eliminating, all conflict; the idea that it would have this practical implication is the principal weapon used by pluralists to discredit it.

We return, then, to the main issue at stake between welfarists and pluralists. If non-welfarist goods are considered item by item, then it is not difficult to make their ethical value seem to depend on the extent to which they make our lives go better for us. The pluralist would have a more convincing case if her list of basic values, to be added to welfare, were less eclectic and piecemeal. This would be true if there were some other evaluative dimension, just as abstract and generic as prudential value, to which appeal was needed in order to capture some of the value of these personal goods. Pretty clearly, aesthetic value will not serve here, since it seems irrelevant to many of these goods. We are therefore led once more to perfectionist value as the only viable candidate. We have already rejected perfectionism as a rival monism, on the ground that any list of foundational values which omits well-being is ethically unacceptable. But here we encounter a more modest and circumspect version of the view. The perfectionist can claim, with some plausibility, to have a rival story to tell about the value of personal goods. Whatever direct contribution they may make to our well-being, they also have intrinsic perfectionist value because their presence in a life *makes it a better life of its kind*. In that case, welfarism does not tell the whole story about how lives can go well or badly, though it does tell an important part of it. It needs to be supplemented by perfectionism, and perfection needs to take its place alongside welfare on the list of foundational goods for ethics.

Now this is, to my mind, as plausible as pluralism gets. At least this version has *some* story to tell (two stories in fact) about how items qualify for inclusion on its menu of basic goods: only equally generic, intrinsic, important, and ethically salient categories of value will qualify, and, it is claimed, there are (at least) two of them. Now the welfarist is once more forced onto the defensive: in order to resist this more focused and stripped down version of pluralism, he must discredit perfectionist value enough to show that it does not deserve to be included even as one item on a list of foundational values for ethics. Once more the ugly, exclusivist face of welfarism is exposed.

In order to make his case against perfection as a foundational value, the welfarist must be able to point to some salient difference between it and welfare. We are supposing that all of the apparatus of ethics is ultimately for the sake of furthering the good. But we must ask: *Whose* good? Who are the bearers of the kind of value which is the point of it all? This question opens up a clear gap between welfare and perfection. If welfare is subjective, then it follows that it can inhere only in subjects—that is, beings capable of a certain kind and level of consciousness. This is why it seems so natural to think of prudential value as belonging to lives: what else could it belong to? As we saw earlier (sections 1.3 and 3.4), a life, or the subject of a life, is also capable of possessing perfectionist value, but so are many other things. In order for something to be a potential bearer of perfectionist value it seems to require only a nature—that is, some answer to the question, what kind of thing is it? An account of the nature of a thing, we are to suppose, will identify certain properties which are essential to it—properties in the absence of which it would not be a thing of *that* kind. From this account it will then be possible to extract criteria for determining how well a particular thing measures up to the standards of its kind. However this very abstract schema comes to be filled out in detail, it will clearly apply across the full range of natural kinds. Inevitably, therefore, many things will be candidates for perfectionist value which could not possibly have a welfare.

It can be tempting to think that the good which is foundational to ethics must be the human good. But this is a restriction which must be defended, lest it seem a mere unthinking speciesism (or, more broadly, natural-kindism). Philosophical debates in environmental ethics have shown how difficult it is to provide the needed defence. For a perfectionist ethics it would surely be impossible. What perfectionism begins by telling us is that a thing's excellence, by the standards of its kind, is intrinsically valuable. What conceivable reason could it then have for narrowing this claim to one particular kind? Why should it be that, while our excellence is worth promoting for its own sake, nothing else's is? The logic of perfectionism seems to drive it in the direction of holding that the good of the members of any natural kind is intrinsically valuable, and that furthering that (general category of) good is the ultimate point and rationale of ethics.

For those who take their environmental ethics seriously this may seem a welcome result. Although individuals remain the sole (or primary) bearers of value, which will displease the more holistically minded, at least this is a step beyond the reflex human chauvinism which characterizes most traditional ethical frameworks. Indeed, it is quite a long step beyond anthropocentrism, since it extends moral standing to every natural object in the world. In this it quite outstrips welfarism, which can confer such standing only on sentient beings. Such a dramatic overturning of the old paradigms can be refreshing, but perhaps it should also induce caution. For consider what perfectionism threatens to commit us to.

The perfectionist programme requires the idea of a natural kind. Let us suppose that this idea is coherent, and that we can assemble some intelligible account of it. Then every particular thing which counts as natural will belong to at least one such kind. This will not only include all organisms, but also inanimate objects such as rocks, oil deposits, lakes and rivers, mountains, planets, and stars. The objects which belong to each of these kinds, we are to suppose, are capable of being evaluated in terms of their own standards of excellence. Now I do not think that this notion is crazy, however difficult it might be to give it a satisfying philosophical explication. I think I have a rough working sense of what it might mean to say that the Alps are superior to the Apennines *as mountains*, where this comparison just points to the fact that they are, well, more mountainous, as opposed to being more scenic or more interesting to climb. And I suppose I can also make sense of thinking that one strain of virus is superior to another *as a virus* if it does better whatever viruses typically do—invades cells more efficiently, or mutates more readily, or whatever. So I think that we can make some sense of natural objects being more or less ideal specimens of their kind, and thus of their having more or less perfectionist value. What is unclear to me is why we should think we have a moral reason to make things better examples of their kind.

In the case of human beings the idea that we should promote their good surely owes at least part of its appeal to the fact that we can do so for their sake or on their behalf. In doing good for someone we are therefore not merely making the world a better place but also doing something *for that particular person*. Now this notion of furthering someone's good for her own sake can be generalized beyond the boundaries of our species; I have a perfectly good sense of what it means to take my cat to the veterinarian for her sake. But it cannot be generalized indefinitely, for not all natural objects have a 'sake' for which we can do things. Therefore, although I can make sense of preserving a mountain as a good specimen of its kind, and might be prepared to contribute some time or money to save it from being strip-mined, my doing so would be for the sake, not of the mountain, but of those creatures whose lives will be enhanced by its preservation. Our ethical sensibilities seem to have much to do with our ability to see things from the point of view of potential victims and beneficiaries. I am prepared to think that mountains and stars can fare better or worse on some objective scale of perfection, but this fact does not give them a point of view on whose behalf I can marshal my services. Having a point of view in this sense seems to require being a subject, but perfectionist value is not confined to subjects.

So far I have assumed that what matters—what must matter—for perfectionists is the good of any natural object capable of belonging to a natural kind. If anything, however, this may understate the distribution of moral standing on a perfectionist theory of value. We also classify artefacts into kinds and grade them in terms of criteria drawn from these kinds. In fact our paradigm bearers of perfectionist value are things with clearly delineated functions; on the natural side we readily think of items such as organs (one of Aristotle's favourite examples), but the world of functional objects also clearly includes such things as tools and purpose-built machines. Although I have to stretch somewhat to imagine the criteria for counting as a good mountain, I have no such problem in the case of a hammer or a dishwasher. But if we have difficulty in thinking that promoting the good of mountains might matter for its own sake, how will we fare in trying this on for artefacts? There are, of course, many good reasons for building better (cheaper, more efficient, less wasteful) machines, but the fact that doing so will be better *for the machines*, or will add to the sum total of perfection in the world, does not seem to be among them.

In environmental debates the unwelcome extension of moral standing to lawn-mowers and oil rigs has sometimes been blocked by pointing out that, while such things have a good, they do not have a good of their own.[32] The point being made is that our standards of excellence for artefacts are determined by our purposes in making them, thus by something external to the things themselves. It is not clear that this distinction really makes any ethical difference (would we lose our standing should it turn out, as many seem to believe, that we were created by a deity for some obscure purpose of her own?). But even if it does make a difference, the lesson to be learned does not seem to be a perfectionist one. Artefacts plainly have a nature from which norms can be derived. Since that is all that perfectionist value requires, why isn't that sufficient? What difference could the genesis of such things make, from a perfectionist standpoint? Of course it is crazy to count tools or machines as mattering in their own right, independently of the contribution they make to our good (or the good of other sentient creatures). But the best explanation of why it is crazy seems to be available only to the welfarist.

Part of the problem with perfection as a fundamental value for ethics is that as a category of the good it settles on just about everything. What it would be like to set about trying to increase it, or to protect it wherever it happens to be, is not easy to imagine. But the scope problem, as serious as it is in its own right, also exacerbates a further difficulty. Excellence or perfection is, as we have seen, relative to kinds. Thus it is possible, in principle at least, to compare things belonging to the same kind in terms of their perfectionist value. However, we are given no resources for carrying out comparisons across kinds. Unless different kinds belong to some common super-kind (what would it be? the category of thing?), it is difficult to see how such comparisons could ever get

---

[32] Cf. Attfield 1981, 1983 and Taylor 1986. Both Attfield and Taylor use this move to justify limiting moral standing to living beings.

a purchase. But in that case perfectionism threatens to be mute in all cases of conflict among different varieties or locations of perfectionist value. When a category of value is distributed so widely, such conflicts will be legion. How are any of them to be adjudicated?

How, indeed, are they even to be conceptualized? So far, I have assumed that each particular thing, whether natural or artificial, belongs to exactly one kind. This assumption was necessary in order to ensure that the perfectionist value of each thing would be measured against one determinate set of criteria. But the assumption is patently false. Even if we have adequate rules for determining what is to count as a kind, it is obvious that every particular thing belongs to many, perhaps infinitely many, such kinds. I am a human being, to be sure, but I am also an organism, an animal, a spatiotemporally extended object, a biped, a vertebrate, a parent, a philosopher, a baseball fan, and heaven knows what else. Presumably, each of these kinds generates its own grading standard, in which case I can be better or worse as human being, animal, parent, etc. Is my level of perfection to be determined just by one favoured category? If so, how is this to be selected? Or by all of them? But then the conflict problem looms again: what makes me a better parent may make me a worse philosopher. The problem with perfectionist value is not just that it is everywhere; there is also too much of it in each particular location.

The superabundance of perfectionist value entails that there will often be no ethical point to promoting or protecting it. This still leaves open the possibility that some particular domain of such value, circumscribed by some extraneous factor, might be foundational for ethics.[33] This possibility would, however, be undercut were there reason to think that there is *never* any ethical point to promoting perfection for its own sake. In pursuing this question I will confine myself to the core case of human good, in order that the issues at stake here stand out as starkly as possible, and that we not be distracted by the quite distinct scope problem.

---

[33] Thomas Hurka has suggested that only the perfection of living things matters (Hurka 1993, 6, 16–17). Even if this scope restriction turned out to be intuitively plausible, it would still be nice if perfectionism could generate some account of why being alive makes this kind of difference. The line of argument explored earlier—that only organisms have a good of their own—seems unlikely to do the job.

We already know that individuals can face a choice between their perfection and their welfare: what makes them better persons may fail to make them better off, if it gives them no satisfaction or fulfilment. When you are choosing between such options for yourself, then the sacrifice of either to the other seems intelligible; we can understand the point of the choice in either case, and we may take the view that it is simply your decision to make. (On the other hand, if you seem to be too willing to sacrifice your well-being in the pursuit of some perfectionist ideal, we may stop being so supportive.) In cases of personal choice, where we are determining the array of goods within our own lives, we all assume that individuals enjoy a broad prerogative within whose limits the balance to be struck between perfection and welfare (and other goods as well) is simply up to them. To stipulate any rigid priority among these goods, whether it favours perfection over welfare or vice versa, seems here an unwarranted intrusion into the sphere of individual autonomy.

But we must also make choices whose impact will fall on the lives of others. If we adopt a welfarist/perfectionist pluralism then we will sometimes sacrifice other people's welfare for the sake of their perfection. But imposing that priority on them seems presumptuous on our part, because of the objectivity of perfectionist value. Their perfection is in no way determined by their interests or concerns. Perfectionist evaluation imposes on an individual standards derived from the species as a whole; it exemplifies the hegemony of the natural kind. But then our preferring the perfection of others to their welfare involves completely overriding any say they might have in the matter. However they may feel about it, whatever the impact on their aims or aspirations, an ideal reflecting the standpoint of the species is to prevail. To put it mildly, this seems to accord little recognition or respect to their individuality, or to their say over the management of their own lives.

Objective values are quite literally alien to us because they emanate from a standpoint which is external to us as individuals, and because their status as values requires no affirmation or endorsement of them on our part. The problem for perfectionism can therefore be generalized: promoting any objective value as a foundational good for ethics will infringe autonomy or individuality. Perfectionists can of course soften the impact of their theory of value by making autonomy one of the items in their conception of the human good. But this is at best only a partial solution, since the relative importance to be assigned to autonomy, in competition with other perfectionist goods, will still be determined from the outside and with no reference to the individual's own priorities. The deep problem for any objective theory is that personal concerns play no role in determining why something (anything) counts as a good for an individual in the first place, or why one thing counts as a greater good than another. Any such theory will therefore be committed in principle to overriding the autonomous choices of individuals concerning their own lives, imposing on them what they themselves value less. Only a subjective theory, which incorporates the individual's authentic point of view into its account of the good, is capable of acknowledging the status of human agents as determiners of their own priorities for their lives.

At the beginning of this section we divided putative non-welfarist foundational goods into two categories: personal and impersonal. This excursion through perfectionism has carried us beyond the former category and deep into the latter. Since most of the fundamental issues have already been canvassed, we will be able to deal with impersonal goods much more briefly. Whereas co-option is the preferred welfarist strategy for personal goods, denial is its only option for impersonal ones. Perfectionism has no difficulty recognizing impersonal goods; its problem is that it recognizes too many of them. Because of the subjective/objective opposition, welfare is in many ways the mirror image of perfection. Since welfare is restricted to sentient creatures, there is no worry that welfarism might distribute moral standing indiscriminately over everything there is. From the vantage point of environmental ethics, welfarism is a halfway house between anthropocentrism on the one hand and various views which aim for a wider distribution of moral standing on the other. That it decisively rejects the former counts strongly in favour of it. The only serious question is whether it draws the circle too narrowly, by excluding too many things from consideration.

There are two possible problems here: first, the fact that welfarism is thoroughly and unashamedly individualist, since only individuals can be welfare subjects; and second, the fact that it countenances only those individuals who are capable of having interests. It is the second limitation which troubles biocentrists like Robin

Attfield and Paul Taylor, who wish to extend moral standing to all living creatures.[34] However, since the only good which we can promote for non-sentient organisms is their perfection, rather than their welfare, this extension now seems unpromising. For reasons outlined above, it also makes it difficult, or impossible, to resist a further extension to all natural things, or even artefacts. We should keep in mind here that to deny intrinsic value to the lives of non-sentient organisms is not to deny them all value. In most cases, we will have (derivative) welfarist reasons for protecting and preserving these organisms, especially when we take into account not just our own interests but those of all sentient creatures. In any case, if we want a more generous distribution of moral standing the only way I can see to obtain it is to return to perfectionism. There appears to be no viable intermediate position between counting only those creatures with interests and accepting that ethical consideration may be merited by just about everything there is.

Resolution of the individualism issue follows essentially the same path. Welfarism implies that collective goods have no intrinsic value; instead, they are worth fostering only to the extent that they enrich the lives of individuals. This result applies to the flourishing of both cultural and natural communities, and therefore runs against the grain of both political communitarianism and environmental holism.[35] Once again, perfectionism is capable in principle of acknowledging the intrinsic value of collective goods, since the flourishing of a collectivity can be thought of as its distinctive excellence. And once again this outcome can only be purchased at the price of an indiscriminate distribution of moral standing. The shared traditions of cultural communities must be validated by showing how they contribute to enriching the lives of the members of those communities, thereby defining one prudentially valuable form of human life.[36] The flourishing or survival of a natural species or of a biotic community, or the integrity and stability of the

[34] Attfield 1981, 1983; Taylor 1986.

[35] Influential formulations of the communitarian view can be found in Sandel 1982 and MacIntyre 1984, ch. 15. In environmental ethics the classic statement of the 'land ethic' is Leopold 1949, 224: 'A thing is right when it tends to preserve the integrity, stability, and beauty of the biotic community. It is wrong when it tends otherwise.' More sustained and philosophical defences of what has come to be known as ecoholism have been offered by Goodpaster 1979, Rolston 1988, and Callicott 1989, among many others.

[36] Cf. Kymlicka 1989a, ch. 8.

ecosystem, must pass a similar test. These are values worthy of our support when, as is usually the case, they are means of ensuring the welfare or survival of sentient beings. Where they are not, they have no ethical value, whether intrinsic or instrumental.

For the more communally or holistically minded, the individualism of welfarism will seem its greatest drawback. By contrast, I regard it as its greatest strength, since the central claim of welfarism —and the source, I believe, of its enormous intuitive appeal— is that nothing which requires ethical notice has occurred unless someone's (or something's) life has been made to go well or badly, or has been affected for better or worse. The localization of welfare in individuals provides a clear (well, a tolerably clear) criterion for the scope of the ethical domain, which is capable of differentiating it from other realms of value (such as the perfectionist or aesthetic). Perhaps axiological individualism is not necessary for this, but it certainly seems to me a promising way of explaining both the range and force of ethics. Moral considerations matter because it matters how well lives are going, and how well the lives of other creatures are going must matter to us *because* it matters (from the inside) to those creatures.

7.3 WELFARIST ETHICS AND POLITICS

We have now constructed a theory of welfare and defended a welfarist theory of the good. Our work is therefore essentially complete. Instead of recapitulating the ground we have already covered, I want to conclude by making a few suggestions about where we might go from here. Suppose that we agree about the nature of welfare and its place in ethics; what difference might that make to our ethical and political theories?

In affirming a welfarist foundation for ethics we have remained studiously agnostic about the further shape of an ethical theory. Consequentialists will build on this foundation by amalgamating the interests of separate individuals into some overall agent-neutral goal, which may be purely aggregative (as in utilitarianism) or incorporate distributive constraints. The maximization of this goal will then serve as the touchstone for developing a deontic structure of rights and duties, justice and fairness, and an aretaic structure of virtues.[37] Deontologists will want to bypass this globalizing step and instead construct a system of duties whose function is to protect individual welfare, mainly (though not exclusively) by prohibiting the intentional infliction of harm. These duties may be exceptionless, or they may be overridable by consideration of overall consequences. Finally, virtue theorists will identify as virtues those dispositions which tend to promote well-being, whether that of the agent or of others.

I do not intend to abandon this agnosticism at this late stage in the argument. The development of a full welfarist ethical theory is a task for another occasion. Instead, I want to consider the possible impact of welfarism on some prominent issues in political theory. First we need to consider briefly the relationship between ethics and politics. The former has been traditionally thought to be prior to the latter: the general norms or principles of ethics apply *inter alia* to the special case of interactions between states and their citizens. However, this ordering has been challenged in recent years on the ground that the values commonly espoused by ethical theories themselves presuppose antecedent social and political arrangements, so that ethics itself is political right down to its foundations. In the face of this challenge, welfarism reaffirms the traditional priority. At least it does so when it adopts, as it should, a subjective theory of welfare, which can be neutral among divergent ways of life and cultural traditions. With one important exception, to be discussed in a moment, this conception of individual welfare is independent of, and prior to, any assumptions about desirable (or undesirable) political structures or cultural traditions. Welfare is in this sense beyond ideology. It can therefore be used as the foundation for building a cross-cultural theory of justice, and of exploitation or oppression.

The important exception concerns the role played within a subjective theory by the requirement of authenticity. If an individual's well-being consists in whatever way of life she endorses *as an informed and autonomous subject*, then welfarism obviously privileges the traditional liberal value of autonomy. But it does so not because autonomous individuals rank higher on some scale of objective value, but rather because where the social conditions for

<hr/>

[37] I have tried to show how this process might go for rights in Sumner 1987, ch. 6.

the autonomous adoption of personal values are lacking, *we cannot know wherein people's well-being consists.* There is therefore a deep affinity between welfarism (when coupled with a subjective theory of welfare) and the liberal conception of the person as self-determining and self-making.[38] Once autonomy has been recognized as a foreground value then it seems inevitable that defence of the traditional liberal freedoms (especially freedom of expression) will become a high priority for a political theory.[39]

This derivation of political liberty from welfarism (assuming that it can in fact be carried out) contrasts with more recent currents in liberal thought, especially in the work of John Rawls. In *A Theory of Justice* Rawls tried to ground principles of justice in the agreement of agents in a hypothetical 'original position', structured by conditions which it would be reasonable for everyone to accept. Partly in response to criticisms that these conditions were biased toward liberal individualism, Rawls has latterly come to reinterpret his theory of justice—what he now calls political liberalism—as 'freestanding', that is, as requiring no grounding in a 'comprehensive moral doctrine'.[40] It can therefore be compatible with the wide range of such doctrines which may be espoused by citizens of a multicultural liberal society. On the other hand, by being disengaged from an ethical foundation, and instead presupposing shared commitments which are peculiar to the liberal democratic tradition, it also abandons all pretensions to universal validity.

A welfarist foundation for liberalism would occupy the middle ground on this conceptual territory. Because welfarism is only a theory of the good, and is therefore compatible with a variety of fully articulated ethical theories, it is not a comprehensive moral doctrine of the sort that Rawls has in mind. Instead, it is the common denominator of many (though not all) such doctrines. On the other hand, neither welfarism nor the subjective theory of welfare embedded in it is self-evident or uncontroversial. (If they were, then we would not have needed to take so long to argue for them.) Even after reading this book, not everyone will be a welfarist or a subjectivist about welfare. Welfarism cannot, therefore, hope

---

[38] See s. 5.2.
[39] As in Mill 1977. For contemporary arguments from the value of autonomy to liberal freedoms, see Raz 1986, ch. 15, and Scoccia 1987.
[40] Rawls 1993, esp. pp. 11 ff.

to offer an argument to liberal ideals from uncontroversial premisses which everyone (even everyone in the liberal tradition) accepts. However, it does capture what seems to me one very powerful idea concerning the relationship of ethics to politics, namely that the state needs to justify its policies by showing how they will make the lives of its citizens go well, and that these citizens are the final authorities on when this condition has been satisfied. If this idea seems intuitively right, then it is a matter of more than parochial interest to determine just how much of liberalism can be established on a welfarist foundation.

One important aspect of liberalism is its acceptance of, or respect for, widely divergent lifestyles. Contemporary liberals have tended to interpret this ideal as one of neutrality among conceptions of the good life, where this means that the state may not favour or promote one such conception on the ground of its intrinsic superiority to the rest.[41] By a 'conception of the good life' liberals have meant some set of values or standards for the conduct of one's life, which determine the appropriate mix of what we have been calling personal goods. They do *not* mean that liberalism must be neutral among competing political moralities; on the contrary, it is one such morality. In order to qualify for neutral consideration, therefore, conceptions of the good must be compatible with a liberal theory of justice (the belief that you will be most fulfilled by a career as a serial killer will not qualify).

In the previous section we remarked the apparent connection between liberal neutrality and value pluralism. One way to defend neutrality is to argue that there are many co-equal personal goods, thus many equally valuable combinations of them. Another is to retreat to scepticism about the possibility of evaluating different lifestyles. However, there is enough affinity between a subjective conception of welfare and liberal neutrality to suggest that the latter could also be given a welfarist justification.[42] From one point of view welfarism is not neutral, since it is one option among many as a theory of the good. But affirmation of welfarism by

[41] The principal advocates of liberal neutrality have been Rawls 1971 and 1993, Lecture V; Nozick 1974; Ackerman 1980; Dworkin 1985, ch. 8; Larmore 1987, ch. 3; and Kymlicka 1989*a*, ch. 5, and 1989*b*. However, commitment among contemporary liberals to the ideal of neutrality is not unanimous; for dissenting views see Raz 1986 and Hurka 1993, ch. 11. They will find support in many classic defences of liberalism, such as Mill 1977.

[42] This affinity is explored in Arneson 1990*a*.

liberals does not violate liberal neutrality in any serious way, since a subjective conception of welfare is itself neutral among all the different ways of life which individuals can autonomously endorse. As Richard Arneson has put it, 'Welfare . . . is a purely formal notion that does not determine the substantive aims that society, valuing each individual's satisfactions, strives to reach.'[43] Once more, therefore, welfarism seems to constitute a middle ground for liberals, this time between pluralism and scepticism. Furthermore, for reasons outlined above it furnishes a defence against the claim that liberal freedoms themselves favour one way of life—that of the autonomous agent—over others.

Liberty, and the neutrality intended to foster it, make up one important liberal value. But liberals are also disposed to defend their political regime on grounds of equality. This equality may be the abstract 'equal concern and respect' advocated by Ronald Dworkin.[44] Or it may be much more concrete, consisting of some form of substantive equality among the citizens of the liberal state. This latter interpretation implicates a theory of distributive justice and raises the question: What is the good of which citizens are to be assured equal shares? Or, as G. A. Cohen has put it, what is the currency of egalitarian justice?[45]

Does welfarism suggest an answer to this question? It might seem to suggest the wrong answer: that liberal institutions should aim to ensure equality of welfare. On a subjective account, some aspects of our well-being (our aversion to pain, for instance) are relatively unaffected by our idiosyncrasies of taste or our freely chosen projects. But others are not: what counts as the best life for you will be strongly influenced by your particular constellation of personal values or aspirations. Suppose that, having convinced yourself that you are the sort of person who deserves the best, you are unable to be satisfied with less than the fastest cars, the flashiest clothes, and the best cosmetic surgery, while your more modest neighbours are able to achieve the same level of well-being with much more limited resources. A theory of justice which requires that resources be distributed so as to ensure equality of welfare will, in effect, enable you to tax your neighbours for the maintenance of

[43] Ibid. 220.   [44] See, for instance, Dworkin 1985, ch. 8.
[45] Cohen 1989. Besides Cohen, this issue of liberal equality has been addressed by Rawls 1971 and 1982, Scanlon 1975, Sen 1980, Dworkin 1981*a* and 1981*b*, and Arneson 1989 and 1990*b*.

your expensive lifestyle. And that seems unfair, not least because (we are to suppose) you too could have chosen to cultivate more humble tastes.

Welfare is an unattractive currency for egalitarian justice. But is it the currency implied by a welfarist theory of the good? There are two reasons for thinking not, one shallow and one deeper. The first reason just reminds us again that welfarism does not itself imply any ethical goal, either aggregative or distributive; *a fortiori*, it does not imply equality of welfare as such a goal. The danger with making this response, and going no further, is that welfarism might then be thought to be entirely silent concerning the currency of egalitarian justice, thus lending liberals no assistance whatever on this question. Instead of giving the wrong answer, it gives no answer at all. We therefore also need the second reason for resisting the straightforward argument from welfarism to equality of welfare.

Here we need to draw attention to an important feature which, like their welfarism, is the common property of all welfarist ethical theories (indeed of all non-welfarist theories as well). Each such theory will provide, in its own way, a criterion of the right: some general specification of what the right thing to do (or be) consists in. However, a theory is not committed to recommending that ethical decision-making always be based directly on this criterion (whatever it may be). The question of how best to meet or satisfy the theory's criterion—how to do the right thing—is a further one, and for various contingent reasons a direct strategy (just apply the criterion whenever you face an ethical decision) is unlikely to be the most successful.[46] Most theories will therefore counsel the adoption of an indirect strategy, consisting of whatever set of rules or dispositions is calculated, given realistic assumptions about the nature of human agents and their circumstances, to increase the likelihood of success in making the right decisions.

The choice of a currency for a conception of egalitarian justice can be regarded as such an indirect strategy. From the fact that making people's lives go better is the ultimate rationale and justification for liberal policies, it does not follow that well-being must figure directly in the formulation of such policies. In principle

---

[46] I have discussed these issues at length, for the special case of consequentialist theories, in Sumner 1987, s. 6.2. See also Railton 1984 and Parfit 1984, Part I.

at least, a welfarist liberal state need never ask itself directly what will best promote the welfare of its citizens (though it will surely often do better if it does). Instead, it can fall back on the value of fostering what we have called standard goods: those goods which correlate reliably with well-being, though their role and importance may vary widely from person to person. It is some mix of these goods which will then constitute the currency of egalitarian justice. What that currency might be—whether Rawls's primary goods, or Scanlon's urgent preferences, or Sen's capabilities, or Dworkin's resources, or Arneson's opportunity for welfare, Cohen's access to advantage, or something else entirely—I shall not attempt to decide. For our purposes, the important conclusion is that welfare might serve to direct liberals to the best currency without itself serving as that currency.

All of the foregoing remarks about possible links between welfarism and liberalism are highly speculative, designed to raise interesting questions for further exploration rather than providing answers to them. They have been motivated by a sense of regret that welfarism, which served in the heyday of utilitarianism as one prominent ethical basis for public policy, has declined in this anti-foundationalist age to the status of a neglected option, even among liberals.[47] This decline has doubtless been prompted both by the widespread abandonment of utilitarianism and by the assumption of simplistic and unattractive conceptions of well-being. With a better understanding of what welfare consists in, and of the various theoretical directions available to welfarists, perhaps the time has come for welfarism to be taken seriously again as a promising foundation for both ethics and politics.

---

[47] Griffin 1986, Part III, is a conspicuous exception to this trend.

BIBLIOGRAPHY

ABRAMOVITZ, MOSES. 1979. 'Economic Growth and its Discontents'. In Michael J. Boskin (ed.), *Economics and Human Welfare: Essays in Honor of Tibor Scitovsky*. New York: Academic Press.

ACKERMAN, BRUCE A. 1980. *Social Justice in the Liberal State*. New Haven: Yale University Press.

Ad Hoc Committee of the Harvard Medical School to Examine the Definition of Brain Death. 1968. 'A Definition of Irreversible Coma'. *Journal of the American Medical Association*, 205: 6.

ANAND, K. J. S., and HICKEY, P. R. 1987. 'Pain and its Effects in the Human Neonate and Fetus'. *New England Journal of Medicine*, 317: 21.

ANDREWS, FRANK M., and WITHEY, STEPHEN B. 1976. *Social Indicators of Well-Being: Americans' Perceptions of Life Quality*. New York: Plenum Press.

ARISTOTLE. 1984. *The Complete Works of Aristotle*. The Revised Oxford Translation. Ed. Jonathan Barnes. Bollingen Series. Princeton: Princeton University Press.

ARNESON, RICHARD J. 1989. 'Equality and Equal Opportunity for Welfare'. *Philosophical Studies*, 56: 1.

—— 1990a. 'Neutrality and Utility'. *Canadian Journal of Philosophy*, 20: 2.

—— 1990b. 'Liberalism, Distributive Subjectivism, and Equal Opportunity for Welfare'. *Philosophy and Public Affairs*, 19: 2.

ATTFIELD, ROBIN. 1981. 'The Good of Trees'. *Journal of Value Inquiry*, 15: 1.

—— 1983. *The Ethics of Environmental Concern*. New York: Columbia University Press.

AUSTIN, JEAN. 1968. 'Pleasure and Happiness'. *Philosophy*, 43: 163.

AYALA, FRANCISCO J. 1970. 'Teleological Explanation in Evolutionary Biology'. *Philosophy of Science*, 37: 1.

BAIER, KURT. 1958. *The Moral Point of View: A Rational Basis of Ethics*. Ithaca, NY: Cornell University Press.

BARRY, BRIAN. 1965. *Political Argument*. London: Routledge & Kegan Paul.

BENDITT, THEODORE. 1974. 'Happiness'. *Philosophical Studies*, 25: 1.

BENTHAM, JEREMY. 1843. *The Works of Jeremy Bentham*. Ed. John Bowring. Edinburgh: William Tait.

—— 1952-4. *Jeremy Bentham's Economic Writings*. Ed. W. Stark. London: George Allen & Unwin.

BENTHAM, JEREMY. 1970. *An Introduction to the Principles of Morals and Legislation.* Ed. J. H. Burns and H. L. A. Hart. Collected Works of Jeremy Bentham. London: Athlone Press.

—— 1983*a*. *Chrestomathia.* Ed. M. J. Smith and W. H. Burston. Collected Works of Jeremy Bentham. Oxford: Clarendon Press.

—— 1983*b*. *Deontology, Together with a Table of the Springs of Action and the Article on Utilitarianism.* Ed. Amnon Goldworth. Collected Works of Jeremy Bentham. Oxford: Clarendon Press.

BERGER, FRED. 1984. *Happiness, Justice, and Freedom.* Berkeley: University of California Press.

BERLIN, ISAIAH. 1969. *Four Essays on Liberty.* London: Oxford University Press.

BRANDT, RICHARD B. 1979. *A Theory of the Good and the Right.* Oxford: Clarendon Press.

BRAYBROOKE, DAVID. 1987. *Meeting Needs.* Princeton: Princeton University Press.

BRINK, DAVID O. 1989. *Moral Realism and the Foundations of Ethics.* Cambridge: Cambridge University Press.

—— 1992. 'Mill's Deliberative Utilitarianism'. *Philosophy and Public Affairs*, 21: 1.

BROAD, C. D. 1971. *Broad's Critical Essays in Moral Philosophy.* Ed. David R. Cheney. London: George Allen & Unwin.

BROOME, JOHN. 1978. 'Choice and Value in Economics'. *Oxford Economic Papers*, 30: 3.

BROWER, BRUCE W. 1993. 'Dispositional Ethical Realism'. *Ethics*, 103: 1.

CALLICOTT, J. BAIRD. 1989. *In Defense of the Land Ethic.* Buffalo: State University of New York Press.

CAMPBELL, ANGUS. 1981. *The Sense of Well-Being in America: Recent Patterns and Trends.* New York: McGraw-Hill.

—— and CONVERSE, PHILIP E. 1972. *The Human Meaning of Social Change.* New York: Russell Sage Foundation.

—— —— and ROGERS, WILLARD L. 1976. *The Quality of American Life: Perceptions, Evaluations, and Satisfactions.* New York: Russell Sage Foundation.

CARLEY, MICHAEL. 1981. *Social Measurement and Social Indicators.* London: George Allen & Unwin.

CASSELL, ERIC J. 1982. 'The Nature of Suffering and the Goals of Medicine'. *New England Journal of Medicine*, 306: 11.

—— 1991. 'Recognizing Suffering'. *Hastings Center Report*, 21: 3.

CHRISTMAN, JOHN. 1991. 'Autonomy and Personal History'. *Canadian Journal of Philosophy*, 21: 1.

COHEN, G. A. 1989. 'On the Currency of Egalitarian Justice'. *Ethics*, 99: 4.

Consultants to the President's Commission for the Study of Ethical Problems in Medicine and Biomedical and Behavioral Research. 1981. 'Guidelines for the Determination of Death'. *Journal of the American Medical Association*, 246: 19.

CRANFORD, RONALD E. 1988. 'The Persistent Vegetative State: The Medical Reality (Getting the Facts Straight)'. *Hastings Center Report*, 18: 1.

DONNER, WENDY. 1991. *The Liberal Self: John Stuart Mill's Moral and Political Philosophy*. Ithaca, NY: Cornell University Press.

DWORKIN, GERALD. 1988. *The Theory and Practice of Autonomy*. Cambridge: Cambridge University Press.

DWORKIN, RONALD. 1981a. 'What is Equality? Part I: Equality of Welfare'. *Philosophy and Public Affairs*, 10: 3.

—— 1981b. 'What is Equality? Part II: Equality of Resources'. *Philosophy and Public Affairs*, 10: 4.

—— 1985. *A Matter of Principle*. Cambridge, Mass.: Harvard University Press.

—— 1990. 'Foundations of Liberal Equality'. *The Tanner Lectures on Human Values*, 11.

EASTERLIN, RICHARD A. 1974. 'Does Economic Growth Improve the Human Lot? Some Empirical Evidence'. In Paul A. David and Melvin W. Reder (eds.), *Nations and Households in Economic Growth*. New York: Academic Press.

EDGEWORTH, F. Y. 1881. *Mathematical Psychics*. London: Kegan Paul & Co.

EDWARDS, REM B. 1979. *Pleasures and Pains: A Theory of Qualitative Hedonism*. Ithaca, NY: Cornell University Press.

EGONSSON, DAN. 1990. *Interests, Utilitarianism and Moral Standing*. Studies in Philosophy, 4. Lund: Lund University Press.

ELSTER, JON. 1982. 'Sour Grapes: Utilitarianism and the Genesis of Wants'. In Amartya Sen and Bernard Williams (eds.), *Utilitarianism and Beyond*. Cambridge: Cambridge University Press.

FEINBERG, JOEL. 1973. *Social Philosophy*. Englewood Cliffs, NJ: Prentice-Hall.

—— 1984. *Harm to Others*. New York: Oxford University Press.

FINNIS, JOHN. 1980. *Natural Law and Natural Rights*. Clarendon Law Series. Oxford: Clarendon Press.

—— 1983. *Fundamentals of Ethics*. Oxford: Clarendon Press.

—— BOYLE, JOSEPH M., JR., and GRISEZ, GERMAIN. 1987. *Nuclear Deterrence, Morality and Realism*. Oxford: Clarendon Press.

FRANKFURT, HARRY G. 1971. 'Freedom of the Will and the Concept of a Person'. *Journal of Philosophy*, 68: 1.

FRIEDMAN, MARILYN. 1986. 'Autonomy and the Split-Level Self'. *Southern Journal of Philosophy*, 24: 1.

GALBRAITH, JOHN KENNETH. 1958. *The Affluent Society*. London: Hamish Hamilton.

GAUTHIER, DAVID. 1986. *Morals by Agreement*. Oxford: Clarendon Press.

GLASSEN, P. 1957. 'A Fallacy in Aristotle's Argument about the Good'. *Philosophical Quarterly*, 7: 29.

GOLDSWORTHY, JEFFREY. 1992. 'Well-Being and Value'. *Utilitas*, 4: 1.

GOLDWORTH, AMNON. 1979. 'Jeremy Bentham: On the Measurement of Subjective States'. *Bentham Newsletter*, 2.

GOODPASTER, KENNETH E. 1978. 'On Being Morally Considerable'. *Journal of Philosophy*, 75: 6.

—— 1979. 'From Egoism to Environmentalism'. In K. E. Goodpaster and K. M. Sayre (eds.), *Ethics and Problems of the 21st Century*. Notre Dame, Ind.: University of Notre Dame Press.

GOSLING, J. C. B. 1969. *Pleasure and Desire: The Case for Hedonism Reviewed*. Oxford: Clarendon Press.

GRIFFIN, DONALD R. 1976. *The Question of Animal Awareness: Evolutionary Continuity of Mental Experience*. New York: Rockefeller University Press.

GRIFFIN, JAMES. 1986. *Well-Being: Its Meaning, Measurement, and Moral Importance*. Oxford: Clarendon Press.

—— 1991. 'Against the Taste Model'. In Jon Elster and John E. Roemer (eds.), *Interpersonal Comparisons of Well-Being*. Cambridge: Cambridge University Press.

—— 1993. 'Dan Brock: Quality of Life Measures in Health Care and Medical Ethics'. In Martha Nussbaum and Amartya Sen (eds.), *The Quality of Life*. Oxford: Clarendon Press.

—— 1994. 'The Distinction between Criterion and Decision Procedure: A Reply to Madison Powers'. *Utilitas*, 6: 2.

HAMPSHIRE, STUART. 1983. 'Morality and Conflict'. In Stuart Hampshire, *Morality and Conflict*. Cambridge, Mass.: Harvard University Press.

HANKISS, ELEMER. 1983. 'Cross-cultural Quality of Life Research: An Outline for Conceptual Framework'. In UNESCO, *Quality of Life: Problems of Assessment and Measurement*. Paris: UNESCO.

HARDIN, C. L. 1988. *Color for Philosophers: Unweaving the Rainbow*. Indianapolis: Hackett Publishing Company.

HARE, R. M. 1964. 'Pain and Evil'. *Proceedings of the Aristotelian Society*, Supplementary Volume 38.

—— 1981. *Moral Thinking: Its Levels, Method, and Point*. Oxford: Clarendon Press.

—— 1985. 'Ontology in Ethics'. In Ted Honderich (ed.), *Morality and Objectivity: A Tribute to J. L. Mackie*. London: Routledge & Kegan Paul.

HARSANYI, JOHN C. 1977. 'Morality and the Theory of Rational Behaviour'. *Social Research*, 44: 4.

HARTLEY, DAVID. 1749. *Observations on Man.* London: Richardson.

HASLETT, D. W. 1990. 'What is Utility?' *Economics and Philosophy*, 6: 1.

HAWORTH, LAWRENCE. 1986. *Autonomy: An Essay in Philosophical Psychology and Ethics.* New Haven: Yale University Press.

HIRSCH, FRED. 1977. *Social Limits to Growth.* London: Routledge & Kegan Paul.

HUME, DAVID. 1978. *A Treatise of Human Nature.* Ed. L. A. Selby-Bigge. Revised by and notes by P. H. Nidditch. 2nd edn. Oxford: Clarendon Press.

HURKA, THOMAS. 1993. *Perfectionism.* New York: Oxford University Press.

HUTCHINSON, D. S. 1986. *The Virtues of Aristotle.* London: Routledge & Kegan Paul.

JEVONS, W. STANLEY. 1965. *The Theory of Political Economy.* 5th edn. New York: Augustus M. Kelley.

KAGAN, SHELLY. 1992. 'The Limits of Well-Being'. *Social Philosophy and Policy*, 9: 2.

KEKES, JOHN. 1993. *The Morality of Pluralism.* Princeton: Princeton University Press.

KENNY, A. J. P., *et al.* 1972. *The Nature of Mind.* Edinburgh: Edinburgh University Press.

KERR, FREDERICK W. L. 1981. *The Pain Book.* Englewood Cliffs, NJ: Prentice-Hall.

KRAUT, RICHARD. 1979. 'Two Conceptions of Happiness'. *Philosophical Review*, 88: 2.

KYMLICKA, WILL. 1989a. *Liberalism, Community and Culture.* Oxford: Clarendon Press.

—— 1989b. 'Liberal Individualism and Liberal Neutrality'. *Ethics*, 99: 4.

LANDESMAN, CHARLES. 1989. *Color and Consciousness: An Essay in Metaphysics.* Philadelphia: Temple University Press.

LARMORE, CHARLES E. 1987. *Patterns of Moral Complexity.* Cambridge: Cambridge University Press.

LEOPOLD, ALDO. 1949. *A Sand County Almanac.* New York: Oxford University Press.

LITTLE, I. M. D. 1957. *Critique of Welfare Economics.* 2nd edn. Oxford: Clarendon Press.

LLOYD THOMAS, D. A. 1968. 'Happiness'. *Philosophical Quarterly*, 18: 71.

LOCKE, JOHN. 1975. *An Essay Concerning Human Understanding.* Ed. Peter Nidditch. Oxford: Clarendon Press.

LOMASKY, LOREN. 1987. *Persons, Rights, and the Moral Community.* New York: Oxford University Press.

LUCE, R. DUNCAN, and RAIFFA, HOWARD. 1957. *Games and Decisions: Introduction and Critical Survey.* New York: John Wiley & Sons.

McDOWELL, JOHN. 1985. 'Values and Secondary Qualities'. In Ted Honderich (ed.), *Morality and Objectivity: A Tribute to J. L. Mackie.* London: Routledge & Kegan Paul.

McFALL, LYNNE. 1989. *Happiness.* New York: Peter Lang Publishing.

McGINN, COLIN. 1983. *The Subjective View: Secondary Qualities and Indexical Thoughts.* Oxford: Clarendon Press.

MacINTYRE, ALASDAIR. 1984. *After Virtue: A Study in Moral Theory.* 2nd edn. Notre Dame, Ind.: University of Notre Dame Press.

MACKIE, J. L. 1974. *The Cement of the Universe.* Oxford: Clarendon Press.

—— 1977. *Ethics: Inventing Right and Wrong.* Harmondsworth: Penguin Books.

MARSHALL, ALFRED. 1961. *Principles of Economics.* Annotations by C. W. Guillebaud. 9th edn. London: Macmillan & Co.

MATLIN, MARGARET W., and STANG, DAVID J. 1978. *The Pollyanna Principle: Selectivity in Language, Memory, and Thought.* Cambridge, Mass.: Schenkman.

MAYR, ERNST. 1988. *Toward a New Philosophy of Biology: Observations of an Evolutionist.* Cambridge, Mass.: Harvard University Press.

MELZACK, RONALD, and WALL, PATRICK D. 1983. *The Challenge of Pain.* New York: Basic Books.

MERRIAM, IDA C. 1968. 'Welfare and its Measurement'. In Eleanor Bernert Sheldon and Wilbert E. Moore (eds.), *Indicators of Social Change: Concepts and Measurements.* New York: Russell Sage Foundation.

MILL, JAMES. 1869. *Analysis of the Phenomena of the Human Mind.* Ed. John Stuart Mill. 2nd edn. London: Longmans, Green, Reader & Dyer.

MILL, JOHN STUART. 1969. 'Utilitarianism'. In *Essays on Ethics, Religion and Society,* ed. J. M. Robson. Collected Works of John Stuart Mill, vol. x. Toronto: University of Toronto Press.

—— 1974. *A System of Logic: Ratiocinative and Inductive.* Ed. J. M. Robson. Collected Works of John Stuart Mill, vols. vii and viii. Toronto: University of Toronto Press.

—— 1977. 'On Liberty'. In *Essays on Politics and Society,* ed. J. M. Robson. Collected Works of John Stuart Mill, vol. xviii. Toronto: University of Toronto Press.

MISHAN, E. J. 1967. *The Costs of Economic Growth.* Harmondsworth: Penguin.

—— 1977. *The Economic Growth Debate.* London: George Allen & Unwin.

MONTAGUE, ROGER. 1966–7. 'Happiness'. *Proceedings of the Aristotelian Society,* 67.

MOORE, ANDREW. 1991. 'A Theory of Well-Being'. Ph.D. Diss.

MOORE, G. E. 1903. *Principia Ethica.* Cambridge: Cambridge University Press.

—— 1922. *Philosophical Studies*. London: Routledge & Kegan Paul.

—— 1947. *Ethics*. London: Oxford University Press.

MYERS, DAVID G. 1992. *The Pursuit of Happiness: Who is Happy—and Why*. New York: William Morrow & Company.

NAGEL, THOMAS. 1979. *Mortal Questions*. Cambridge: Cambridge University Press.

—— 1986. *The View from Nowhere*. New York: Oxford University Press.

NARVESON, JAN. 1967. *Morality and Utility*. Baltimore: Johns Hopkins Press.

NELKIN, NORTON. 1986. 'Pains and Pain Sensations'. *Journal of Philosophy*, 83: 3.

NISSEL, MURIEL. 1984. 'Indications of Human Betterment'. In Kenneth E. Boulding (ed.), *The Economics of Human Betterment*. London: Macmillan.

NOZICK, ROBERT. 1974. *Anarchy, State, and Utopia*. New York: Basic Books.

—— 1989. *The Examined Life: Philosophical Meditations*. New York: Simon & Schuster.

NUSSBAUM, MARTHA. 1988. 'Nature, Function, and Capability: Aristotle on Political Distribution'. In Julia Annas and Robert H. Grimm (eds.), *Oxford Studies in Ancient Philosophy*, Supplementary Volume. Oxford: Clarendon Press.

—— 1993. 'Non-relative Virtues: An Aristotelian Approach'. In Martha Nussbaum and Amartya Sen (eds.), *The Quality of Life*. Oxford: Clarendon Press.

Organization for Economic Co-operation and Development. 1973. *List of Social Concerns Common to Most OECD Countries*. Paris: OECD.

—— 1982. *OECD List of Social Indicators*. Paris: OECD.

—— 1986. *Living Conditions in OECD Countries: A Compendium of Social Indicators*. Paris: OECD.

OVERVOLD, MARK. 1980. 'Self-Interest and the Concept of Self-Sacrifice'. *Canadian Journal of Philosophy*, 10: 1.

PARFIT, DEREK. 1984. *Reasons and Persons*. Oxford: Clarendon Press.

PARTRIDGE, ERNEST. 1981. 'Posthumous Interests and Posthumous Respect'. *Ethics*, 91: 2.

PENZ, G. PETER. 1986. *Consumer Sovereignty and Human Interests*. Cambridge: Cambridge University Press.

PERRY, RALPH BARTON. 1926. *General Theory of Value*. Cambridge, Mass.: Harvard University Press.

PIGOU, A. C. 1932. *The Economics of Welfare*. 4th edn. London: Macmillan.

POWERS, MADISON. 1994. 'Repugnant Desires and the Two-Tier Conception of Utility'. *Utilitas*, 6: 2.

RAILTON, PETER. 1984. 'Alienation, Consequentialism, and the Demands of Morality'. *Philosophy and Public Affairs*, 13: 2.
—— 1986. 'Moral Realism'. *Philosophical Review*, 95: 2.
RAWLS, JOHN. 1971. *A Theory of Justice*. Cambridge, Mass.: Harvard University Press.
—— 1975. 'Fairness to Goodness'. *Philosophical Review*, 84: 4.
—— 1982. 'Social Unity and Primary Goods'. In Amartya Sen and Bernard Williams (eds.), *Utilitarianism and Beyond*. Cambridge: Cambridge University Press.
—— 1993. *Political Liberalism*. The John Dewey Essays in Philosophy, no. 4. New York: Columbia University Press.
RAZ, JOSEPH. 1986. *The Morality of Freedom*. Oxford: Clarendon Press.
RILEY, JONATHAN. 1988. *Liberal Utilitarianism*. Cambridge: Cambridge University Press.
RIPSTEIN, ARTHUR. 1993. 'Preference'. In R. G. Frey and Christopher W. Morris (eds.), *Value, Welfare, and Morality*. Cambridge: Cambridge University Press.
ROLSTON, HOLMES, III. 1988. *Environmental Ethics: Duties to and Values in the Natural World*. Philadelphia: Temple University Press.
ROSE, MARGARET, and ADAMS, DAVID. 1989. 'Evidence for Pain and Suffering in Other Animals'. In Gill Langley (ed.), *Animal Experimentation: The Consensus Changes*. Basingstoke: Macmillan Press Ltd.
RYLE, GILBERT. 1949. *The Concept of Mind*. New York: Barnes & Noble.
—— 1954. *Dilemmas*. Cambridge: Cambridge University Press.
SACKS, OLIVER. 1985. *The Man Who Mistook his Wife for a Hat*. London: Pan Books.
SAMETZ, A. W. 1968. 'Production of Goods and Services: The Measurement of Economic Growth'. In Eleanor Bernert Sheldon and Wilbert E. Moore (eds.), *Indicators of Social Change: Concepts and Measurements*. New York: Russell Sage Foundation.
SAMUELSON, PAUL A. 1938. 'A Note on the Pure Theory of Consumers' Behavior'. *Economica*, NS 5: 17.
—— 1947. *Foundations of Economic Analysis*. Cambridge, Mass.: Harvard University Press.
—— 1948. 'Consumption Theory in Terms of Revealed Preference'. *Economica*, NS 15: 60.
SANDEL, MICHAEL J. 1982. *Liberalism and the Limits of Justice*. Cambridge: Cambridge University Press.
SCANLON, T. M. 1975. 'Preference and Urgency'. *Journal of Philosophy*, 72: 19.
—— 1993. 'Value, Desire, and Quality of Life'. In Martha Nussbaum and Amartya Sen (eds.), *The Quality of Life*. Oxford: Clarendon Press.
SCARRE, GEOFFREY. 1992. 'Utilitarianism and Self-Respect'. *Utilitas*, 4: 1.

SCITOVSKY, TIBOR. 1976. *The Joyless Economy: An Inquiry into Human Satisfaction and Consumer Dissatisfaction*. Oxford: Oxford University Press.

SCOCCIA, DANNY. 1987. 'Autonomy, Want Satisfaction, and the Justification of Liberal Freedoms'. *Canadian Journal of Philosophy*, 17: 3.

SELLARS, WILFRID. 1956. 'Empiricism and the Philosophy of Mind'. In Herbert Feigl and Michael Scriven (eds.), *Minnesota Studies in the Philosophy of Science*, vol. i. Minneapolis: University of Minnesota Press.

SEN, AMARTYA. 1979. 'Utilitarianism and Welfarism'. *Journal of Philosophy*, 76: 9.

—— 1980. 'Equality of What?' In Sterling McMurrin (ed.), *The Tanner Lectures on Human Values*. Cambridge: Cambridge University Press.

—— 1980–1. 'Plural Utility'. *Proceedings of the Aristotelian Society*, 81.

—— 1982. *Choice, Welfare and Measurement*. Oxford: Basil Blackwell.

—— 1984. *Resources, Values and Development*. Oxford: Basil Blackwell.

—— 1985a. *Commodities and Capabilities*. Amsterdam: North-Holland.

—— 1985b. 'Well-Being, Agency and Freedom'. The Dewey Lectures 1984. *Journal of Philosophy*, 82: 4.

—— 1987a. *On Ethics and Economics*. Oxford: Basil Blackwell.

—— 1987b. *The Standard of Living*. Ed. Geoffrey Hawthorn. Cambridge: Cambridge University Press.

—— 1993. 'Capability and Well-Being'. In Martha Nussbaum and Amartya Sen (eds.), *The Quality of Life*. Oxford: Clarendon Press.

SHELDON, ELEANOR BERNERT, and MOORE, WILBERT E. (eds.). 1968. *Indicators of Social Change: Concepts and Measurements*. New York: Russell Sage Foundation.

SIDGWICK, HENRY. 1962. *The Methods of Ethics*. 7th edn. London: Macmillan.

SMART, J. J. C. 1973. 'An Outline of a System of Utilitarian Ethics'. In J. J. C. Smart and Bernard Williams, *Utilitarianism: For and Against*. Cambridge: Cambridge University Press.

SMITH, JANE A., and BOYD, KENNETH M. (eds.). 1991. *Lives in the Balance: The Ethics of Using Animals in Biomedical Research*. Oxford: Oxford University Press.

SPARSHOTT, FRANCIS. 1994. *Taking Life Seriously: A Study of the Argument of the Nicomachean Ethics*. Toronto Studies in Philosophy. Toronto: University of Toronto Press.

STOCKER, MICHAEL. 1990. *Plural and Conflicting Values*. Oxford: Clarendon Press.

STRAWSON, GALEN. 1989. *The Secret Connexion: Causation, Realism and David Hume*. Oxford: Clarendon Press.

STRUMPEL, BURKHARD (ed.). 1974. *Subjective Elements of Well-Being*. Paris: OECD.

STRUMPEL, BURKHARD. 1976. 'Introduction and Model'. In *Economic Means for Human Needs: Social Indicators of Well-Being and Discontent*. Ann Arbor: Institute for Social Research.

SUMNER, L. W. 1981. *Abortion and Moral Theory*. Princeton: Princeton University Press.

—— 1987. *The Moral Foundation of Rights*. Oxford: Clarendon Press.

TATARKIEWICZ, WLADYSLAW. 1976. *Analysis of Happiness*. Tr. Edward Rothert and Danuta Zielinskn. Warsaw: Polish Scientific Publishers.

TAYLOR, CHARLES. 1982. 'The Diversity of Goods'. In Amartya Sen and Bernard Williams (eds.), *Utilitarianism and Beyond*. Cambridge: Cambridge University Press.

TAYLOR, PAUL W. 1986. *Respect for Nature*. Princeton: Princeton University Press.

TELFER, ELIZABETH. 1980. *Happiness*. London: Macmillan.

THALBERG, IRVING. 1978. 'Hierarchical Analyses of Unfree Action'. *Canadian Journal of Philosophy*, 8: 2.

THOMSON, GARRETT. 1987. *Needs*. London: Routledge & Kegan Paul.

TRIGG, ROGER. 1970. *Pain and Emotion*. New York: Oxford University Press.

VINE, BARBARA. 1994. *Asta's Book*. London: Penguin Books.

VON NEUMANN, JOHN, and MORGENSTERN, OSKAR. 1953. *Theory of Games and Economic Behavior*. Princeton: Princeton University Press.

WHITING, JENNIFER. 1988. 'Aristotle's Function Argument: A Defense'. *Ancient Philosophy*, 8: 1.

WICKSTEED, PHILIP H. 1933. *The Common Sense of Political Economy and Selected Papers and Reviews on Economic Theory*. London: Routledge.

WIGGINS, DAVID. 1985. 'Claims of Need'. In Ted Honderich (ed.), *Morality and Objectivity: A Tribute to J. L. Mackie*. London: Routledge & Kegan Paul.

WILKES, KATHLEEN V. 1978. 'The Good Man and the Good for Man in Aristotle's Ethics'. *Mind*, 87: 348.

WILLIAMS, BERNARD. 1979. 'Conflicts of Values'. In Alan Ryan (ed.), *The Idea of Freedom: Essays in Honour of Isaiah Berlin*. Oxford: Oxford University Press.

WINCH, D. M. 1971. *Analytical Welfare Economics*. Harmondsworth: Penguin Books.

YOUNG, ROBERT. 1986. *Personal Autonomy: Beyond Negative and Positive Liberty*. New York: St Martin's Press.

INDEX